Dear Reader:

The book you are about to [read is a] St. Martin's True Crime L[ibrary, what the New York] Times calls "the leader in t[he field." St. Martin's brings] you a fascinating account of the latest, most sensational crime that has captured the national attention. St. Martin's is the publisher of perennial bestselling true crime author Jack Olsen (SON and DOC) whose SALT OF THE EARTH is the true story of how one woman fought and triumphed over life-shattering violence; Joseph Wambaugh called it "powerful and absorbing." DEATH OF A LITTLE PRINCESS recounts the investigation into the horrifying murder of child beauty queen JonBenét Ramsey. FALLEN HERO is the *New York Times* bestselling account of the O.J. Simpson case. Fannie Weinstein and Melinda Wilson tell the story of a beautiful honors student who was lured into the dark world of sex for hire in THE COED CALL GIRL MURDER.

St. Martin's True Crime Library gives you the stories *behind* the headlines. Our authors take you right to the scene of the crime and into the minds of the most notorious murderers to show you what really makes them tick. St. Martin's True Crime Library paperbacks are better than the most terrifying thriller, because it's all true! The next time you want a crackling good read, make sure it's got the St. Martin's True Crime Library logo on the spine—you'll be up all night!

Charles E. Spicer

Charles E. Spicer, Jr.
Senior Editor, St. Martin's True Crime Library

Treading lightly in his polished black police shoes, his hand firmly placed on the grip of his gun, the officer adopted a tiptoe-like step as he rounded the doorway and descended the two steps into the modest maid's galley, a room no more than nine feet wide.

He involuntarily jumped back when he spotted a dark-haired man lying in a pool of purplish-red blood. The man's face was pressed into the cold wood floor. His muscular, jean-clad legs were extended straight out behind him, as if he had fallen forward with a thud. The only sound came from the portable television that sat on the kitchen counter . . .

A WOMAN
SCORNED

Lisa Pulitzer

St. Martin's Paperbacks

A WOMAN SCORNED

Copyright © 1999 by Lisa Pulitzer.

Cover photographs © AP/Wide World Photos.

ISBN: 0-312-96833-7

Printed in the United States of America

St. Martin's Paperbacks edition / March 1999

10 9 8 7 6 5 4 3 2 1

To my husband, Douglas Paul Love,
and our baby girl, Francesca Danielle

ACKNOWLEDGMENTS

I am deeply grateful to all the people who helped me bring this book to completion.

I thank Charlie Spicer, my editor at St. Martin's Press, his editorial assistant, Dorsey Mills, and associate publisher John Rounds for their unstinting support, encouragement, kindness, and patience.

I am particularly grateful to my literary agent, Madeleine Morel of 2M Communications, Bill Contardi of the William Morris Agency, Douglas Pulitzer of the Pulitzer Law Firm and Celeste Phillips of Levine, Sullivan and Koch.

My gratitude to Sheriff Joseph Higgs, Captain Fred Pfeiff, and Sergeant Gary Healy of the Fauquier Sheriff's Office, Kevin Casey and Jackie Burton of the Commonwealth Attorney's Office, and Blair D. Howard, P.C.

Without the expert help and encouragement of author Cynthia Blair, I could never have seen this project through to its completion.

A special thanks to author Joan Swirsky for her invaluable insights, and to copy editor Richard Onley, news editor Dick Belsky, photographers Linda Martin and Sarah Libby Greenhalgh, and journalist Mike Sluss.

Gratitude to Amy Beth Wapner, a special friend, and Daniel Pagnani, a gem of a medical doctor.

To all of the friends, teammates and business associates of Roberto Villegas and Susan Cummings who helped me to understand this complicated story, I give my heartfelt thanks.

And to my mother, Elaine Matthews, a big hug for her

love and support during a most hectic and joyous time.

Most important, eternal love to my husband, Douglas Paul Love, whose late-night editing sessions saved the day. Without him, my life would not be as fabulous as it is.

AUTHOR'S NOTE

This story is based upon research of numerous court files, and numerous interviews with law enforcement officers, witnesses, and other principals. The dialogue that I present is similarly reconstructed from the testimony at trial and other court hearings, as well as by and upon the many interviews that I conducted.

Nobody's memory is perfect, and thus the dialogue in this book is not necessarily direct quotes, but is as faithfully reconstructed as human memory will allow for.

"I favour a low profile and always remember my dad's motto: 'Be more than you seem.' "

Portion of a letter written to the author by Susan Cummings from her cell at the Fauquier County Jail on June 23, 1998

A WOMAN
SCORNED

CHAPTER 1

"NINE-ONE-ONE, WHERE'S YOUR EMERGENCY?" Dispatcher Michael Zeets answered the Sunday morning phone call from the Fauquier County Sheriff's Office Emergency Communications Center.

"Ah, yes, I need. . . . I need to report a . . . a shot man and he's dead," the female caller declared in a calm, even tone.

Zeets noted the contrast between her lyrical French accent and the dispassionate delivery of such grisly information.

"Where at?" The uniformed dispatcher leaned forward in his seat, running his fingers impatiently through his dark blond hair. Glancing at the calendar on the wall, he noted the date was September Seventh.

"He's at Ashland Farm and . . ." The woman paused.

"What's the address?" Zeets strained to decipher what the caller was saying, no easy task given her accent. It was much too early in the morning for this—especially on a Sunday, but the report of a murder was not exactly typical.

"8714 Holtzclaw Road." The woman sounded oddly composed as she gave her location with cool detachment.

"8714 Holtzclaw Road?" Zeets repeated. He checked the clock on the wall, noting it was 8:51 a.m.

Zeets was new on the job and did not recognize the street address. His office was located in the historic Old Town section of Warrenton, nestled in the heart of Virginia's hunt country. He was unfamiliar with many of the little-used gravel roads that wound their way through the quiet farming district outside of town. Most people had no reason to go there unless they were visiting one of the horse country's well-heeled residents. The police were no exception.

Still, even a rookie like Zeets was well aware that families like the Curriers, the du Ponts, the Kennedys, and the Kent Cookes, as well as philanthropist Paul Mellon, owned estates in the gently-rolling foothills of the Blue Ridge Mountains. Mellon, he knew, was the largest land holder in Fauquier County. But it wasn't only old money that had put roots down in what was one of the most exclusive residential areas in the nation.

Relative newcomers included *Washington Post* publisher Donald Graham, as well as some of Hollywood's familiar faces, like actor Robert Duvall, and comedian Dick Smothers, who had come in search of quiet refuge in a pastoral setting.

One name Zeets hadn't heard before was Susan Cummings. It wasn't until days later that he would learn that her father was the wealthy international firearms dealer, and former CIA agent, Samuel Cummings.

"Yes, Ashland Farm." The woman confirmed her address for the dispatcher, never abandoning her eerily calm tone of voice. "And, ah, I spoke to . . . Sergeant Healy about a week ago and . . . and, ah, he knows the man."

Zeets readjusted his large frame in the cushioned armchair, then pushed back the thick frames of his gold-rimmed glasses. He noted the calmness in her voice.

"Okay, what's his name?"

"Ah, Roberto Villegas." She pronounced it "Vijegas," drawing it out dramatically. To Zeets it sounded almost theatrical. "V-i-l-l-e-g-a-s."

The heavy-set dispatcher leaned forward in his chair as she spelled the last name, printing it carefully on the official police form. He was still finding it difficult to understand her continental inflection. As far as he could tell, her accent sounded like a blend of French, German, and British.

"Okay, did you find him or . . . ?"

"He tried to kill me." The voice at the other end of the receiver made the announcement flatly.

"Okay." Zeets made a point of remaining calm. "Did you shoot him?"

"I . . . I had a gun, yes," the woman stammered.

The burly deputy paused for a split second, trying to digest the incredible admission.

"Did you shoot him?" he asked again, aware that one of the department's tape recorders hummed quietly in the background documenting all 911 calls.

"I . . . I need to talk to my lawyer." The female caller stumbled over her words.

"Okay, that's fine. I just . . . he. . . . You say he's dead?" Zeets realized he was barely making sense. That was what came of trying to do two things at once: keeping the caller talking on the line while reaching for a microphone to dispatch police cruisers to the scene.

"He . . . The man is dead," the woman replied.

"Okay." The dispatcher inhaled deeply.

"What's your phone number there, ma'am?"

He quickly jotted down her reply.

"Okay. And what's your name?" Zeets asked, scribbling the information onto a white, lined pad.

"My name is Susan . . . S-u-s-a-n . . . Cummings . . . C-u-m-m-i-n-g-s."

As she spelled it out, Zeets jotted the name next to the telephone number. He noted the strange pronunciation of her name: "Su-ZAHN."

"Okay, ma'am, can you hold on one second? I'll go ahead and send somebody out there."

"Thank . . . Thank you."

Zeets flipped the small black foam mouthpiece of his telephone headset up and away from his mouth, as he reached for the radio. Grabbing the palm-sized microphone from its holder on the console in front of him, he spoke into the radio handset, addressing the patrol units in the field. Then he turned his attention back to Susan Cummings.

"I need . . . I need you to stay on the phone with me though, okay?"

"Okay," she replied.

"Okay, hold on just one second." He switched back to

the radio, and again addressed the deputies in the field.

"Okay, ma'am, where is he located at?"

"He's located in the second kitchen."

"In the second kitchen?" The dispatcher was intrigued.

"Yes." Zeets noticed that the caller offered no further explanation.

"Okay, is anybody else in the house with you or anything?"

"Nobody at this time," she declared in a soft, clear voice.

"Okay, ma'am, I'm also . . . because you say he's dead or whatever . . . I still have to . . . I still have to send an ambulance out there, too, okay?"

"I understand . . . I understand."

"Okay, hold on one second." The wheels of Zeets' chair squeaked along the floor as he reached forward for the mike and radioed to the patrol units cruising the streets of Fauquier County.

"Come in, Unit Twenty-eight," he said in an assured tone. He read the notes he'd made into the gray plastic handset to Sergeant Cuno Andersen, who was motoring along Springs Road just outside of Warrenton. Adjusting the tiny black knob on the switchboard, the dispatcher tuned the radio frequency so he could next communicate with the Warrenton Fire and Rescue Squad, routing an ambulance to the scene.

"Okay, ma'am," he said, returning to Susan Cummings. "Where's your house located on Holtzclaw Road?"

"It's right off 211 going west on Route 681." The caller's voice continued to exhibit the same evenness.

"Okay, how far down is it?" Zeets studied the street map spread out across the top of his desk.

"It's about two and a half miles."

"Two and a half miles?" he echoed, running his index finger along the black line labeled Holtzclaw Road. "Is it on the right-hand side or left-hand side?"

"The left-hand side."

"Okay, hold on one second." Cupping his right palm over the telephone receiver, the baby-faced dispatcher clarified the directions for the patrolmen hunting down the correct estate.

"Ma'am, coming off of uh . . . Springs Road . . ." He was still uncertain about the mansion's exact location and continued to question the caller for more precise details.

"Yes?"

". . . how do you get there from Springs Road? Is it . . . 'cause that's the way the deputies are coming."

"Ah, I think it's ah. . . . I don't know . . . it's called Holtzclaw Road. . . . Holtzclaw. . . . I don't know the . . ."

Zeets sensed that the woman was becoming unnerved by all the confusion over the exact directions.

"Okay, I'll get it. . . . I got it right here on the map. . . . Hold on a sec . . ." Zeets fumbled with the unwieldy street map, meanwhile struggling to keep the woman talking on the line. "Can you tell me, ah . . . has he been over there before or . . . ?"

"He . . . he's here every day." Her voice was almost a whisper.

"Okay. And you've been having problems with him?"

"Yes, I have."

"Okay. Where's the weapon, ma'am?"

"It's . . . it's on the floor in the kitchen."

"Okay. I just wanted to make sure you don't have it when the deputy shows up 'cause you might be a little antsy when he gets there, so you just want to make sure that you don't have it."

"No, it's . . . it's on . . . it's on the floor," she reassured him.

Six minutes had passed since Zeets answered the 911 call to the Fauquier County Sheriff's Office, and deputies were still unsure of where to turn.

"We got the address. . . . Holtzclaw Road . . ." the dispatcher shouted over the mike to Sergeant Andersen.

"Is somebody coming soon?" Susan was beginning to sound impatient.

"Yes, ma'am," he replied politely. "They're coming right now."

"Right."

"But I gotta keep you on the phone 'til they get there."

Even as he spoke, Zeets had already shifted his attention to the deputy out in the field.

"How are you doing ma'am?" Zeets asked the caller, realizing he'd been silent for too long.

"Not very good."

Now he heard distress in her voice. "Okay, we'll have somebody there shortly. They're getting ready to turn on Holtzclaw Road now."

"Thank you very much."

A silence followed. Zeets was about to reassure her again when he heard her say, "Diana. . . . Diana, please come here. Don't go in the kitchen. Roberto is dead. . . . I'm on the phone, please, Diana."

Zeets noticed that she sounded more concerned about the possibility of this woman seeing the dead body than she did about the bloody scene. It occurred to him that this "Diana" might go into the kitchen and contaminate the crime scene.

"Right. Make sure nobody goes into the kitchen," Zeets insisted.

"No . . . my sister just walked in," the caller explained.

"Okay."

"The cops are coming right away, Diana." Zeets could overhear the woman addressing her sister. "Sit down. Sit down."

He was getting worried. His deputies were still struggling to locate the residence—and now he was faced with the prospect of the mysterious Diana entering the kitchen and disturbing the crime scene.

"Make sure nobody goes in there," Zeets cautioned Susan again.

"No . . . nobody . . . nobody," she reassured him calmly.

"Now you say. . . . Is there anybody with your sister or is it just you and your sister now?" Zeets nervously toyed with his ballpoint pen as he tried to assess the situation.

"Just my sister and myself at this time."

"Okay." He held his hand over the receiver as he relayed the woman's address to the patrol officers crawling along Holtzclaw Road in search of the home.

"Ma'am, what was your first name again?" Zeets backtracked to the beginning of his conversation with the caller.

"Susan. . . . S-u-s-a-n."

"Okay."

"Diana . . . don't go in the kitchen." Zeets grew increasingly worried when he heard the caller caution the sister a second time.

"This is Unit Twenty-eight." It was the sergeant in the field radioing Zeets that he had somehow managed to overshoot the house and reached the end of the block. "Ask her if it's a stone house."

"Ma'am, is your house the stone house?" Zeets directed his question to Susan.

"Yes, it is."

"Okay, ma'am, I need you to come out the front door and meet the deputy," Zeets instructed, wondering whether Sergeant Cuno Andersen was about to confront a victim— or a perpetrator.

CHAPTER 2

SERGEANT CUNO ANDERSEN DROVE ALONG HOLTZCLAW Road at a slow crawl, peering out the window until he spotted the white-pillared entranceway of the grand old estate.

Squinting as he approached the two stone columns, he made out the numbers 8714 and 8712 posted in gold near the top of the colonnades. He swung left, then charged up the driveway. As he pressed hard on the gas pedal, a spray of loose pebbles near the bottom of the driveway spit out from beneath the police car's tires.

It was just after 9 a.m. when he steered his police cruiser up the tree-lined approach. Passing a lush thicket of evergreens, silver maples, and bristly green hedges along the windy blacktop driveway, he slowed after a few hundred yards to negotiate the sharp turns of the narrow pathway. As he rounded the bend, he caught sight of the majestic eighteenth-century stone manor perched on top of a gentle rise.

He craned his neck upward, taking it all in. The dignified two-story main house was made of gray stone, with no fewer than four red-brick chimneys rising upward on the sloping slate roof. Atop one section of the house, crowning the wing like a gleaming tiara, was a sparkling white widow's walk that overlooked the 350-acre Ashland Farm. Freshly-painted black shutters with tiny cut-out hearts, a common decorative motif in Virginia horse country, lent a whimsical air to the otherwise stately manor house.

But the main house was just one of a half-dozen buildings

dotting the grassy slopes. An immaculate giant white barn stood to the right, the indoor riding arena with its slanted steel roof visible from the driveway. Several small guest cottages were nestled around the barn. Off to the other side was a small white stable where a handful of horses grazed lazily.

Rough-hewn wooden fences zigzagged across the property demarking separate grazing areas for cows and other farm animals as well as the multitude of sleek thoroughbred horses. An assortment of vehicles—tractors, pickups, and beat-up cars—were parked at odd angles around the farm. Two shiny trucks, one black, one white, were parked outside the mansion.

The estate was the quintessential Virginia horse farm. The craggy fields, the low hedges, even the man-made pond all contributed to the effect of large sums of money spent with enviable casualness.

Sergeant Andersen pulled his cruiser up to the side door of the house, then switched off the ignition. He reached across to the passenger seat and grabbed his ten gallon hat, pressing it firmly on his head as he stepped out of his patrol car. He was vaguely aware of the balmy Indian-summer breeze on his clean-shaven face.

Blue lights whirled on top of the car as he reached back inside, this time through the open driver's-side window. He tugged at the handset of his police radio to contact the Emergency Communications Center one last time.

"I'm outside the house," Andersen told Zeets, who he knew was still on the line with the Cummings woman.

"Ma'am," Zeets said, holding the telephone receiver to his mouth, "I need you to come out the front door and meet the deputy."

"Okay," Susan answered flatly. "I. . . . I'll hang up now."

"Okay, that's fine." Zeets lingered on the line a little longer, listening for confirmation that she had obeyed his instructions. When he heard the dull buzz of a dial tone, he disconnected the call and focused his attention on the other patrol units in the field.

Sergeant Andersen strode confidently up the shrub-lined

path toward the impressive glass-enclosed porch, squinting from the bright sun that reflected off the slate walkway under his feet. Although he was the first deputy to arrive on the scene, he had heard his colleagues on the radio saying that they were already on Holtzclaw Road. He just assumed it was a matter of minutes before they were on the scene to back him up.

Making his way to the front door, he was careful not to disturb the profusion of red and pink flowers that sprouted from the azalea bushes along the walkway. He could hear the faint clatter of the black window shutters gently rattling in the warm breeze. Looking beyond the mansion, he caught sight of a small fence-laced corral where several graceful horses stood alert in their stalls. The animals whinnied, no doubt startled by the flash of police lights.

Climbing the steps leading to the glass foyer, Andersen held his right hand over his holstered 9mm and kept his eyes fixed on the heavy wood-framed door. Even so, he started when all of a sudden it was flung open. An attractive blonde, tall and slender with highlighted hair pulled back into a neat ponytail, stepped out onto the porch.

Though a glass door separated them, the deputy instinctively took a step backward as the woman started to walk toward him.

"Stop," he commanded.

"They're in here," the statuesque woman told him excitedly.

"Who's in here?" the officer asked, confused.

Andersen got no reply, just a blank stare.

"Where is the shooter?" he demanded, watching as the woman began to turn away. It was then that he noticed a shadowy figure behind her.

His hand was instinctively traveling toward his gun when the second woman came clearly into view. She was a brunette, dressed casually in faded Levi's and a crisp white sleeveless turtleneck. Thick locks of her dark wavy hair covered much of her long, bony face.

Andersen studied her striking features: high cheekbones devoid of makeup, wide brown eyes rimmed with dark circles. Aside from her slight build, he quickly concluded that she bore little resemblance to the attractive flaxen-haired woman who stood in front of her.

"Step away from the door," he barked.

As the two women backed away, the officer saw crimson ribbons of blood dripping from the arm of the dark-haired woman. He watched as beads of the fresh liquid oozed from wounds on her left forearm.

"What happened to you?" he demanded abruptly.

The reed-thin brunette stood motionless, not meeting his gaze. Instead, she kept her eyes down, directed at the walkway. She did not say a word.

The deputy studied her angular face, trying to read her blank expression.

"What happened?" the shift supervisor repeated forcefully, looking down the length of his long, chiseled nose. When he got the silent treatment a second time, he turned back to the blonde. She, too, gave no response. She seemed to be staring off at some object far in the distance and it was unclear to the deputy what she had witnessed, if anything. As he waited for an answer, he could feel himself losing patience.

"Turn around," he shouted at Susan. Yanking her arms behind her back, he unsnapped a pair of shiny silver handcuffs from the pouch on his gun-belt. Droplets of blood from the cuts on her left arm fell onto his hands as he clamped the metal restraints around her slender wrists. Deliberately, he wiped his fingers along the back of her Clorox-white T-shirt, leaving smudges of red blood on the ribbed cotton fabric.

"Where's the victim?" The officer directed his question to the trim blonde. Although the 911 caller had already informed Dispatcher Zeets that the victim had been shot and was dead, he realized that the information might be incorrect, and he needed to be sure that the man was not clinging to life and in need of medical attention.

The streaky-haired blonde addressed the deputy. "They're back in here, back in the kitchen," she said in a deep, husky voice, moving back toward the house and motioning him to follow her as she turned right toward the living room.

The deputy had been transferred to the street beat after five years in the Criminal Investigations Division of the sheriff's department, where he had worked narcotics and followed up on suspicious fires. He had extensive training in emergency medicine from his days as a volunteer with the Warrenton Fire and Rescue Squad, and was prepared to administer medical attention to the victim if it was needed.

Following the fair-haired woman into the house, the officer remained right on her heels as she rushed through the salon, which was elegantly, although sparsely, furnished with a few couches and a smattering of antiques. He was taken aback by the large number of cats dozing all over the living room, languorously snuggled in the cushions of the overstuffed chairs.

Sergeant Andersen kept the pace as the first woman hurried through the spacious living room, and into a library, where shelves of books and paintings covered the walls.

While his twenty years as a police officer had exposed him to the lives of the wealthy again and again, and he'd witnessed both their impressive displays of opulence and their unexpected eccentricities, he had never encountered anything quite like this. Despite the home's enormous size, there were no more than a half-dozen pieces of furniture in the maze of rooms he rushed through. In fact, he noted that the only rooms that were furnished in a normal fashion were the library, with its classic, mural-style wallpaper depicting a hunting scene, and the formal dining room, with a long, elegant table and ornate wooden chairs.

Andersen followed the blonde woman into a long hallway and watched as her silky hair fell around her narrow shoulders as she raced along. It was there that he spotted the rows of colorful first-, second-, and third-place ribbons displayed on the walls of the passageway. He assumed, correctly, that hey were trophies won over years of competing in horse shows.

The odd trio made its way deeper into the home, accompanied by the sounds of the metallic jangling of the handcuffs that hung from the brunette's bony wrists. As they went further back, he noted that the rooms became smaller. The deputy was led through a series of dark, alcove-like entryways.

As he followed along, the sudden sound of a soft voice startled him. Realizing it was the handcuffed woman who had begun conversing with her sister in a foreign language, one he did not understand, he halted the exchange.

"Cut it out," the officer demanded. "Speak in English."

There was silence.

Continuing down the lengthy corridor, the three came upon a landing area with two steps that led down to another of the sprawling home's many wings. Without warning, the woman in the lead stopped abruptly in front of the officer and pointed her long, thin finger down the pair of stairs to a second breezeway.

Andersen nodded for her to continue. The rubber soles of his black shoes creaked on the shiny new green-tiled floors as he chased after her down the greenhouse-style enclosure, pausing to quickly check each of the small rooms that led off the corridor to the right. He bent to turn the old-fashioned doorknobs, rotating each as he went. Some of the knobs were loose and felt as if they would fall off in his hand. Other doors were swollen shut and he had to throw his shoulder against them to force them open.

One room, so large it might have been designed to be a ballroom, and distinguished by a lustrous wooden floor, was completely bare. Standing at attention just inside the door of another room was an authentic life-size suit of armor.

Passing a small bedroom, the officer peeked in and then turned his gaze back to the sparkling-clean oversized windows of the breezeway. Stone walls framed the gardens outside. Beyond them, he could see a horse corral where several lithe animals were grazing a grassy field.

As they rushed along, Deputy Andersen realized that the airy tunnel-like hallway connected the gracious main house to a less formal wing with a "mud room" that was used by visitors to wipe their feet and hang their coats, and a laundry room where feminine garments hung from rope clotheslines and bags of kitty litter cluttered the floor.

As they approached the end of the hall, the officer slowed

down, detecting the sound of muffled voices. Reaching for his gun, he started when the blonde woman stopped abruptly, and then moved aside to let him pass her.

Sergeant Andersen slowed his pace even further. His eyes gravitated to a dark-colored semi-automatic pistol that lay on the floor of the narrow corridor just outside a small pantry. The deputy recognized the gun as a Walther P-1, the German-manufactured firearm that was imported into the United States by the company he knew Sam Cummings had founded in the mid-1950s. One empty shell casing was on the ground in close proximity to the weapon, and another lay just beside the door hinge.

Glancing back at the blonde, the sergeant paused momentarily before instructing her to go back outside to retrieve the other deputies. Turning to the one in the handcuffs, he barked an order.

"You sit here." He commanded the waif-like brunette to take a seat on one of the shiny wooden steps that led down into the small sunken kitchen.

Treading lightly in his polished black police shoes, his hand firmly placed on the handgrip of his gun, the officer adopted a tiptoe-like step as he rounded the doorway and descended the two steps into the modest maid's galley, a room no more than nine feet wide.

He involuntarily jumped back when he spotted a dark-haired man lying in a pool of purplish-red blood. The man's face was pressed into the cold wood floor; his eyes were frozen open, and staring. His muscular, jean-clad legs were extended straight out behind him, as if he had fallen forward with a thud. The only sound came from the portable television that sat on the kitchen counter.

The deputy cautiously approached the body as Susan Cummings sat quietly watching from the top of the stairs, limp strands of wavy dark hair falling loosely about her face. He stared down at the man's lifeless body. It was sprawled between two kitchen chairs in a twelve-inch puddle of dark blood that seemed to create a halo around his head. The officer noticed that the fluid had soaked through much of the victim's dark red polo shirt. He also saw that two bullets had ripped through the back of the blood-stained garment, leaving two gaping holes in the cotton fabric.

Climbing back up the two steps to the hallway, the shaken officer turned back to view the narrow room. His eyes darted from left to right as he methodically scanned the rivulets and sprays of blood that were dripping and spattered on the pale-yellow walls, and that had stained the entire mid-section of the pantry door. Lifting his hat from his head, the officer wiped away beads of sweat from his brow and ran his fingers through his stubby light-brown hair as he stared down at Susan.

Again, he descended the steps. Bending down on one knee, he crouched over the motionless figure, pressed two fingers to the victim's carotid artery, and held them there, checking for a pulse. He felt nothing, and moved his fingers slightly, again trying to detect a vibration. As he listened, his gaze traveled upward to the small, country-kitchen table where breakfast plates and a bag of uneaten pastries still cluttered the linoleum tabletop. The window behind the table was open, but no breeze permeated what now felt to him like an airless room.

For Sergeant Andersen, the remains of the morning meal and the voices coming from the tiny television set on the counter provided an eerie backdrop to the grisly discovery. The officer swallowed hard as an unsettling feeling swept over him.

Turning his attention back to the motionless body, he withdrew his fingers from the man's neck, satisfied that there was no pulse. He rose to his feet and slowly backed out of the cramped six-by-eight-room, taking care not to disturb any of the evidence. The spongy soles of his size-eleven shoes made swishing sounds on the glossy parquet floor as he climbed back up the steps to the hallway and positioned himself at a vantage point that allowed him to watch Susan and also keep an eye on the body.

All of a sudden, he heard voices coming from the other end of the hall. He glanced up to see Deputy Jim Tulley running in his direction. The well-built, dark-haired officer was being led there by Diana Cummings.

"Take her outside," he ordered Tulley, pointing at Susan.

"Yes, sir," the deputy responded, grabbing Susan by the arm and pulling her to her feet. Sergeant Andersen watched as the young officer escorted the shackled woman and her out-of-breath sister back through the maze of rooms.

"Call for a medic!" Andersen yelled after his colleague.

As Tulley stepped out onto the walkway, a third sheriff's car pulled up to the house, its whirling blue police lights adding a theatrical touch to the unfolding drama.

Deputy Tulley waved to his colleague Shawn Walters as he walked the sisters to the edge of the lawn where his vehicle was parked. An early September breeze wafted across Ashland Farm as Tulley grabbed the radio handset and communicated with Dispatcher Zeets, telling him to send emergency medical personnel to the scene.

"Right," Zeets confirmed the request.

"This is communications, you are requested to move up to the house," Zeets now radioed the volunteer emergency medical team that had been ordered to "stage" at the corner of Holtzclaw Road and Route 211 and wait for further instructions.

"Okay," said Chief William Grimsley, who sat idly behind the wheel, watching the house from the driver's seat of his ambulance.

As the medic pulled away from the corner, Deputy Walters parked his police cruiser along the edge of the driveway of Ashland Farm. It was a little after nine when the compactly-built officer jumped out of his vehicle. Rays of warm morning sunlight reflected off the shiny badge that was pinned over his left shirt pocket. He glanced at the two women standing together on a grassy patch of lawn in front of the house.

He reached inside the glove box to grab the black rope handle of his Polaroid 600 series. As he checked the camera for film, an ambulance motored up the driveway and stopped alongside Walters' police cruiser. The officer waved to the ambulance driver and then dashed off toward the house.

"Sergeant Andersen!" he shouted in a piercing voice as he hastened down the long, tiled passageway.

"I'm down here!" Andersen yelled back.

Walters followed the sergeant's voice, continuing through the maze of rooms until he spotted the barrel-chested police officer through the floor-to-ceiling windowpanes of the second hallway.

"Bring your camera in here and start taking pictures," Andersen stood leaning against the wall outside the tiny pantry, his arms folded across his chest.

"Yes, sir." The wiry officer raised his hand in salute and acknowledged his order.

Andersen watched as Deputy Walters photographed the weapon that lay on the floor at the bottom of the three stairs near the doorway that led to the kitchen, and the two empty shell casings that lay just beside it.

"Take a picture of the victim," Andersen instructed the deputy, nodding toward the doorway of the tiny room. His watch read 9:07 a.m.

Clutching his camera, Walters followed his superior into the cramped quarters. His jaw tightened when he spotted the dead man lying on the floor with the ring of blood around his head. Pressing his right eye against the viewfinder, the deputy documented on film the top of the man's scalp, which was pressed up against a corner of the wall, his face turned to the left. The shutter clicked again and again as Walters snapped a series of pictures that recorded the position of the man's body. The deputy focused the camera to show that the victim's left arm was down by his side, and his right arm was bent at the elbow and tucked underneath his broad chest.

Each time the dark-haired officer clicked the black button of his camera, a date was recorded in the lower left-hand corner of the photo. It was the wrong date—September 6— but it would serve to help police differentiate the photos taken by Walters from those that would be snapped later in the day by Investigator Michael Lamper.

At Sergeant Andersen's direction, Walters took at least a dozen pictures. Even so, he did not photograph the two empty shell cases that lay on the floor of the breakfast room, a point that Susan's defense attorney would harp on at the trial.

As he completed the roll of film, Warrenton Rescue Chief William Grimsley, Jr., was outside grabbing an emergency first-aid kit and an oxygen tank from his white truck.

Chief Grimsley was the first medic to arrive on the scene. He had been to countless rescue calls during his twenty-two years of service. Three years earlier, the officer, who liked to be called "Butch" was promoted to chief of Warrenton's southern end.

Clutching the first-aid equipment under his arm, the volunteer rescue worker hurried up the path that led to the front door, nodding to Deputy Tulley and the blonde woman who stood there as he ran by. She pointed toward the living room as he brushed lightly past her.

Once inside the sprawling house, the medical technician roamed the first floor, not sure where the victim lay.

"Hello?" he shouted as he wandered through the library, hoping the deputy inside would point him in the right direction.

"This way!" an officer called back from the rear of the home.

"Keep talking!" the medic yelled back.

"Keep coming this way!" Andersen was guiding his old pal to the bloody kitchen as Sergeant Walters continued to record the crime scene. The sergeant recognized Butch Grimsley's voice from the years they had worked together on the town's emergency rescue squad. He was relieved that the chief would be making the D.O.A. call.

"Take a picture of the gun." Sergeant Andersen turned his attention back to Deputy Walters, who was nervously photographing the grisly murder scene.

Straddling the pistol between his legs, the deputy clicked off several shots of the weapon before Sergeant Andersen reached down and locked the pistol so it could not be fired anymore. As he pulled on the metal safety slide, the gun released no bullets. He knew that meant the firing chamber had been emptied.

Meanwhile, Grimsley was descending the small staircase that led to the service quarters.

"Hey, Butch." Andersen raised his head to greet his former colleague.

"Ugh!" the medic grunted as he fell forward after catching his foot on the edge of a loose piece of the parquet floor. The disengaged wood chip jutted up from the floor just outside the doorway where the menacing black pistol lay in plain view.

"I've already checked his pulse," Andersen told the paramedic. "Just call it from the door."

During his twenty years in law enforcement, Andersen had been to many crime scenes and was only too aware that key evidence could be contaminated if too many police personnel entered the scene. The sergeant did not want Grimsley to enter the room and disturb any of the evidence. It was clear to him that the victim was dead, and he saw no reason for the medic to check the body again.

Following the sergeant's orders, Grimsley positioned himself at the edge of the doorway. The chief medic, whose face was characterized by broad features and chiseled cheekbones, leaned his muscular torso into the room to get a better view of the dead man. He grimaced as he peered down at the circle of blood around the victim's head.

A commotion coming from the kitchen drew his attention to the small TV at the opposite end of the room, which was blaring a commercial advertisement. Scanning the counter, the rescue chief spotted an empty leather knife sheath resting on the linoleum to the left of the double sink. Lowering his gaze, his eyes fixed on the gaping bullet holes that had penetrated the wall just next to the pantry door, and the two gaping puncture marks in the victim's blood-soaked shirt.

As part of the police record, Grimsley would draw a bare-bones sketch of the crime scene that afternoon, and another more detailed drawing—that differed from the ones made by the sheriff's deputies on the scene—three days later. His diagrams would later become a subject of debate at the trial of Susan Cummings when her lawyers would argue that police had altered the evidence.

CHAPTER 3

DEPUTY WALTERS STATIONED HIMSELF IN THE FOYER ADjacent to the side door of the house. It was the door that Susan and her sister routinely used to enter and leave. The officer flipped open the front cover of his notebook to begin the painstaking process of recording the names of everyone who entered and left the home. Keeping this all-important crime scene log is a standard part of all murder investigations, and Walters, eager to be as meticulous as possible, intended to follow departmental procedure to the letter.

Roberto's limp, lifeless body remained untouched, lying on the kitchen floor between two white, rail-back chairs. Both Sergeant Andersen and Chief Grimsley were finishing up the unpleasant task of pronouncing the victim dead.

Outside the mansion, the sun was heating up the blacktop driveway where Deputy Jim Tulley stood next to his police car. He was charged with guarding Susan Cummings, who was locked in the back seat. He took notice of the kaleidoscope of wildflowers—black-eyed Susans, phlox, bull thistles, and small red morning-glories—as he waited for further instructions.

Deputy Jim Jones ambled over to join his colleague on the driveway. With his neatly-combed mustache and slight but well-toned build, Jim Jones resembled Dennis Weaver.

Jones, a handsome deputy with close to two decades of police experience, had just arrived. He had already been inside to peruse the crime scene and had returned to the driveway on orders from Sergeant Andersen to photograph Susan's injuries.

Jones flung open the door to his police cruiser and pulled out his camera. A pudgy gray cat scurried between his legs as he ambled back over to the driveway where Susan and her sister were now standing. In fact, Jones had been dodging cats ever since he'd gotten there. They were all over the place. He could swear he'd already spotted at least a dozen.

Ambling over to Susan, the deputy raised his camera and instructed the still-bleeding woman to turn to the side so he could capture her wounds on film. Her wrists were still shackled when he focused his lens on her slender arms and clicked off a series of pictures of her injuries. The officer was glad that his subject was wearing a sleeveless tank top; the shirt made it easier for him to document her lacerations.

As Jones moved the camera closer to chronicle the cuts from a different angle, he could hear the crunch of footsteps on the pebbly gravel behind him.

A young medic placed his equipment on the ground and waited for the officer to complete his photos. Chance Kimbel's navy blue rescue uniform differentiated him from the sheriff's officers, who were clad in the county's official tan slacks and brown shirts.

Kimbel studied Susan's arm as she obediently posed for the camera. He had joined the Warrenton Fire and Rescue Squad when he was only fifteen years old. During his seven years on the job, he had seen his fair share of mortal injuries. Hers appeared minor.

Deputy Tulley tugged on a branch of a bristly evergreen bush as he stood watching Kimbel remove several pieces of gauze and a jar of sterile water from his medical bag.

"Okay, I'm done. You can clean her up," the camera-wielding Jones declared, turning to the emergency medical technician who was crouched on the grass beside him setting up his supplies.

Kimbel looked up from his first-aid kit and nodded to the deputy. Sliding his satchel nearer to Susan, the rescue worker grabbed a moist pad and began wiping the blood that had dried in thin lines along his patient's upper arm. As he removed the caked-on clumps of darkish red scabs that had begun to form along her forearm, more than a dozen slash marks became visible.

Chance counted at least five scrapes on her upper shoulder, and more than ten on her mid-arm. He noted that his patient hardly flinched as he rubbed the wet gauze pads on the thin cuts that ran from the top of her arm to just above her elbow.

"Do you have any other injuries?" Chance Kimbel inquired in a concerned tone, parting his lips to reveal an innocent, boyish grin.

"No," Susan answered.

"Are there any other areas that need to be treated?" Kimbel asked one more time.

"No," the woman repeated her response, never once mentioning the thin scrapes that would appear on her face the following day.

The next evening, Susan would visit a local doctor, who would observe the lacerations that crisscrossed each other just under her eye to form an almost crucifix-like shape on her right cheek.

Her lawyer would later say that he'd noticed the cuts when he met with her at the adult detention center on the afternoon of the shooting. Police would point to the mug shot that had been taken several hours after that meeting and argue that it revealed no facial lacerations.

Chance Kimbel knelt on the grass and packed away his first-aid supplies. He saw no need for further treatment. In his opinion the lacerations did not even require bandaging.

Grabbing his camera for a second time, Deputy Jones moved forward and fired off another round of photos, this time of Susan's freshly-washed wounds. He didn't even have to focus—the camera was automatic. Positioning the 130-pound heiress so that she faced away from the house, the officer snapped more pictures of her treated injuries.

As Jones snapped away, the front door of the mansion unexpectedly flew open. Out of the corner of his eye, he saw Sergeant Andersen barrel out of the house and on to the walkway, holding onto the brim of his hat as he dashed past

Jones and headed toward his police car. He quickly glanced back at the two Cummings sisters to ascertain their location before continuing on his way.

The sun's rays glinted off the authoritative gold star emblazoned on the side door of Andersen's police car as he radioed communications officers manning the switchboard on West Lee Street, and detailed the situation. Resting his foot on the car's steel doorframe, he kept his eyes fixed on the murder suspect as he spoke into the handset.

Deputy Tulley ambled over to the sergeant's police car, and whispered to him that Susan Cummings had just asked to speak to Sergeant Gary Healy, the head of the Criminal Investigations Division.

"Okay," Andersen nodded, wondering how the heiress knew Sergeant Healy. Turning his attention back to the dispatcher, he asked that his superior officers be notified and requested that a medical examiner be sent to collect the body of Roberto Cerillio Villegas.

CHAPTER 4

As uniformed deputies unfurled the bright-yellow plastic crime-scene tape and began draping it around the perimeter of the main house, the telephone was ringing at the residence of Sergeant Gary Healy.

The head of the major crimes unit for the Criminal Investigations Division never expected to be contacted—he wasn't on call—and it was Sunday morning, a time when the county was usually at its quietest.

"There's been a shooting at Ashland Farm," the dispatcher told Healy.

"Who's been shot?" the sergeant asked. He was not surprised when he heard the dispatcher's answer.

"A man, Roberto Villegas," Zeets told him. "Sergeant Andersen instructed me to contact you, sir. He's at the scene."

It was police protocol to alert the sergeant in charge of the Criminal Investigations Division whenever a felony offense was committed in the county. But there was another reason that Healy was being called to this murder scene.

"Sergeant Andersen said the shooter is requesting to speak with you, sir." The dispatcher waited as Sergeant Healy grabbed a pen to take down directions to the estate.

Climbing into his car, the veteran law-enforcement officer remembered back to his closed-door meeting with Susan Cummings just two weeks before.

*   *   *

Sergeant Healy had been sorting through his case files when the secretary buzzed him, telling him that there were two women to see him about a domestic matter. Rising from his chair, he ambled down the carpeted hallway to the waiting area of the Criminal Investigations Division. There, he found Miss Cummings and a second woman standing near the copy machine. Showing them to one of the interview rooms at the rear of the office complex, he maintained a friendly demeanor as they made themselves comfortable in two of the wooden chairs placed around the small table in the center of the room.

The investigator was proud of the immaculate new office space that he and his colleagues had taken over earlier that year. It had come as a surprise when Sheriff Higgs announced that he had allocated the comfortable upstairs offices to his division.

As soon as the sheriff learned that the county's personnel department was planning to vacate the upstairs space and move to another building, he made the announcement that he would allot the desirable space to his most senior men. In addition to providing private offices for the lead investigators, the sheriff saw to it that badly-needed new additions were made: a fully-equipped, state-of-the-art forensics laboratory, several more interview rooms, and a small line-up room where suspects were routinely brought to be scrutinized by crime victims.

As he opened the cover of his notepad, Healy offered the two women coffee. Adjusting his ample frame in the hard-backed chair, he jotted down the date—August 20—at the top of his notepaper. Then, he listened as the older woman began to speak. She introduced herself as Jane Rowe, and her friend as Susan Cummings. Jane explained that she was employed as a nurse at a nursing home in the nearby town of Marshall, and that Susan lived at Ashland Farm. The two had become friends through their association with the game of polo. They were there, Jane said, to file a complaint with the sheriff's office.

Sergeant Healy fixed his attention on the pleasant fortyish woman as she crossed her legs, repositioned her body in the straight-back chair, and began to chronicle Susan's troubles. She seemed sincere in her concern for her friend, and it was clear to the investigator that she believed that she was doing the right thing by coming down to the police station to provide Susan with moral support in her time of need.

"I've come here with Susan today because she is in fear of her life," Jane told the officer. "This guy Roberto Villegas has been abusive to her, and he says he will kill her before he'll lose her."

Clearing her throat, she launched into a lengthy story. In a firm, confident voice, she spent nearly five minutes recounting for the investigator how Susan had confided in her at a polo party in late July.

As Healy took notes, she told the investigator how this year's mid-summer polo bash was held at the home of Steve Seager, a prominent veterinarian and the Great Meadow Polo Club's veterinary advisor. Dr. Seager's nineteen-year-old son, Adair, had been playing polo since the eighth grade and was a member of the intercollegiate polo team at Texas A&M. His young daughter, Fiona, just fifteen, had also joined the Great Meadow team.

The Irish-born veterinarian and his blonde wife Doris had recently moved to The Plains and, as a gesture of southern hospitality, had offered their home to club members for the annual outdoor social event and barbecue. It was there that Susan told Jane that her Argentine boyfriend, Roberto Villegas, had been berating her with abusive language and spewing terrifying verbal threats of bodily harm, even murder.

Sergeant Healy took a long sip of his now-lukewarm coffee and fixed his gaze on the heavy-set, bleached-blonde Rowe as she explained that Susan had joined a group who had gathered under one of the colorful striped awnings in the house's rear yard to enjoy the delicious spread of food and cocktails being served. Roberto, she said, was off mingling with other guests.

Jane Rowe's eyes grew narrow and her tone breathless as she recalled her reaction to seeing Susan standing alone beneath the tent. Not only did she hold herself apart from the rest of the jovial party guests; the expression on her face was incongruously distraught.

Jane pointedly walked over, determined to find out what was wrong. She reported that when she expressed concern, Susan, who usually said little about her personal affairs, burst into tears.

She said the heiress admitted to her, as well as to a few of the other women who were standing nearby, that things were not only reaching a crisis point in her relationship with Roberto, but that she was afraid of what he might do. She said that Susan told her that she was trying to end her affair with the Argentine polo star but that Roberto had been intimidating her with threats.

As the party-goers looked on in surprise, Susan had tearfully confessed that she was not sure how to handle the situation.

As Healy listened to Rowe's recollections, he shifted his glance to Susan. He sensed that something wasn't right. In the first place, it struck him as odd that Susan herself remained silent during Jane's long discourse. Second, he noted that something about her demeanor didn't add up.

Healy had been a law-enforcement officer for nearly three decades. He had begun his career as an officer on the U.S. Park Police in Washington, D.C., then after two and a half years, moved to the large suburban Fairfax police force. Until 1993, when he formally retired, he investigated major crimes like robberies and homicides in the considerably more populated suburban area. He had conducted countless interrogations during his twenty-seven years on the force, delving into a wide range of complicated crimes. Even after his official retirement, when he tried his hand at the sporting goods business, he found that he missed the challenge and excitement of solving crimes. After a short stint as a uniformed officer in the patrol division of the Fauquier Sheriff's Office, he learned that a position had opened up in the Criminal Investigations Division, and jumped to grab it. He had risen quickly to the position of Sergeant of Major Crimes, overseeing the other ten investigators in the division.

The forty-nine-year-old detective had earned himself the

nickname "the Green Folder Fairy" because of the color-coded filing system he implemented as a way of sorting the never-ending stream of incident reports that landed on his desk each week. Green was the color designated for burglary and larceny cases. Every Tuesday, he tossed dozens of incident reports on the desks of the other detectives, adding additional cases to their already burdensome inventory.

There were invariably more green folders than any other color. The previous year, for example, the tally of 217 burglaries and 450 larcenies far outnumbered any other single category of crime. Even though in recent months, rapes and murders were climbing, the nickname stuck.

Through his almost three decades of experience, Healy had learned to pick up on subtle clues, and during his meeting with Susan and Jane, his instincts were telling him to proceed with caution. If Susan Cummings is the one who's being threatened, why is she not speaking on her own behalf? he wondered.

"Excuse me, ma'am," Healy interrupted Jane Rowe politely. Like all the other members of this Southern police force, he was in the habit of addressing everyone he spoke to with an almost chivalrous courteousness that his counterparts in other sections of the country might find quaint. "I really need to hear from Miss Cummings herself in order to properly assess the situation."

He directed his focus on Susan. She was perched on the edge of her chair, giving the impression that she was as fragile as a small bird. Yet, while she was slender, she was also tall, at five-feet, seven-inches. It was her fine bone structure that made her appear delicate. Her skin contributed to that look; her face had a waxen quality that struck Healy as almost doll-like. Her thick, dark, wavy hair was disheveled, pushed behind her ears but occasionally falling over one eye.

Healy suspected that there was more to her than what was on the surface. He sensed that while she tried to appear guileless she was actually quite cunning. He was equally suspicious of her move to enlist the aid of someone like Jane, who seemed pliable to him.

Susan sat up straight in her chair. With her head tilted

slightly to one side, she glanced at Sergeant Healy momentarily, then turned her eyes to an imaginary point just beyond the officer.

Speaking in a low voice, her pronunciation colored by a heavy European accent, she began to recount the details of her affair with Roberto Villegas, who was a member of the polo team she owned. She said they had been seeing each other for about two years.

Jane continually interrupted, taking on the role of interpreter as if Susan were incapable of expressing herself in English. Susan, too, seemed to play into that role, hesitating and searching for words and sometimes acting as if she hadn't understood something Healy had said.

The heiress related that Roberto had been physically abusive to her on at least one occasion and that he had threatened to kill her if she should ever try to leave him.

Healy observed that while Susan appeared concerned on the surface, her presentation of what should have been extremely painful incidents seemed oddly forced, as if she were putting on an artful performance for the investigator's benefit.

He also puzzled over the absence of a security system on Susan's property. With all of her wealth, she was perfectly able to hire security guards—or even a personal body guard if she truly felt it was warranted.

"His words are, 'I will put a bullet through your head and hang you upside down to let the blood pour on your bed,'" Susan continued in the same soft, accented voice that Healy had to strain to hear. "Drowning me has also been mentioned several times."

The investigator paused to think about what he had just been told. It sounded to him as though Susan was describing a love affair between an employee and herself that was not going the way that she had hoped. Either she had tired of him, he thought, or, a more likely possibility, Villegas was tiring of her. Perhaps the polo pro had even gone so far as to find another woman and Susan was reacting like a woman scorned.

Sergeant Healy nodded in acknowledgment as he jotted

down some notes on his lined writing tablet. He glanced at his watch and saw that forty-five minutes had passed.

"Let's go see a magistrate right now," the sergeant advised Susan, slapping his hands on the top of the table and rising to his feet. "Because he's already assaulted you once, we can get you a restraining order."

Her reaction surprised him.

"No," she said crisply. "I don't want to do that."

Sergeant Healy wondered how hard to press her. He had expected a woman in her situation to respond favorably to the opportunity to protect herself from the possibility of another assault. Yet, it was clear from the expression on her face that the recommendation made her uncomfortable.

"It's not that complicated," he explained, wondering if that was what was standing in her way. "All you have to do is go with me or another deputy before a magistrate and explain that he assaulted you. The judge signs the order immediately."

"No, no," she insisted.

"All right then, here's something that doesn't involve you directly," the investigator suggested. "You can fill out a trespass notice. Somebody from the sheriff's office takes it to the judge and we can serve it on him without you being involved at all."

Healy explained that once the notice was filed in the court, she could post a "No Trespassing" sign outside the estate. If Roberto Villegas ever stepped onto her property, all she would have to do was dial 911 and deputies would already be authorized to arrest him on the spot for violating the notice.

Once again, Susan refused.

Sergeant Healy hesitated. He would never have expected a woman in this situation to be so resistant to taking action. He found himself wondering why she had even bothered to report her concerns to the police in the first place.

Once again Jane Rowe stepped in as Susan's spokesperson.

"Isn't there something else that can be done to get him out of her life?" she asked in exasperation.

Jane glanced at Susan as if waiting for her cue. "We know that Roberto Villegas is wanted in several other parts of the country for other crimes. Can't you just check it out?"

Sergeant Healy blinked in disbelief, but said nothing.

When he hesitated, she pressed him. "Couldn't you get him on one of the other warrants out for his arrest?"

"All right," he drawled. "Let's see what we can find."

Healy stood up slowly, looking from Susan to Jane and back to Susan. It wasn't at all customary to check on somebody's past offenses based on some arbitrary request, but he was already involved in the case and would at some point be required to make inquiries into Villegas' past. Besides, he was curious about the real story behind Roberto Villegas. If the polo-playing playboy really was the monster that Susan and Jane were saying he was, the computer should tell him soon enough.

The sergeant walked down the carpeted hallway to the area where the nationally-linked crime-data computer was set up while Susan and Jane waited in the interrogation room. He was still plagued with the feeling that something was very wrong here. Punching in the letters of Roberto Villegas' name, he waited, his eyes fixed on the computer screen as the machine scanned the endless list of criminals from all around the country.

The words popped up on the screen. "No hits found."

It took a few seconds for their meaning to register. Then Healy's mind began clicking away. Susan and Jane had acted certain that Villegas had a criminal record. They insisted that he had a history of abusive behavior—and a rap sheet to back it up. Yet his name was coming up clean. Why? As he walked back down the hallway, he was overcome with a feeling that there was a game being played here.

"Nothing's coming up," Sergeant Healy reported, watching their faces closely.

He saw the two women exchange surprised glances.

While he wanted to believe what was being told to him, it was becoming more and more difficult to ignore the uneasy feeling he was getting from the interplay of the two women who sat before him. His conviction would have been even stronger if he had known that Susan had already tried to rid herself of the polo player in an even more drastic way: she had tried to get him deported. She had used her connections to look into Roberto's immigration papers with the express intent of trying to send him back to Argentina.

By this point Susan wasn't the only one who wanted documentation of this meeting. Sergeant Healy felt strongly that a report needed to be filed and kept in the active police records in case there was a follow-up incident.

"I'd like you to make a statement for the record," Sergeant Healy told Susan firmly.

Sneaking a glance at Jane, the dark-haired heiress agreed.

Healy handed her the standard police complaint form, a one-page questionnaire. On the front were spaces for basic information, including name, address, Social Security number, and occupation.

Susan listed her job as "horsewoman," and then went on to complete the rest of the form. In her neat, cursive handwriting, she detailed her experiences with Roberto:

Roberto Cerillio Villegas is the man I have been dating since Spring of 1995. Within the last six months, he has began [sic] to show signs of aggression towards me. With threats to kill me. His words are "I will put a bullet through your head and hang you upside down to let the blood pour on your bed." This is only one example of such strong destructive language. Drowning me was also mentionned [sic] several times and it seems this is becoming a daily discussion. These various threats always follow after a very minor disagreement on my part. For example, I will say I do not have time for you Roberto have I [sic] lot of work to do. He always react [sic] negatively to my demands or personal wishes. He is overpowering, short-fused, non tolerant, changes his moods quickly and admits that [sic] is "the crazy type." He insists on marrying me and wants two children because he says "The world needs more people such as himself to teach everybody a lesson (What lesson I do not know?) [sic] His words are also, "I will show you and these little

Rednecks over here what a real man is. I will teach them who is the boss and after you go Susan I will kill a few cops and the Rednecks before I put a bullet in my head.

Unrelated to any incident involving myself he mentioned he had shown aggressive behavior towards a bystander in the state of Florida. There in a shopping mall, he had just parked his truck next to another car and when he oppened [sic] his door he slightly struck the door of the other vehicle. The owner of the car involved happened to be in the car and stepped out and remarked to Roberto about the minor damage. Roberto, quickly after responding to the man using fowl [sic] language, took his black flashlight and violently struck the man, knocking him unconscious. Roberto said I left without looking back·and went about my business as usual.

Roberto Cerillio Villegas as far as I know is struck with a mental condition, one that can be very dangerous for the people surrounding him at a critical moment. I have offered to let him go not to be involved with me anymore. I have tried to be his friend and understand him. He refuses to let go. The game of polo is what associated us.*

The sound of a car horn startled the investigator and forced him to stop thinking about Susan's visit to his office two weeks before. He was already approaching the Cummings estate and he'd know soon enough why Susan wanted to talk to him.

Route 211 was quiet as it always was on Sunday morning. Sergeant Healy braked and turned left onto Holtzclaw Road. He took another quick left which put him on the driveway leading to the main house of Ashland Farm. The narrow path was already lined with marked police cars and rescue vehicles.

He noted that, despite all the traffic, there were no other unmarked police cars, meaning that he was the first investi-

*Susan Cummings' statement to Police Sergeant Gary Healy of the Fauquier County Sheriff's Office on August 20, 1997.

gator to arrive on the scene. His well-trained eyes evaluated the activity that was going on outside the manor. He'd never actually been on the Cummings property before and was taken aback by the vastness of the young heiress's estate.

Lights flashed from the tops of the three patrol cars, and the radios squawked with the dispatcher's voice fading in and out among the static. Several uniformed officers stood conversing on the driveway.

Healy spotted Susan Cummings seated in the back of a police cruiser. A second woman, a blonde, stood next to the car.

As he turned off the car's ignition, he noticed Deputy Tulley standing at the edge of the lawn, authoritatively guarding the two women. He was just getting out of his car when one of the officers walked over to him.

"Susan says she wants to talk to you," the deputy informed him. Healy eyed her across the lawn. After their bizarre meeting two weeks earlier, he didn't know what to expect.

As he made his way across the driveway, the sergeant noted the impeccably-maintained gardens, mature shrubs, and century-old trees that surrounded the mansion. He could see that Susan had stepped out of the police car, and was waiting for him on the driveway.

It wasn't until he was just a few feet away from her that he noticed the scratches on her left arm. Whatever suspicions had been lurking in the back of his mind suddenly crystallized the instant he laid eyes on the bleeding scrapes. A multitude of thin red bands ran down the pale, tender flesh of her left inner arm, beginning at her shoulder and extending only as far as the crook of her elbow. They were in groupings of twos and threes and were of equal length and depth.

While Healy overheard someone comment that she was claiming that Roberto had tried to kill her, his impression was that these surface slashes were not consistent with the defense wounds he was used to seeing when someone had been attacked. Instead, they appeared to be superficial cuts so shallow that they could well have been made by brushing against a rosebush. In fact, he was surprised that they were bleeding at all, and suspected that she had squeezed them in order to keep the blood flowing for the officers' benefit. Had they really been inflicted in the way she was claiming, they would have been deeper.

To him, it looked as if the wounds had been self-inflicted. Not only were they uniform in length, they were all perfectly parallel. Their positioning also made them suspect. Healy knew defense wounds would have been jagged and irregular, the result of having reflexively jerked away from her attacker.

"Mr. Healy, I'd like to talk with you." Susan addressed him in the same soft, calm voice that he'd heard during their meeting at the police station. "I feel I can trust you, but I'd like to talk to my attorney first."

Healy knew perfectly well that as soon as she had mentioned her attorney, his hands were tied. He would now need a search warrant to take the investigation further. Without one he was not allowed to question her or search the premises. While getting one was not difficult, it still meant that he had to go back to the police station and fill out the necessary paperwork, then contact the judge who was on call to obtain the required signature.

He was, however, allowed to survey the crime scene. Walking purposefully toward the house, Healy greeted Walters, who was still keeping the crime-scene log at the front door. The investigator followed the deputy's directions into the living room and through the long corridor to the servants' quarters.

He found Roberto's body lying lifeless in the corner of the small kitchen. It looked as though he had been seated at the kitchen table when he was shot because of the position of the corpse. His legs were stretched out underneath the table, and it looked to Healy as though the victim had fallen right out of the chair.

After studying the body for a few seconds, he scanned the room with a cold, purposeful eye, looking for clues that would tell him something of the events that had preceded the shooting. His eyes traveled to the mound of chewed breakfast roll that sat between the edge of the table and the

plate. The plate itself was empty, but there were flakes of
pastry scattered about the top of the table. Healy surmised
that the regurgitated mass that lay at the edge of the table,
just in front of the victim's plate, was the final mouthful of
the croissant that Roberto had been munching on when the
bullet struck.

Three placemats from the arms manufacturer, Rossi,
nearly covered the surface of the table. And a magazine lay
open just in front of Roberto's plate. From the way the pe-
riodical was positioned, it appeared as though the polo player
had been reading from it when Susan had entered the room.

My God, Healy thought, Susan Cummings used the sheriff's office to try and cover her tracks. She killed this guy.

The sergeant shook his head, wondering if the Argentine
polo player had had any idea what he was getting himself
into the first time he met Susan Cummings.

CHAPTER 5

SPARKS FLEW THE FIRST TIME SUSAN LAID EYES ON THE dashing Argentine polo star. She spotted the darkly-handsome sportsman in the dusty polo arena while taking a polo lesson at Great Meadows, a sprawling equestrian center in the town known as The Plains, a few miles from her rambling horse farm.

Class was already underway, but she was having trouble focusing on the day's lesson. She couldn't stop herself from staring at the man galloping by on his dark-brown pony. He wasn't like the other men she routinely saw around Great Meadows. His thick black hair, his liquid brown eyes, his wide toothy grin, suggested an earthy sensuality rarely exhibited by the upper-crust element who usually frequented such places. She felt an immediate attraction and wondered who he was.

As he made contact with the heavy ball, she watched his hips rise up from the saddle, and the heels of his hand-tooled, Western-style boots press down in the stirrups. The fabric of his sexy, skin-tight riding pants was stretched taut outlining every contour of his lower body.

The thwack of the stick against the white ball and the sounds of hoofs thumping on the firmly-packed earth beneath him added to his image as a skilled horseman.

Glancing around the corral, she realized that, while the dark-haired man was one of several sportsmen practicing in the 150-by-300-foot playing field, he was the only one who had a crowd of spectators gathered along the fence watching him ride.

Whack! Susan glanced up with a start. Embarrassed that she failed to return the polo ball that one of the other students had just sent flying in her direction, she realized that at least for now she had better concentrate on the class.

Her initial interest in polo was sparked one June morning in 1994. She was sipping tea at a tiny table in the small maid's galley that she preferred to her home's more expansive main kitchen, and idly leafing through the local paper, when her eyes were suddenly drawn to an advertisement about the upcoming polo season. She scanned it at first, then put down her cup and focused her attention on the blurb.

One line in particular caught her attention. According to the ad, the nearby Willow Run Polo School, just a few miles from her home, offered lessons.

"Hmm, polo would be very interesting," she thought, raising her cup again.

That very morning, she jumped into her black Toyota Turbo and sped to the rustic riding center to sign up for lessons. She was bored with the traditional horsy activities of the local hunt country set, the dressage and point-to-points, just as she had tired of so many of the other activities she had dabbled in since graduating from college fourteen years before. Although she'd earned a bachelor's degree in the arts and humanities at Mount Vernon College, the private, all-girl college she'd attended in Washington, D.C., her real interest was in caring for animals—especially horses.

While she was a proficient rider and often accompanied her sister to the local foxhunts that Jacqueline Bouvier Kennedy had participated in and made famous years before, they were becoming routine. Even the prestigious and more demanding hunters' and jumpers' competitions, with all their pomp and pageantry, had lost their glow.

Susan yearned for something more exciting to fill her long, empty days.

And there was something else that contributed to her restlessness. Even though she had lived among the moneyed members of the Virginia hunt circle for close to a decade and a half, she never really fit in with the aristocratic crowd. Perhaps it was because she hadn't been born in Virginia as so many of her set were. Her beginnings were much more exotic and international.

Susan and her twin sister Diana were born on July 21, 1962, in southern France, to billionaire Sam Cummings and his Swiss bride, Irmgard Blaettler. The fact that Susan was the daughter of the largest private arms merchant in the world was ultimately to affect every aspect of her life.

The one-time CIA agent had made millions buying and reselling surplus weaponry, first for the U.S. government, and later for his own company, Interarms, which he founded in 1953.

His career as an international firearms dealer made him one of the richest men in the world. At the high point of his career, Sam Cummings' company controlled more than ninety percent of the world's private trade in guns and reported gross annual sales of $100 million. The arms merchant operated his business from bureaus in Virginia, England, Denmark, South Africa, and Austria, and he stored his supplies in depots in England and the United States. At one time, he had more than 700,000 weapons, enough to supply a small armored division, stockpiled in a complex of converted tobacco warehouses that he owned along the banks of the Potomac River in Alexandria, Virginia.

Cummings' good fortune allowed him to provide for his wife and twin daughters on a grand and luxurious scale, quite unlike what he'd experienced during his own childhood. Sam was born in Philadelphia on February 7, 1927, to Samuel and Lilla Cummings. Sam's father had inherited a fortune from his own father, Samuel George, who struck it rich selling bottled mineral water to the rapidly-growing population of the expanding cities of the New World. For a while, life was more than comfortable, with servants, and cars, and a grand old estate in the wealthy suburb of Ardmore, just outside the City of Brotherly Love.

When Sam was two years old, his sister, named Lilla after their mother, was born. This was a particularly joyful period for the family. The wealth Sam Senior had inherited was a fortune that enabled him to live luxuriously without ever having to work. And his mother was comfortable and secure in the life she enjoyed, with a cook, a chauffeur, and a full-time maid.

But disaster struck in 1929. The stock market crashed and the family was left without a penny. Overnight, the maids, the automobiles, even the family house were gone.

Sam's father was forty-one when he was forced to seek employment. The former heir to the Cummings fortune eventually landed a low-level position in an electrical supply shop, and then in a restaurant until it abruptly closed its doors.

Sam's mother, Lilla, was more resourceful. Knowing that many families were losing their homes through foreclosure proceedings, and fearful that her own family might someday have no place to live, she came up with a plan to generate some cash. Boasting her talents to restore and flip houses for a profit, she negotiated a deal with the bank that would allow it to reduce its portfolio of unsold houses, while simultaneously providing her family with a place to stay. The idea was simple: let her family live in one of the bank's vacant properties while she renovated it and then marketed it on the bank's behalf.

Surprisingly, the bank agreed, and the Cummingses were granted the key to the first of their many residences. The problem was, the arrangement obliged the family to move time and again, from one ramshackle house to another. Sam and his sister were forced to live with the constant banging of hammers and the noxious smells of wet paint and plaster. The arrangement was not ideal, but it did afford the family a decent place to live and provided a means for their mother to earn an honest income.

But her success also meant that the family was forced to change addresses two or three times a year. Sam and his baby sister lived in more than three dozen houses over the next decade and a half.

Sam and his sister learned to adjust to life among the constant construction and moves. But their father never accepted the hand that fate dealt him. Having to go to work at a mundane job—a turn that he always felt was grossly unfair—was slowly destroying him.

When he was just eight years old, young Sam experienced what he would later describe as the most upsetting event of his entire life. Returning home one Saturday from an afternoon matinee that he attended with his little sister, he found his mother troubled and distraught. He listened carefully as she told young Sam and six-year-old Lilla that their father was ill. His condition, she said, was so serious it required that he be admitted to a nearby hospital. The next morning, when the children awoke, their mother told them that their father had died.

Not only was it the most devastating news that Sam Cummings would ever hear, it would also affect every aspect of his life from that point on.

It wasn't until some time later that his mother provided the details of Sam's father's death. She revealed the fact that their forty-nine-year-old father had fallen ill after lunch that Saturday afternoon in 1935. She said that he had gone upstairs to the bedroom for a little rest, and when she went to the master suite to check on him, she found him dead of a massive heart attack.

Even at the tender age of eight, Sam had no doubt that his father's passing was caused by the humiliation of losing his fortune at an age when he should have been slowing down, and then having to go out and earn a day's pay.

After his father's death, Sam's mother worked hard to support the family. She continued with her business of renovating and reselling houses, and her efforts were met with great success. She earned enough money to send Sam and Lilla to the finest private schools in Philadelphia. Sam attended the Episcopal Academy, a sprawling campus dotted with imposing ivy-covered stone buildings, located in Merion, on the edge of Philadelphia's prestigious Main Line. His sister was enrolled nearby at The Baldwin School, one of the country's most exclusive academies for girls.

When Sam was fourteen, the family moved to Washington, D.C. It was 1941, and the United States had just entered the Second World War. Sam's mother sensed that the real-estate market in Philadelphia was about to collapse. Now that war was here, money was scarce. She realized that housing would be more desirable in the nation's capital where people would flock for government jobs. There, in the shadow of the Capitol building, the family continued its gypsy-like existence, changing residences every six to nine months, until Sam graduated from Central High School in 1945.

Even more important than his formal education, Sam had learned the importance of hard work and tight budgeting from his mother. And, while heart-breaking, the circumstances that led to his father's death—coupled with his mother's unflagging drive to protect and care for her family—would shape the way Sam Cummings approached his own life. These lessons would carry him to the heights of success in his later dealings as an arms merchant.

His discovery of an antique machine gun at the age of five also played a major role in carving out his future.

The youngster was passing a deserted American Legion post on his way home from school one afternoon when he spotted a German MO8/15 that most likely had been carried back to the States by a soldier as a souvenir from World War I. When Sam's efforts to lift the forty-pound machine gun proved unsuccessful, he enlisted the help of an older person who toted it home for him.

To the dark-haired boy, the weapon had more meaning than just a plaything, it was a way to fill his long afternoons. His family's financial woes meant the broad-faced youngster had few games to play with, and dismantling the weapon and putting it back together provided him with the challenge and the thrill that other kids derived from playing with model cars.

As Sam got older, his fascination with guns did not wane. Instead, he sought to possess other firearms and readily swapped books, trinkets, and anything else of value in order to acquire them.

By the time he was eighteen, he had amassed a small arsenal that consisted of antique muskets, pistols, rifles, and handguns—and learned everything there was to know about them. He taught himself how to take them apart and how to reassemble them. He knew what they could do, and he knew how to use them.

Sam was recruited into the U.S. Army near the end of 1945, and was assigned to Fort Meade in Maryland. Before leaving home, he stowed his prized gun collection in a chest in his mother's Washington basement after first rubbing every piece carefully with liniment to preserve it.

Sam was sent to Camp Lee near Richmond, Virginia for basic training. Next came NCO candidate school, where he received instruction to become a sergeant. The military training facility at Camp Lee was one of the first in the nation to become racially integrated. It was there that Sam met Charles Lewis, one of only a handful of black Non-Commissioned Officers in the Army. The bright, young officer shared Sam's fascination with firearms, and the two spent hours discussing the different makes and models. Sam would later recruit his army buddy to join him at Interarms as his first employee.

While in the service, Sam spent a great deal of his spare time learning all he could about the various types of firearms. His superiors found him so proficient that they later charged him with the task of training new recruits about weaponry.

By 1946, the war had come to an end. The first lots of post-war scrap were arriving on the mainland, and the slender, dark-haired man tried his hand at his first official business transaction. He successfully sold a carload of German army helmets that he found in a junkyard near his camp. He had spotted the cache of armor among the articles that were arriving on ships from Europe. Striking a bargain with the scrapyard owner, Sam purchased the helmets for fifty cents apiece, and then hauled them to nearby Maryland. There, he sold them for eight times the purchase price. It would be the first of his many successful dealings.

In addition to obtaining a greater knowledge of weapons, Sam's time in the service also qualified him for G.I. benefits, which paid for his undergraduate education at George Washington University. While earning a degree in economics and politics, the handsome young student lived at home with his mother in Washington. He continued to dabble in the less-than-lucrative trade of surplus firearms, spending his week-ends searching the area for discarded weapons or guns in need of repair that he could purchase at a reduced price. In his spare time, he taught himself all he could about the way the weapons worked and made a point of learning about the models that were most appealing to American hunters and gun enthusiasts.

Like his mother, with her talent for turning a profit ren-ovating otherwise unsaleable homes, Sam had become a mas-ter at repairing and reselling antique and abandoned firearms—an expertise that would come in handy on his first trip abroad.

It was 1948, and Sam, then a junior at George Washington University, had been selected to spend a summer semester at Queens College, Oxford University. Upon completion of the term, he and several friends decided they would travel the continent and allotted themselves a budget of a dollar a day. Before his departure, Sam had gone to his mother's basement and retrieved his gun collection which he sold to earn the money to foot the bill for the trip.

Excitedly, the three students loaded their sleeping bags into the beat-up old Ford they'd purchased in England and boarded the car ferry en route to Denmark. In order to get to the Scandinavian country, they would have to drive through Germany, but they were told that they would not be permitted to stop. As they got underway, they were unpre-pared for the devastation that they would soon encounter. Steering along the European roadways, the young men were taken aback by the total destruction that had befallen the cities and the countryside.

Their budget of a dollar a day soon proved too little, as the price of gasoline had skyrocketed. Europeans were re-quired to produce petrol tickets in order to qualify for gas rations. The young students compensated for their lack of funds by selling their rations to the lines of Frenchmen in need of gas. To save even more money, the men decided they would sleep in the abandoned German bunkers that dot-ted the landscape of Normandy and Northwest France.

As they motored along, they were astounded by what they

found abandoned in the battlefields. Stockpiled inside the concrete reinforced bunkers were guns, ammunition, cartridges, and grenades that had been left there by troops who once occupied the area.

Navigating the narrow back roadways of France, Sam and his friends stared out the car windows in silence. Lining the streets were rusting hulks of German tanks, armored cars of heavy plate steel, lethal-looking howitzers, and other pieces of artillery that had never been collected by the French Army. The men parked along the road, then walked the grassy battlefields, astonished by the multitude of weapons that lay scattered about. There were Mausers, Luger pistols, and machine guns that appeared to be in good working order.

Sam shook his head in disbelief. He was awestruck by the caches of arms he was seeing heaped on top of the knolls of gravel that had been set up along the sides of the roads. The army had created them for farmers to use to discard the weapons they discovered while tilling their soil, and it appeared to Sam that they had been forgotten or left for scrap.

Imagine the money I could make if only I could import these weapons to America where they're in demand by sportsmen and collectors, Sam thought to himself as his eyes scanned the abandoned arsenals.

Picking through the piles of discarded guns, the students selected a machine gun to carry back to the States as a souvenir. Tying it to the top of their auto, they continued on to Denmark, returning once more through Germany and down to the sunny Riviera, where Sam Cummings would eventually make his home. There, by the Italian border, they saw more abandoned artillery.

Again, Sam calculated their value on the American gun market. He sighed, knowing there was no way he could take them back to the United States. But that didn't stop him from thinking about them when he returned to America to complete his undergraduate studies.

Upon his graduation from George Washington University in 1949, Sam recognized that he needed to find a job to help him pay the cost of law school. He was aware that his G.I.

benefits would barely cover the tuition for his first year at George Washington Law School. He also knew that his bachelor's degree in politics and economics was not going to open a lot of doors for him in a city where jobs were now scarce.

Preparing himself a résumé, the ambitious young law student boasted that he was an expert in firearms, and then mailed off his *curriculum vitae* to a handful of government agencies and private arms companies. He even visited the FBI, the CIA, the Secret Service, and the National Rifle Association. His applications were all turned down.

Finally, the United States Chamber of Commerce gave him a position as a filing clerk in their legislative offices. The part-time job paid twenty dollars a week, and afforded Sam ample time to complete his school work.

Soon, he was elevated to a more visible position that gave him access to the lobbyists on Capitol Hill. The new role paid sixty dollars a week, and allowed the struggling law student to sit in on Congressional hearings and committee meetings. In fact, he was in the Capitol building on the day that President Harry S Truman announced that the United States would enter the Korean War, and was haunted by the eerie silence that fell upon members of the House of Representatives when the declaration was read.

Just seven days after the war began, Sam was summoned by the CIA. They had kept his résumé on file, and were now interested in his expertise as an arms expert. His interview lasted for several hours, and was an experience that most people would have found rather intimidating.

Seated across the table from three intelligence officers, the twenty-one-year-old student aced an inquisition that would have caused even the most proficient of weapons experts to sweat. In a cool, even tone, the slender, confident man fielded question after question, and at points, astonished the panelists with what he knew. His answers were so on-target that the seasoned agents found themselves wondering how a person so young could have come upon his seemingly endless breadth of knowledge about a subject of such a sensitive nature.

With little hesitation, Sam was recommended and ultimately hired. He was assigned to a post in the small-arms division of the Office of Scientific Intelligence, and was given a salary of $3,000 a year. Unlike his job with the Chamber of Commerce, this position would be full-time, leaving him little time to tend to the demands of his law-school studies.

Putting his education on hold, Sam immersed himself in his new assignment. His task would be to identify the weapons that had been captured by American soldiers in Korea and shipped back to the bureau for inspection. He would also be asked to pin down the names of the guns that had been photographed in the hands of Communist soldiers. The pictures had been secretly snapped by American spies, and Sam had little difficulty classifying the bulk of them as Russian guns from the Second World War.

He had spent a good portion of his free time learning about artillery, first as a teenager, and later as an officer of the U.S. Army, and found his new assignment relatively simple. One of the benefits of the job was the access he was given to the Agency's extensive files, which enabled him to obtain data on any weapon, piece of ammunition, or other related topic that piqued his interest.

Sam had been at the Agency for several months when a memorandum was placed on his desk. Glancing at the packet, he saw it was a report prepared by members of embassies in Western Europe. The subject was surplus weapons from World War II.

Skimming the pages, Sam could hardly believe what he was reading. He raised an eyebrow as he scanned the responses to questions about whether there was still German weaponry left over in Europe. On page after page, officials were reporting that they had no knowledge of any abandoned German war booty in the battlefields of their countries.

Sam knew there was a hidden reserve of guns and tanks, and cases upon cases of unused ammunition. He had seen it for himself during his tour of the continent, and could not understand what would prompt the officials to unanimously respond to the contrary.

Shaking his head in disbelief, Sam sat down at his desk and composed a memo to his superiors. In it, he detailed all that he knew, and all that he'd seen on his trip through Europe as a student some years earlier.

Several weeks passed before the young arms expert was summoned to see Allen Dulles, the deputy director of the CIA. Others in the agency were stunned when they learned that Sam had received orders to see Dulles in his office.

After all, the deputy executive officer was recognized as the world's foremost spy. He had orchestrated all of the American counterintelligence operations carried out in Europe during the Second World War, and within months would be elevated to director of the Central Intelligence Agency.

But Sam was not intimidated. In fact, he entered the meeting with an air of confidence that impressed the senior agent. Taking a seat across the desk from Dulles, the twenty-four-year-old weapons expert respectfully told him exactly what he had seen during his tour of the European continent.

The information was enough to persuade the deputy director that the report from the European embassies was indeed filled with inaccuracies. Within days, Sam would be sent on a secret mission to buy up the abandoned German war booty. The United States government wanted the arsenal to arm the Chinese Nationalist Army for a Communist invasion.

It would be his first covert operation—and the only one he would ever admit to publicly. The undercover assignment would provide Sam with his first taste of the international arms trade and would set the stage for him to return to Europe to do business on his own behalf as president of the international arms company that he would found the following year.

Sam's identity would be disguised, and his credentials falsified. Posing as a Hollywood movie producer, the lanky young man in his polyester suit was told to approach European governments with a story that was fabricated for him by the Central Intelligence Agency.

He was instructed to say that he was in Europe to purchase German war booty for the infinite number of war movies that the American film industry was preparing to produce. The Agency had given him impeccable credentials, an unlimited line of credit, and an accomplice named Leo Lippe to help authenticate his story.

Sam was amused by his new "business partner." He not only appeared naïve and simple-minded, he had no experience with guns. Except for his credentials as a prominent Los Angeles cinematographer, Sam found his cohort laughable in his showy suits and flashy neckties. He wasn't surprised to learn that Leo had never been abroad.

In chatting with his new associate, Sam discovered that Leo Lippe's only association with the Central Intelligence Agency was a business deal he had brokered with the Office of Strategic Services. During the transaction, the cinematographer had befriended several members of the Agency. The representatives appreciated Lippe's integrity, and believed that his knowledge of the movie industry would help Sam answer any questions that were put to him by wary government officials. There was another thing that set the two men apart when they headed abroad: Sam knew the real purpose of their trip, but Lippe did not.

The CIA provided the men with American import licenses and letters of credit, and then sent them off to the airport where they boarded a plane for Europe. Their mission was to buy the hundreds of thousands of guns and the millions of rounds of bullets that lay discarded in the overgrown battlefields of England and in the countryside of the European continent.

While it began in London, just like Sam's vacation three years before, the CIA-sponsored trip bore little resemblance to Sam's previous visit abroad. Then, his mode of transportation had been a beat-up Ford Anglia and his budget was a dollar a day. This time, he would travel in style, being chauffeured in limousines and sporting pockets overflowing with cash—all to bolster his image as a Hollywood big wig who was there to purchase surplus weaponry for an equitable price.

To further support the men's grandiose claims, the

Agency gave them carte blanche to stay at the finest hotels. Leo and Sam, however, felt the first-class accommodations would be a waste of money and opted for more modest lodgings. Sam's desire to pinch pennies would continue long after he left the CIA.

The men set themselves up in a Geneva hotel, and for the next year, trekked across the continent, visiting France, Switzerland, Scandinavia, Belgium, the Netherlands, Spain, Portugal, and Italy. Much to their amazement, their story was never questioned by representatives of any of the European governments—with the exception of the Swiss. And even with their one failure, they managed to walk away with dignity, Leo in his tacky designer duds and Sam in a cheap department store knock-off.

The trip would prove invaluable to Sam Cummings, who would return in later years to purchase the abundance of arms that remained behind for his own company, International Armament Corporation, or Interarms.

Sam's success would qualify him for another assignment— this time a trip to Central America. The U.S. government wanted him there to oversee a deal between the Costa Rican government and Western Arms, a private arms company based in California.

Arrangements had been made for the West Coast firm to purchase the thousands of small arms and millions of rounds of ammunition that the Costa Rican government was selling. Sam was sent to San Jose to supervise the transaction and make sure the weapons did not end up in sinister hands. While there, the dashing young man met his first wife, Inka Graetz, a pretty airline stewardess he would marry in New Orleans on Christmas Eve, 1952.

With two successful missions under his belt, Sam had to decide whether he wanted to continue working with the Central Intelligence Agency, return to law school, or try his hand in the private sector of military surplus. He had learned a lot from his dealings in Europe and Central America, and he felt ready to branch off on his own. Returning to Washington, he enlisted the help of his mother in finding him and his new bride a place to live.

Lilla Cummings suggested a modest timber-frame house with a view of the Potomac River. The only problem was that the home was in a less-than-desirable neighborhood of Georgetown.

For Sam, the affordable price of $10,000 more than made up for the questionable location. He quickly settled in and began the task of setting up his arms firm, the International Armament Corporation.

No stranger to the art of deception, Sam came up with a way to make his firm sound bigger than a one-man operation. Although he planned to operate the company from his home, buying fancy stationery and listing a Post Office box as his official address, he did not want his clients to suspect that he was the sole proprietor of a business that trafficked in multi-million-dollar arms deals.

To further promote his illusion, Sam printed up business cards that identified him as the ''vice president'' of the company to which he'd given such an important-sounding name. The less-than-presidential designation was Sam's way of misleading prospective clients into believing that there were senior, more experienced associates operating above him.

He chose the saying *Esse Quam Videre* as the motto for his newly-formed company. The adage, which means ''To be rather than to seem to be,'' was the motto of the Episcopal Academy he had attended in Philadelphia as a youth. Derived from a line in Aeschylus's *Seven against Thebes,* the verse translates to mean ''His resolve is not to seem the bravest, but to be the bravest.''

No doubt, Sam's decision to use the motto figured into the firm's marketing efforts. But it also provided an insight into Sam's persona. Friends and associates described the arms merchant as a modest man who was confident in his own abilities and showed little concern about what others thought of him.

The next step was to contact world leaders and buyers for the military to purchase their surplus weapons. While Sam waited in Georgetown for a reply to his correspondence, his pretty young bride returned to her job as a flight attendant.

Wedded bliss did not last long. Inka's busy transatlantic

schedule and Sam's constant trips abroad to purchase arms for his newly-formed company made it impossible for the two to spend any real time together.

After only two and a half years of marriage, the couple called it quits. The breakup was amicable and left Sam with plenty of free time to build his weapons empire.

During the next five years, he set out on the road to establish himself as the world's largest private arms merchant. His first successful deal was with the Panamanian government. Sam purchased the 7,000 small arms that Colonel Bolivar Vallarino, the commanding officer of the country's National Guard, wanted to get rid of. He negotiated a price of $25,000 for the load, and then set about finding a buyer to come up with the cash.

He found a taker in Cecil Jackson of Western Arms. Sam had worked with Jackson when he was employed by the CIA, and was sent to oversee the arms deal between the California-based company and the Costa Rican government.

He had learned the art of negotiation from his former missions, and hammered out a price of $66,000 for the shipment. After he paid an additional sum to haul the cargo to Washington, he was left with a profit of $20,000. The sum allowed him to continue to expand his business, eventually striking deals with governments around the world.

In 1968, when the Gun Control Act was approved, Cummings slyly cashed in on the ban of imported military weapons to the United States. Just weeks before its passage, he secreted nearly three-quarters-of-a-million firearms in his Alexandria warehouse, and then sold them to collectors and huntsmen for a grossly inflated price.

Over the next three decades, his company supplied weapons by the shipload to some of the world's most hated dictators. Haiti's François "Papa Doc" Duvalier, the Dominican Republic's Rafael Leonidas Trujillo "Molina," and Cuba's Fulgencio Batista were counted among his clientele.

When Cuba's Batista fled the country, Sam Cummings boarded a plane for Havana to demonstrate his new line of assault rifles for a new customer, Fidel Castro. He supplied

M-1 rifles for a CIA-organized coup in Guatemala, armed both sides of wars and revolutions, and bought guns off the bodies of dead servicemen for resale on the worldwide market.

He was the subject of a book, *Deadly Business: Sam Cummings, Interarms, & the Arms Trade* written by journalists Patrick Brogan and Albert Zarca. He also turned up disguised as a fictional character in a John le Carré novel. And author Frederick Forsyth used Sam Cummings as the model for one of his characters, an international arms dealer, in his book *The Dogs of War*.

When he met Irmgard Blacttler, the stunning brunette was employed as an accountant at a hotel in Geneva. Cummings admired the exacting Swiss woman. Even her brusque efficiency, which he found typically Swiss, was appealing to him. Shortly after he married her in 1960, the couple moved to the picturesque principality of Monaco and rented a flat in the tiny country's capital, Monte Carlo.

The spacious apartment was worlds away from the modest wooden home he had once owned in Georgetown. It afforded Sam and his new bride sweeping views of the glistening Mediterranean. The couple was also just steps away from the high-priced boutiques, expensive jewelry shops, and high-rise hotels that dominated the landscape of Europe's gambling capital, where the sweet smell of roses and lavender perfumed the air.

Their home was not far from The Rock, as the western quarter is nicknamed. The tiny section of Monaco, which is literally a huge boulder jutting out of the calm blue waters of the Mediterranean, is known for the medieval town at its apex, two hundred feet above the sea. It is even better known because of its famous residents, His Highness Prince Rainier III and his lovely princess, Grace Kelly, who lived in the Prince's Palace perched in the center of the centuries-old village. Sam and his wife never tired of the ceremonious changing of the guard, which took place each afternoon in the Place du Palais, just in front of the medieval and Renaissance-style castle.

But the world-renowned Casino, the pomp and circumstance of Monaco's royal family, and the jet-setting lifestyle were not what drew Sam Cummings to the garish 478-acre principality, which is snuggled between Nice and the Italian border. He was not a gambler, and he made a conscious effort to avoid alcoholic beverages. He rose early and never stayed out late. And unlike many of his middle-aged colleagues, he made a concerted effort to exercise whenever he could find the time for a dip in the sea.

Sam was attracted to The Rock because of the opportunity it provided him to save a bundle of money in the tax-free haven. But while his interest in the area was largely based on practical considerations, his choice served to provide a fairy-tale setting for the early years of his twin daughters, years in which their childhood playground was shared with the world's wealthiest, most beautiful, and most powerful people.

CHAPTER 6

THE OLD CLICHÉ ABOUT "BEING BORN WITH A SILVER spoon in one's mouth" does not begin to describe the world that greeted Sam Cummings' twin baby girls.

Shortly after Susan and Diana (pronounced Su-ZAHN and Dee-AHna in French) celebrated their first birthday, the family purchased a magnificent fourteen room flat at 2, rue des Giroflées. The grand apartment was located in the posh eastern end of the half-mile-square principality, twenty-one kilometers from the Italian border, adjoining the southern-most edge of France. Their residence was not far from the celebrated Casino that had been a focal point in the town for more than a century.

From their fashionable address on the French Riviera, the young girls regularly passed the Place du Casino to get to the main boulevard that ran along the sea. Though they had grown accustomed to the magnificent site, tourists regularly flocked there to gawk at the sprawling rococo-style gambling center and perhaps risk a few francs on the red and black numbers of the establishment's many roulette tables. It wasn't unusual to see great numbers of Lamborghinis, Rolls Royces and Mercedes Benzes parked in the immaculate square outside the baroque building.

When it was first erected back in the 1850s under the direction of Charles Grimaldi III, a descendant of the country's ruling family, the Casino attracted no clientele. Charles had come up with the brainstorm of helping finance his government—which was badly in need of revenue—while avoiding taxing his subjects, by building a gambling facility. Yet, one problem that he failed to anticipate was that there were no carriage roads or railroads leading to the tiny principality, making it nearly impossible for wealthy Europeans to reach the gorgeous elaborately-decorated establishment, with its gilt-edged rococo ceilings and gold-leaf trim.

When the doors finally opened in 1856, only one person showed up that first day to place a bet, and he won two francs. But all that changed dramatically the following year. The railroad extended its lines to Monaco. Englishmen began descending on the jewel of a city, drawn to it not only by the temperate climate, but also by the opportunity for excitement and unique entertainment.

Within months, the Casino was drawing hordes of customers. Its seemingly overnight success prompted Charles III to abolish all direct taxes. He never anticipated that relaxing the duty would have an unexpected side effect: attracting countless businessmen who were looking for ways to hide the fruits of their elaborate operations.

Like so many businessmen before him, Sam Cummings had hoped that his move to Monte Carlo would allow him to shelter the profits from his multi-million-dollar arms deals. His decision to move to Monaco raised concern among officials in the principality. They feared he would set up a munitions factory and warehouses there. But the fast-talking American managed to assure them that all he intended to do was operate a small office in the luxurious quarters he had purchased for his new family.

Indeed, he could not have picked a more scenic spot. From the apartment's expansive picture windows, his daughters could count the exquisitely-maintained yachts of the super-rich that were anchored in the commercial harbor, La Condamine, just off the coastline. And if they looked out of the huge glass window in their father's corner office, they could see the jagged mountains of the magical island of Corsica—the birthplace of Napoleon Bonaparte—in the distance.

It was here on this lovely stretch of rocky terrain high above the sea that Susan and her twin sister Diana spent their childhood. It was a fairy-tale existence: Grace Kelly was their real live princess, and Grace's daughters, Stephanie and Caroline, were their contemporaries.

Every day, on their way to the beach, the girls passed trendy outdoor cafes and swank French boutiques. Familiar names adorned the signs above the shops—names like Chanel, Givenchy, and Yves Saint Laurent. At the shore, the twin sisters frolicked in the surf alongside the topless women who lay stretched out on the boulders that lined the rocky shoreline, or enjoyed a swim with their father in the tiny private cabana he rented for himself at the water's edge.

Yet, their time together was a rarity. During their early years, the girls were unable to spend much time with their dad. He traveled often for business, remaining absent for weeks or even months at a time.

When he did return home, the girls loved to accompany their father on his daily routine. Like him, they woke before 8 a.m. and went to the Boulevard du Larvotto for an early morning swim.

The private beach, made even more beautiful by the addition of pure white imported sand, attracted some of the world's most striking women. Neither Susan nor Diana paid much heed to the way the model-thin beauties paraded nonchalantly across the man-made seashore in nothing but G-strings. Topless sunbathing was the fashion in Monte Carlo, just as it was on all the beaches of the French Riviera.

While their father paddled around in the salty blue waters, the girls played in the sand near their mother. Irmgard, who liked her friends to call her Irma, also came along on the morning outings. She was a stylish but remote woman with thick dark hair that fell just below her shoulders. With her husband frequently away on business, she assumed the role of primary caretaker and disciplinarian to her winsome twin daughters.

In the afternoons, the family returned home for lunch. The Cummingses exchanged waves with the other residents, as well as the shopkeepers and owners of the exclusive boutiques, as they ambled along the windy side streets that were lined with lemon, orange, and banana trees. Everyone in town knew Monsieur and Madame Cummings and regularly made a fuss about the couple's adorable twin daughters.

In fact, in this country of only 5,000 Monegasque nationals, the girls had made quite a hit. Whether they were swimming in the sea, swinging in the playground, or strolling in the warm Mediterranean sun, their appearance elicited oohs and aahs from passersby. The fraternal twins, in their fancy, well-pressed dresses and white lace knee socks, were invariably the center of attention.

At home, the toddlers were taught to speak two languages fluently. They conversed with their American-born father in English and with their Swiss mother in French, with French becoming their primary tongue. They later mastered a third language, German. But well before they learned to converse with others, the two girls had developed their own secret language—one that only they could understand.

Their mother had been told that the cryptic communication the girls had developed was not at all remarkable between twins. It was called "twin talk" and was a phenomenon with children who had shared a womb.

Unlike a single baby who tends to mimic the sounds and speech of his parents, twins tend to mimic each other because they spend so much time together. Sometimes they establish such a close connection that they lose interest in communicating with other people, and in rare cases, they develop words and phrases that make sense only to them.

Susan and Diana's secret way of speaking, using made-up words that were unrecognizable even to their mother, enabled them to enjoy a unique connection. Not even with their closest friends and lovers would the girls ever be able to converse in such an intimate manner.

Scientists have long been fascinated by the emotional closeness shared by twins and the unique way in which they communicate. Numerous studies have been done on the topic, including those at the University of Minnesota, where a registry keeps track of more than 8,000 pairs of twins.

Unlike identical twins, where a single egg is fertilized and then divides into two equal parts, resulting in babies that are of the same sex and identical genetic inheritance, non-identical or fraternal twins occur when two separate eggs are fertilized. In theory, at least, fraternal twins such as Susan and Diana should be no more alike than any other siblings. Yet, researchers have consistently pointed to the bonds and similarities that fraternal twins share.

It is not unreasonable to suspect that Susan enjoyed—even treasured—the special connection she shared with her fraternal twin sister. Research has shown that this type of intense closeness can provide children with a great sense of security. But, studies also suggest that being so close can also lead to jealousy and competition.

Simply by observing young mothers wheeling their babies in a park, the average person can see that certain infants seem to capture more interest and attention. When the people of Monte Carlo saw the little Cummings' girls strolling down the boulevards of their enchanted town, was it Diana who they focused on, who inspired their smiles? In spite of their sameness, their bond, and their shared language, did Susan think that her sister was treated differently? Thought to be prettier? Appreciated because she was the more gregarious and outgoing one? If so, was she jealous?

Perhaps Susan felt that Diana possessed something extra—a certain sparkle—that she herself would never be able to acquire.

Irmgard Cummings, the girls' watchful Swiss mother, was no doubt aware that her skinny, shy daughter was not socializing as well as her confident, more outspoken sister. Did it trouble her that Susan spent hours locked away in her room while Diana was out having fun with her friends? That her beautiful brown-haired little girl preferred the solitude of her frilly, lace-covered bedroom to the bustle of the beaches and play areas that Diana and her friends frequented?

Often, parents of twins think there is less of a need for their children to go out and mix with others. In many cases, they mistakenly believe that making new friends is not as important for twins who already have each other to play with. As children, Susan and Diana were inseparable, and their mother noticed that they preferred to stay near home and play by themselves.

But researchers have found that the more twins play solely with each other, the more troublesome it can be for them to make friends later on.

When twins do try and join a group of children at play, often times there can be problems. In some instances, the twosome may act too eager and their abrasive manner may be disruptive to the other children who fear the twins are trying to take charge. Or they can appear awkward and find themselves neither liked nor accepted by the bunch. Upset by the rejection, they may chose to remain on their own.

Irma Cummings seemed aware that her girls faced some of the behavioral obstacles common to many twins. Because they were the same sex, it is possible that they encountered people who unwittingly confused them and called them by the wrong name, even though they didn't look alike. To avoid the mixup, people may have referred to them simply as "the twins," a label that has hindered some pairs of twins from adventuring out beyond the intimate circle of people who can easily tell them apart.

Irmgard Cummings confided in one journalist that on many occasions she peeked her head into Susan's doll-filled chamber and tried to persuade her seemingly lonely child to be part of the world.

"Susan, why don't you go out and have a little fun?" she told the reporter that she asked her daughter, worried that Susan's reluctance to socialize with others might create problems for her later on in life.

In Switzerland, the family owned a sprawling summer chalet in the sleepy mountainside village of Villars. When the days got hotter and the streets of Monte Carlo grew crowded with tourists, the family packed up their belongings and headed for the lavish Swiss villa nestled high in the Bernese Alps.

To get to the remote mountain town, the family often traveled the tail end of the treacherous Lower Corniche—a heart-stopping two-lane roadway that is barely wide enough for two cars to pass. The route is carved into the cliffs some three thousand feet over the River Verdon and snakes along the coastline of the French Riviera to the Italian Alps. The highway had claimed the lives of many travelers over the years, the most famous of whom was Grace, Princess of Monaco.

Life in the sterile Swiss village, less than fifteen miles from the popular ski resorts of Diablerets and the Dent du Midi, was considerably less glamorous than the action-packed, high-style existence of the sunny Riviera. Yet, here the girls were able to frolic freely. They spent much of their time playing with the dogs and cats at a neighbor's barn, where they also took riding lessons.

The protected mountainside getaway also enabled their mother to return to her native land whenever she felt the urge and provided their father with a quiet place to conduct his business away from the heat, humidity, and raucous summertime crowds of trendy Monte Carlo.

The girls' father worked undisturbed in the small office he created for himself in one of the servants' rooms on the first floor of the magnificent chalet. Here, as in Monaco, Sam chose to live without any household help. He didn't even have a secretary; instead, he preferred doing all his paperwork by himself. So it wasn't surprising that in the chalet, as in the Monte Carlo apartment, he converted the maid's quarters into his own home office.

The Cummingses regal residence, adorned with white gingerbread trim and a sloping slate roof, sat perched high atop a cliff in the breathtaking, eternally snow-capped Alps. Its large picture windows afforded the girls dramatic views of white-peaked mountains, lush green vineyards, and the lovely Rhone Valley below. The chalet had been built for the head of a wealthy French family and was landscaped with graduated gardens and lofty pines.

In summer, a stream babbled across the acreage, which is accessible only by a dizzying road that snakes its way up the mountain from the village's principal thoroughfare.

Yet even the pastoral setting of Villars, such a dramatic contrast to the glittering glamor of Monte Carlo, did little to mask the differences between the twin girls.

The wide-eyed brunette may have found solace with her father, who enjoyed the fact that young Susan was interested in target shooting and fast cars, activities that were usually more appealing to boys.

But Sam was often on the road—six months out of every twelve—or locked away in his corner office, preoccupied with important business matters. Susan was well aware that his work demanded that he spend much of his time seated behind his solid wood desk, speaking to clients with equal fluency in English, French, or German on the telephone. The small corner room was filled with artifacts that he had collected over the years. A steel suit of armor stood near the long conference table, and an authentic antique cannon was placed just beside his bureau. The office walls were hung with pictures of famous eighteenth-century skirmishes. Memorabilia pertaining to Napoleon Bonaparte dotted his desk.

In fact, from the room's expansive window, her father enjoyed gazing out at of the French dictator's birthplace. But the vista disappeared when a large apartment building was constructed nearby. Of course, Susan's father easily had the means to relocate his family, but his gypsy-like childhood left him unwilling to make any more changes.

When her father wasn't busy putting together multi-million-dollar arms deals, he would take his twin girls on walks or to a shooting range, where he taught them how to fire guns at the age of five.

These occasions offered one of the rare opportunities for the girls to have their father to themselves. But Sam was not one to indulge in heart-to-heart talks. Instead he encouraged his children to be independent and resorted to mottos that he felt had served him well. One of his favorites, *Esse Quam Videre*, the slogan he had given to his arms company, was the one that Susan was to draw upon for years.

But how did she interpret this adage? Susan quoted it often, but what did it mean to her? That no matter what you appear to be—rich, privileged, spoiled, sheltered—that the image was unimportant? And that what was really important was being "more" than your image? Rich but also philanthropic? Privileged but also humble? Spoiled but also kind-hearted? Sheltered but also imaginative? That image was always subordinate to substance? Did this adage sustain Susan when she felt unimportant or that she didn't measure up to Diana?

On the surface, the interactions between the distracted Sam Cummings and his eager little daughters may have seemed to be characterized by a certain coolness. But the girls loved and admired him and, in later years, even as adults, Susan and her sister lapsed into a form of baby talk with their father, cooing and babbling in an almost childlike fashion.

It seemed that Diana had inherited her effortless social skills from Sam Cummings and that Susan was more like her mother, reserved and detached, more apt to hide her feelings behind a cool exterior.

Research into the behavior of twins suggests that jealousy between twins may be exaggerated when one child is constantly aware of the attention being given to the other. Studies have shown that this jealousy can erupt into aggression, even violence.

Psychologists have found that often a twins' temperament determines the way in which others behave toward him or her. For instance, if one twin is more of a chatterer, or finds it difficult to wait her turn, a parent may pay more attention to her, which could explain why the other twin may be less talkative.

In some twin relationships, children will actually assume "roles" that often continue even when the other twin is absent. One twin may act the leader, while the other may assume the role of the follower; one may be the talker, and the other the listener; one may be well-behaved while the other may play the part of the troublemaker.

Susan's realization may have set the tone for a lifetime of unspoken rivalry between the twins.

Diana always seemed to claim the spotlight. After all, it was only natural for an attractive, talkative girl to enjoy the attention she received. Even so, Diana's friends must have sensed that it wasn't easy for the prettier twin to bask in the compliments of others knowing that her sister was not sharing in her glory. Did Diana spend her lifetime compensating for her guilty feelings by being unfailingly "devoted" to

Susan? No one will ever know for sure, these imponderables will never be ascertained.

At the age of nine, Susan became aware that her parents were speaking about which nation to choose as their home. She listened as her father related that he'd recently learned something upsetting: the girls' citizenship had been called into question, and was, perhaps, even in jeopardy. Sam explained to his wife that because his daughters had been born abroad, they were subject to a new ruling by the United States Supreme Court. The highest court in the nation had decided that children born to Americans abroad could not obtain a U.S. passport unless they spent a minimum of three consecutive years in the United States between the ages of fifteen and twenty-six. Nobody in the family had even remotely entertained the idea of moving to the United States. While Susan's father checked into other alternatives, his daughters were left to wonder about a new life in a new country. Soon they found that they would not be eligible for citizenship in their mother's homeland of Switzerland because they had been born abroad. Even citizenship in their birthplace of Monaco was out of the question because of strict legal rules that required that children born to foreigners living in Monaco have a lineage of five consecutive generations.

This stunning twist of fate afforded both Sam Cummings and his children British passports. And after his triumph, he hired a Washington attorney to assist those with similar situations, helping other Americans born abroad win protection. His efforts even won an amendment to the 1971 Supreme Court ruling that permitted children born outside the United States to inherit the citizenship of their American parent. This legislative addition enabled Cummings to obtain dual British and American citizenship for both his daughters.

With the battle over a country now behind them, the girls were once again able to enjoy their summers in Villars. But as they neared their teens, the quiet charm of the sleepy Swiss village began to lose its luster.

Finally, one summer, when it came time to pack up for the five-hour ride to their summer getaway in the Alps, the twins urged their parents to allow them to remain in Monte Carlo, where the real action was just getting underway. Older, and more interested in what the trendy resort town had to offer, Susan and Diana convinced their parents that spending the season in the steamy summer climate of the French Riviera would be fun.

There, they argued, they could people-watch in the bustling square in front of the Casino, where haughty European women, fashionably attired in expensive couture dresses, accompanied the wealthy high rollers up the carpeted front steps of the gold-leafed Casino. Or they could join the scantily-clad sunbathers lying sprawled on the rocky beaches, and watch the darkly handsome men in Rayban sunglasses drive their expensive convertible sports cars up and down the main drag.

The girls' parents reluctantly agreed to split their time between Villars and Monte Carlo for the sake of their children. Yet, while the twins enjoyed a certain amount of social freedom, their father remained extremely protective of his beloved daughters. While Cummings' position as a high-powered arms merchant thrust him into the public eye, he strove to shield his daughters from the glare of the media as much as possible.

To this end, he sent them to prestigious private schools, which may have kept them from learning many of life's important lessons. But once again, her father's attempts at protecting her could not save Susan from ''real life.''

In fact, her teen years presented Susan with a whole new set of vulnerabilities. She may have been aware that even though she and Diana shared the same background, the same family, and the same classroom, it would seem that Diana invariably fared better, fitting in more comfortably at school and enjoying more popularity.

Diana, no doubt, had also sensed the differences between herself and her twin very early on. She certainly knew, as all siblings do, which of the two was the smarter, the prettier, and the more popular. This kind of awareness often leads to guilt, and just as often to the kind of over-protectiveness that a stronger sibling exerts over a weaker one.

Like most girls who are blessed with the gift of popularity, Diana may not have wanted to give up an inch of her turf. Her attempts at helping her sister may have been nothing more than her own efforts to mask the uneasy feelings she had about always triumphing over her sibling.

In high school, boys were suddenly on the scene and, once again, Diana was the star, wearing the pretty dresses and the beautifying makeup, getting the smiles, the flirtatious remarks, the dates.

Susan, who was more insular, like the Swiss side of the family, didn't seem to have the knack for attracting boys. She was more of a tomboy, and did not own a dress or a stitch of makeup. While Susan Cummings had enough money to buy herself anything in the world, the one thing she couldn't seem to acquire was the attention of a special boy.

Despite their early reservations, both Susan and Diana ended up crossing the Atlantic and coming to the United States. It was the furthering of their education that brought them to the East Coast—and their father's roots. It was no coincidence that the small, all-girl school they attended, Mount Vernon College in Washington, D.C., was later affiliated with George Washington University, their father's alma mater.

The shy brunette spent four uneventful years at the liberal arts college, always feeling comfortable and safe behind its manned security gates.

Susan studied alongside the daughters of ambassadors and diplomats, finally leaving the beautiful campus with its green hills and dense trees with a bachelors degree in arts and humanities.

If Susan had had to work for a living, things probably would have turned out differently. Her real passion—and her only one—was for animals. Had her situation been different, she might have attended one of the country's top veterinary schools. But with her father's generous allowance, she never had the need to establish her own career.

Instead, after graduation, she moved from one cozy environment to another. Susan and her sister, both twenty-two years old, moved to Ashland Farm, the sprawling 350-acre spread her father had purchased to serve as his American residence. Although their father owned a lovely apartment in nearby Old Town Alexandria, just blocks from his Interarms office complex, the girls did not want to remain in the urban environment of the capital city.

Instead, they preferred the wide open spaces, an abundance of plants and trees, and plenty of animals to the concrete sidewalks of urban life.

The grand estate dated back to the 1700s and had served as a stagecoach depot. The Holtzclaw family had acquired the land through a grant issued by Lieutenant Governor Alexander Spotswood in 1724, and took up residence there until the 1920s. One section of the main house was completed by 1889, and then was remodeled and expanded by architect William Lawrence Bottomley in 1929. Between 1861 and 1864, the Confederate Army stationed watchmen at Ashland Farm. The property's main house was converted into a federal medical dressing station for Civil War soldiers. According to legend, a cannon full of gold was buried on the property, but had never been located.

In 1984, Cummings purchased the Ashland Farm estate, along with an even larger tract, Le Baron Farm, in neighboring Culpeper County, for his twin daughters. He paid $1.5 million for both parcels, a real bargain by local standards.

Like Ashland, Le Baron Farm is graced with an impressive mansion and is surrounded by more than eight hundred acres of woodlands. In spite of the availability of two separate residences, Susan and Diana chose to remain together and settled on the Ashland Farm property.

Diana, always playing the role of the nurturing sister, gave Susan the big, empty, isolated mansion that her parents had once lived in. She, meanwhile, moved into the small, unpretentious guest house nestled in a pasture several minutes' walk down a blacktop path from the main house.

Susan and her sister immersed themselves in the farming activities at Ashland.

Susan rose every morning by 5 a.m. to begin her daily ritual. First, she would go to the rear laundry room just down the hall from the servants' kitchen to get pet food for the array of strays—all cats—she had rescued from the animal shelter. She visited the SPCA at least once a month, looking over the new animals to see if there were any more abandoned felines for her to add to her household.

She had amassed nearly two dozen, some of them once badly abused. The animals adored her and followed her from room to room as she went about her daily routine. Her two favorites were Geppetto, a one-eared cat she'd rescued from the pound, and a scrawny black feline with singed fur that told of the abuse it had suffered at its previous owner's hands.

Next, she ambled past Diana's cottage to the big white barn where she tended to her stable of horses.

Susan also kept cows at Ashland Farm. Whenever there was a birth, she spent hours bottle-feeding the new-born calves, as she did the foundling ponies. She found tranquility and seemed to prefer the company of animals to human companionship.

Susan's sister shared her love of horses, and spent a good deal of her time around the barn. In a setting where one's horsemanship was as important as the size of one's bank account, Diana routinely entered her animals in steeplechase events and enjoyed the same foxhunts as Jacqueline Bouvier Kennedy had led years earlier.

Despite Susan's love of horses, social interaction played a large role in the area's competitions. Once again, this was an area where Diana outshone her. For example, Diana loved to hold tailgate parties after participating in the local steeplechase and other such events. Opening the back of her truck, she would lay out an elaborate spread of picnic food and drinks and soon be presiding over an impromptu party.

On the rare occasions when Susan took part, she hovered in the background, unable to bring herself to make small talk in the raucous party atmosphere.

Diana's gregariousness was reciprocated. She was frequently invited to have dinner at the homes of the other members of the horsy set. But her host rarely suggested she bring her twin sister along. Some members of their social set found that being around a young woman with so few social graces made them uncomfortable. Susan's habit of avoiding eye contact and her reluctance to join in any conversation made them hesitant to include her name on their social rosters. Through the sport of polo, the heiress did become acquainted with several women. Among them was Jane Rowe.

But while Susan rejected the social aspects of horse culture, her love of working with the animals themselves was sincere. She enjoyed competing in a variety of equestrian events. She particularly enjoyed the discipline of dressage, which is very much like a dance on horseback.

She also enjoyed "jumpers," which requires clearing a number of fences without regard to style, only time, and "hunters," which is more concerned with form and style than speed.

Susan, however, stopped short at foxhunts. While her sister Diana yearly joined the prestigious Loudoun and Rappahannock County hunts, Susan's love of animals prevented her from even considering chasing after foxes.

Perhaps her interest in polo was a natural extension of her love of animals and sportsmanship. Or perhaps it was something more. Maybe, for this woman who had always considered herself an outsider, the romantic sport offered an even greater promise: a way to express the passion she felt was missing in her personal life.

CHAPTER 7

SUSAN STEERED HER TOYOTA TURBO ALONG ROUTE 17, admiring the rolling green hills and expansive estates that dotted both sides of the countrified four-lane highway. On the passenger seat beside her lay the weekly newspaper that she had been reading earlier that morning. It was folded back to the page that featured an article about the newly-opened Willow Run Polo School.

The warm May sun reflected off the windshield as Susan pressed down hard on the gas pedal and sped past the Fast-food restaurants and miniature strip malls that were sprouting up along a small segment of the rural roadway.

While Susan enjoyed the act of driving, her love of automobiles went far beyond that. Sam Cummings had been her mentor in the area of collectible cars, providing one more link between father and daughter.

Ever since she was a little girl, she had shared her father's love of high-performance autos. Of the two sisters, Susan was the tomboy. She preferred wearing pants to dresses, never adorned her face with lipstick or eyeshadow, and liked to accompany her father to the shooting range to work on her marksmanship.

But when it came to automobiles, both father and daughter shared a consuming interest. Out of all the acquisitions Sam Cummings' wealth afforded him, he took particular pleasure in his luxury foreign cars. When friends would come to visit him in Villars, and requested directions to his villa, he invariably told them, "It's too complicated, I'll meet you in the town square. Look for me, I'll be driving a Volkswagen.''

When they arrived for the rendezvous, Sam's visitors would find him waiting for them behind the wheel of a shiny Porsche. "How do you like my Volkswagen?" he would yell from the driver's seat.

Like her father, Susan had a great appreciation for expensive cars and enjoyed spending hours talking about them with other devotees. She was especially proud of her most recent purchase, her Toyota Turbo, and found great pleasure in its speed and performance.

Squinting her eyes against the glare of the afternoon sun, Susan slowed her car, then signaled left to cross the oncoming traffic of Route 17. Gripping the steering wheel, she piloted her shiny black sports car along the rocky two-lane road until she spotted the freestanding mailboxes that marked the entrance to Willow Run. The school was located next to the impressive farm of Bill Ylvisaker, a founding member of the Great Meadow Polo Club, and adjacent to the home of Susan's friend, Jane Rowe.

Turning left into the driveway, the slender heiress drove several feet and then pressed on the brake as she crossed the tiny dirt bridge that traversed the property's babbling creek. Her eyes widened with excitement as she spotted the school's enormous clapboard barn and the incredible view of the majestic Blue Ridge Mountains that rose up behind it. As she neared the rustic red structure, she admired the cluster of sleek polo ponies that poked their heads over the brown rail-and-post fence that corralled them.

Setting the parking brake on her Turbo, Susan stepped out of the automobile and adjusted the seat of her light-tan riding pants. The graceful branches of the weeping willow trees danced in the breeze as she ambled toward the entrance to the barn. It appeared that the exterior had just been given a fresh coat of red paint. As she neared the wooden structure, her eyes were drawn to the pair of polo mallets that hung above its lofty stable doors.

Peeking her head inside, Susan saw stacks of neatly-rolled hay piled in front of the stalls where chocolate-brown ponies stood chewing on dried grass. She smiled at the horses, noting that they were much smaller than the ones she was accustomed to riding at Ashland Farm.

As she stepped onto the barn's worn concrete floor, a short, olive-skinned man jumped up from the redwood picnic table just outside the barn and followed her inside.

"I'd like to sign up for polo lessons," Susan told him in a soft whisper.

"Sure, follow me."

The groom escorted her to a rear office where she was introduced to Juan Salinas Bentley. The handsome polo instructor from Eaglepass, Texas, had been teaching at the Willow Run Polo School since it opened in 1992. The previous year, he had won the prestigious United States Polo Association's President's Cup at a tournament in Lexington, Kentucky, the biggest club-level polo competition in the country. Still basking from his success as a member of the Rappahannock team, he returned to Virginia, carrying the Cup and bringing with him to Fauquier County one of his winning teammates, Roberto Villegas.

Juan was unusual because he was one of the few American-born polo instructors in a sport dominated by Argentines. He spent summers in Warrenton, the hometown of his wife, Tammy, and traveled to the west coast of Florida for the winter polo season.

The year 1992 marked a turning point for the sport of polo in and around Warrenton. Juan was the first instructor to be hired at the new polo school. A few miles away, Peter Arundel, the son of wealthy publisher Arthur Arundel, was poised to open the Great Meadow Polo Club.

Nine years earlier, the senior Arundel, a former member of the CIA, and several of his friends had purchased a large, open tract in the area known as The Plains from a developer who wanted to build five hundred houses on the wet, low-lying property. The Plains was centrally located roughly halfway between the equestrian centers of Warrenton and Middleburg.

Arthur Arundel and his partners trucked in large quantities of sand and filled in an area that had once been home to nothing more than crayfish. They went on to establish the world-renowned Great Meadow equestrian center there, complete with facilities for hunters, jumpers, and steeplechase competitions. Great Meadow soon became home to the prestigious Virginia Gold Cup Steeplechase races, attracting crowds of 50,000 to 60,000 from across the country.

But the one thing the sprawling horse center did not have was a facility for polo. Interest in the sport was growing along the East Coast, but because of the vast tract of land required to play the sport and the large number of ponies necessary for a game of field polo, enthusiasts were limited to the private playing fields of wealthy patrons.

One of those who wanted to bring the sport to Great Meadow was Peter Arundel, an avid polo player, who took over the Times Community Newspapers from his father. An animated young man with dark, wavy hair and a youthful grin, he grew up foxhunting and eventing. He learned to play polo at a polo school in Potomac, Maryland. Over the years, some of the world's most recognized personalities had competed on the grassy polo grounds of Potomac. Among them were Charles, the Prince of Wales and actor Sylvester Stallone.

The junior Arundel and his wife Brady lived in Middleburg with their two young children and were eager to find a place nearby where Peter could play polo.

At first, he and other polo aficionados wanted to build a standard-size polo field at Great Meadow, in part because they wanted to share the game with a more diversified crowd. Their argument was that local equestrians could foxhunt in the winter, steeplechase in the spring and fall, and play polo in the summer. But he and his supporters ran into opposition from those who argued that the venture would be prohibitively expensive for most equestrians.

The trouble was that traditional polo is played on a Grassy field 300 yards long and 160 yards wide—equal in size to nine football fields—and requires four players to use at least six ponies during a game, one for each of the six periods or "chukkas."

Responding to the complaints, the group suggested the

creation of a polo arena measuring only 150 by 300 feet, roughly one-ninth the regulation size. The advantages of the arena were twofold: much less land would have to be set aside for the facility, and, even more important, only three players and two ponies would be needed to play a four-chukka game.

Peter Arundel and his supporters had hit on a winning plan and construction soon began. The new arena would be one of only a handful currently operating in the United States and would host a game that differed from traditional field polo in that it was faster-paced, like hockey, and required players to use a softer, inflatable ball in place of the sanctioned hard ball.

To make arena polo more accessible to the general public, the young newspaper publisher also founded the Willow Run Polo School, just down the road from Great Meadow. He hired Juan Salinas Bentley to help get it off the ground.

Juan divided his time between Willow Run Polo School, which housed the ponies but was not yet fully equipped for polo instruction, and the polo arena at Great Meadow, where the students trained and competed. Classes were held on Tuesday and Thursday evenings under the stadium lighting.

When Susan Cummings voiced a desire to learn the game, Juan signed her up for the standard package of ten lessons. He was immediately encouraged by her horsemanship, but found her timid behavior in the arena puzzling. Each time he shouted a command in her direction, Susan's face would drop and she looked as though she was going to cry. From her reaction, it appeared to Juan that she was interpreting his feedback as a scolding and seemed upset that she was somehow being singled out. He expected the seemingly frail woman to quietly drop out, but much to his surprise, she continued to attend. After completing her first ten lessons, she signed up for another ten, and continued to play through the end of the season.

The following May, when Susan returned to the Willow Run Polo School, she found Jean Marie Turon inside the giant red barn. He had replaced Juan Salinas Bentley, who left Great Meadow at the end of the 1994 season for another playground of the rich and famous, the tony Hamptons on Long Island's East End.

Turon, an Argentine polo instructor with dark continental looks and piercing brown eyes, had just completed his morning polo classes and was getting ready to exercise his ponies when the willowy woman with the soft French accent appeared in his office.

His hands tucked loosely in the front pockets of his blue jeans, Jean Marie leaned against his desk and stared at the slender woman in the tight riding pants as she began to talk. She spoke so quietly that he strained to hear her words over the whinny of the ponies that were standing in the stalls a few feet behind her. It was only after he moved closer to her that he was able to hear her well enough to understand that she was interested in signing up for another series of polo lessons.

The instructor with the dense mustache and shock of brown hair had spent the previous winter in Palm Beach, Florida. He had come to the United States from Argentina some years before and after traveling the U.S. polo circuit for several seasons, had found a welcome climate in the Virginia hunt country.

In between drags on his Marlboro, he discussed the course of instruction with Susan. He told her that he charged sixty dollars per class, and then signed her up for lessons two times a week. The school was now equipped with wood horses to help students learn the fundamentals of swinging the mallet while in a stationary position. But the bulk of the instruction was still held across the highway in the polo arena at Great Meadow.

When Susan returned for her first day of class, Jean Marie was immediately impressed by her strong riding abilities. But he noticed she had difficulty hitting the ball and wondered if she'd be able to develop the special talents necessary to play polo competitively.

During his years as an instructor he'd seen many promising students fail to acquire the ability to precisely control the ponies in the arena. He tried to impress upon his pupils that one of the most fundamental aspects of the game was to get the animal to stop on a dime, and then immediately turn and gallop off in another direction after the ball.

Many of his students found it difficult to work the ponies so hard. They felt comfortable riding and being around horses from their other equestrian pursuits, but polo was fundamentally different in that they had to be willing to push the horse to its physical limits time and again. Jean Marie observed that many Americans could not bring themselves to work the ponies as hard as they had to; they seemed more inclined to treat the animals like household pets.

He could tell from the way that Susan handled the horses that she had had years of training, but he was still skeptical about her ability to make the transition from the more refined pursuits of dressage, hunters, and jumpers. She seemed fragile and soft-hearted, and it remained to be seen whether she would be able to make the difficult leap to competitive polo.

Right from the beginning, Jean Marie observed that Susan was very dedicated to the sport. He noted that she spent extra time hanging around the barn, grooming and exercising the animals, and that she also showed up at the school for additional lessons.

But it soon became clear that polo was not the only thing on his student's mind. He believed the demure soft-spoken woman had taken a romantic interest in him. Her flirtations didn't come as any great surprise. Jean Marie had grown accustomed to the playful come-ons of female students. He politely shrugged off Susan's solicitations as nothing more than a harmless crush.

It wasn't until she began showing up as early as 8 a.m. and hanging around the barn until well after closing that he began to question her intentions. He was struck by the long hours she spent with the polo ponies and found it troubling that she lingered into the evening, well after everybody else had already gone home.

"Doesn't she have anything else to do?" Jean Marie wondered to himself.

He knew she was a woman of considerable means, and that she lived on a grand estate on the outskirts of Warrenton. It seemed odd that someone of her age and social standing would choose to spend so many of her nights cleaning stalls and caring for horses.

Jean Marie soon realized that Susan's attendance at Willow Run seemed to coincide with each of the five days he taught classes there. On some nights, he even found her hanging in the horse stalls until nearly 10 p.m., continuing to groom ponies that had already been tended to, and seemingly looking for chores around the barn.

"Susan, it's time to leave," he would have to direct her. It was late and he wanted to go home.

"Okay, Jean Marie, I am just finishing up," she promised.

Soon, rumors began to circulate among the workers at Willow Run that Jean Marie and Susan were engaged in a romantic affair. In spite of his repeated denials of any involvement with the thirty-three-year-old, his polo companions were convinced that "something" was going on: if not an affair, at least a casual fling. After all, a romance would help explain Susan's mysterious behavior and her persistent presence.

Jean Marie continued to dispute the scuttlebutt around the barn, but his attempts were all but thwarted when he learned that Susan had signed up for instruction at the Alta Mera Polo School in Charlottesville, where he worked as an instructor on Saturday and Monday afternoons—his two days off.

"Why don't we go together in one car?" Susan suggested, cornering Jean Marie in the small tack room inside the barn.

The instructor stepped back, not quite certain how to respond. Taking a long, deep puff of the cigarette he had smoked right down to its filter, he stared at Susan. He didn't really want to travel with her, since he knew being seen driving with her would fuel even more gossip.

At the same time, he thought about how nice it would be if he could take a nap during the thirty-minute journey. His busy training schedule left him little time to rest between lessons, and he was often exhausted by the end of each week. Stamping his cigarette out on the red vise that sat on top of his workbench, the Argentine instructor proposed a compromise.

"Let me pay for the gas," he countered.

"No way, I'll use the gas from the farm," she replied, explaining that she had her own private gas pump at Ashland Farm.

"Well, okay, let's try it," Jean Marie agreed reluctantly.

Hopping into the passenger seat of the shiny black sports car one Saturday afternoon, Jean Marie felt uneasy. He kept his eyes away from Susan, instead staring out the car window as she steered past the weeping willow trees that graced the school's grassy pasture. As they drove down the dirt road and across the small, rambling creek near the entrance area to the property, the instructor fastened his seatbelt.

Aside from his nervousness, he didn't like how fast Susan was driving. As they headed down Route 17, his discomfort increased as he noted the way she disregarded the speed limit and paid little heed to the police cars that were parked along the sides of the road with their radar detectors pointed at oncoming traffic. Jean Marie couldn't believe that Susan didn't even slow down when she saw one in her rear-view mirror. Instead, she continued at a rapid pace, usually ten to twenty miles above the speed limit. Her flagrant attitude toward police officers, and her seeming disrespect for people in positions of authority, troubled the polo instructor. When an officer did signal her to pull over to the side of the road, Jean Marie watched as she graciously accepted the speeding ticket and then threw it in her purse, knowing she would pay the fine later.

Gripping the door handle for balance, the polo instructor lit up a cigarette, realizing it was going to be difficult for him to close his eyes while she was driving at such high speeds. He sighed, knowing he would now have to engage in conversation with this peculiar woman.

As they pulled into the driveway of the Alta Mera Polo School, Jean Marie waved a hello to his friend, Christy.

Christy was the manager of the rustic riding center, and she and Jean Marie had negotiated an agreeable arrangement.

The deal put thirty dollars in Jean Marie's pocket and twenty five dollars in hers for each student who signed up at Alta Mera for lessons. For that sum, Jean Marie provided hourly polo instruction, and Christy supplied the horses and the use of her barn.

Introducing Susan to his business partner, Jean Marie ambled over to the stable to prepare the ponies while Susan and Christy headed for the office to go over the price of the lessons.

Jean Marie had been traveling to Charlottesville with Susan for just a short time when he noticed a discrepancy in the money he was receiving from Christy for his instruction. At the end of each lesson, he counted his cash, and for some unexplainable reason, his earnings kept coming up short. He found the difference curious, but was unsure how to approach Christy about the matter. He hadn't really been paying close attention to the number of students enrolling each afternoon, and he was aware that Christy's cousin was among those taking instruction.

Maybe she was not charging her relative for the classes, Jean Marie thought to himself, and reluctantly decided to let the matter go.

The following day, he was presented with yet another dilemma. This time, Susan was insisting that he take over the wheel of her sports car on their rides to Alta Mera.

"I would like you to drive," she told Jean Marie in her soft, accented voice.

Great, he thought. This arrangement was not working out the way he had planned.

Jean Marie hesitated, not quite sure what to do. He didn't really want to drive her car; that would defeat the whole purpose of his initial acceptance of the invitation, to catch a few winks of sleep. And the new proposal would put him in a position of having to engage in conversation with Susan.

Striking a compromise, the polo instructor agreed to drive the sports car in one direction, if Susan would take over the wheel on the return trip.

"Okay, Jean Marie," Susan said in her controlled, emotionless manner. "That sounds fine."

That Saturday, the five-foot-eight instructor climbed into the driver's seat of Susan's car. Arranging his slender frame into the supple leather upholstery, Jean Marie checked the part of his thick, brown hair in the rear-view mirror, and then readjusted the car's side-view mirrors as Susan got in next to him.

Pressing lightly on the gas pedal, Jean Marie steered the Toyota out of the school's driveway, and headed for Route 17. He felt uneasy about the way the automobile reacted when he pressed on the accelerator. It made him nervous that he did not have to step very hard in order for the car to exceed the speed limit.

It didn't take long for Jean Marie to notice the flashing blue lights in the car's rear-view mirror. Looking down at the speedometer, he noticed that he was exceeding the limit by almost fifteen miles per hour. Clenching his teeth, the polo instructor signaled to the officer with his right blinker and slowed the car along the grassy embankment of the four-lane roadway. Graciously, he accepted the summons, but inside he was annoyed. He had not been cited for a traffic infraction since his last speeding ticket in 1988, and felt angry that he would now have a violation on his otherwise clean driver's license.

A few days later, the two were again cruising along Route 17. The sun was high in the sky, and the temperature outside was nearing eighty degrees. Turning to Jean Marie, Susan smiled and leaned over.

"Jean Marie, don't you love my car?" She looked over at the trainer, who sat straight up in the driver's seat, his fingers tightly gripping the black leather steering wheel.

"No," he curtly replied. His sexy, continental accent seemed a stark contrast to the angry tone in his voice. "I hate it!"

An eerie silence fell over the car as Jean Marie continued his rampage.

"First," he said, "because I got a speeding ticket while I was driving it. And second, it's black, and it's too hot in the summer."

Jean Marie shifted his eyes to Susan and watched her face

as she slowly digested his harsh words. For the rest of the ride, she did not utter a sound.

Her odd stillness left him feeling uneasy. On repeated occasions, he had tried to read her emotions. No matter what had transpired, he noticed that her facial expression never changed. Even when she was angry with him, he would never know it until the following day. Instead of confronting him directly, Susan would express her displeasure by not showing up for her polo lesson the next afternoon.

This time, nearly a week passed before she returned to Willow Run. Jean Marie and several of the grooms were seated at the redwood picnic table outside the wooden barn when she pulled up behind the wheel of a brand new Toyota Turbo.

Holding his cigarette tightly between his thumb and index finger, the Argentine instructor raised it to his lips and took a long, deep drag as he watched Susan park her new white sports car alongside one of the horse trailers. He smiled to himself, realizing that she had traded in the shiny black one for the exact same model—only this one was white.

This incident wasn't the only one that Jean Marie found surprising. Another time Susan caught him off guard by asking if he would be interested in going to Sarasota with her to play polo. She said she knew that many of the players remained in Virginia until the end of September and then headed south to join teams in Sarasota and Palm Beach for the winter season, and she wondered if Jean Marie would like to accompany her to the Sunshine State.

Flabbergasted, he listened politely as Susan outlined her proposal, telling him that she would provide the trailer for his ponies, and even pick up the cost of their room and board.

Jean Marie shot her a look.

"First of all," he started in his smooth, Spanish accent, "if you want to be a sponsor, you are supposed to pay for the horses, the trailer, and the truck."

"We can go together," Susan interrupted. "We can use your horses, and I'll buy the truck and trailer. I can find you an apartment or we can just share one."

Jean Marie stared at her. He marveled at the way she could misread situations.

She obviously did not understand that he was not interested in her in a romantic way, and that he was not looking for a free ride to Florida, whatever the terms. Besides, he had a girlfriend.

It was not the first invitation she had extended to Jean Marie. During the course of the summer, Susan had offered her indoor riding arena to him, explaining that he could use the equestrian ring at Ashland Farm to teach classes, or for polo matches, if he so desired. She was proud of the facility that she and her sister had built and took great pleasure in giving tours of the rink to guests of the farm.

Out of curiosity, Jean Marie visited the 350-acre property. He even played polo in the indoor arena. To observers, it was unclear whether he was really there on business or whether his visit was more of a social call. Whatever the reason, he declined the use of the arena, telling Susan that the ring was not regulation size.

By this time, Jean Marie was growing worried. Susan was now enrolled in every one of the polo classes that he was teaching. To make matters worse, he and his girlfriend, Jennifer, were alarmed that she kept turning up unexpectedly at the bars and restaurants they frequented.

It made Jean Marie uneasy that she sat across from them at the local eateries, staring in their direction as they downed a few cocktails and enjoyed a bite to eat. Reluctantly, he admitted that her continued presence was giving him the creeps, and was putting him in the awkward position of having to reassure his girlfriend that she had no reason to worry.

It was not long before Jean Marie heard a rumor that Susan had taken up with one of the Mexican stablehands working at Willow Run. Word around the polo school was that a young groom from Mexico had been out with the heiress several times.

Jean Marie was surprised at Susan's choice in men, and even more astounded when he heard that the barn worker had been the one to call it off. To his amazement, he learned that the broad-faced stablehand hadn't liked the way Susan steered him toward the least expensive items on the restaurant menus and often mentioned the large sums of money her father was sending her.

There was a game going on in the Great Meadow polo arena in late June when Jean Marie and his students arrived at the popular equestrian center. As part of the training, many of Jean Marie's students were encouraged to attend the afternoon and evening polo matches to watch the professionals compete as a way of learning more about the game.

On the playing field, Jean Marie spotted his pal, Roberto Villegas. Roberto had borrowed several of his horses, and a few of the stable boys from Willow Run had volunteered to act as his grooms.

It amazed Jean Marie that the guys always jumped to help the polo pro with the ponies, even though they rarely got paid for their time. They told him they really didn't care that Roberto had no money. For them, it was enough of an honor to be working with the polo club's top-scoring player.

Besides, they knew that Roberto always repaid them with an authentic "asado," a traditional Argentine barbecue where meat is cooked in a pit. After the matches, he never failed to show up at Willow Run with a carload of meat and all the trimmings to put on an outstanding outdoor barbecue. For him, it was the most enjoyable part of the entire event.

Jean Marie was standing on the sidelines watching the game with two of his students—one of them Susan Cummings—when Roberto ambled over.

"This is Roberto Villegas." Jean Marie turned first to introduce the polo pro to Susan Cummings and then to the other pupil who stood by his side.

The slender instructor lit up a cigarette and watched as Susan awkwardly smiled at Roberto. He was amused by her attempt to engage him in conversation.

"Are you Argentine?" she asked the handsome polo player.

"Actually, I am, but I'm made in Taiwan." Roberto

parted his thick sensual lips to reveal a sparkling-white grin, and a dimple creased in his right cheek.

Jean Marie laughed at the silly joke and glanced over at Susan. He was accustomed to Roberto's offbeat sense of humor, but he noticed that his remark had taken Susan by surprise. The joke seemed lost on her.

Jean Marie smiled as the frail brunette stood awkwardly next to her pony, staring down at the dirt beneath her boots as she tried to regain her composure. It was at that moment that Roberto interrupted with another nonsensical line.

His kooky comment came as no surprise to Jean Marie, who, over the years, had been on the receiving end of an endless stream of Roberto's jokes and pranks.

In fact, not much time had passed since Roberto had invited nearly sixty people to Jean Marie's house for a barbecue that he said he was putting together for his polo buddy's birthday.

The only problem was, Jean Marie had no idea about the party and was stunned when carloads of invited guests began appearing at his door around 7 p.m. He later learned that Roberto had told the party-goers that he would be the one to provide the lambs for the asado. As part of the hoax, Roberto did not even show up at the gathering until nearly 11 p.m. When he did arrive, he was empty-handed, but had no problem joining in the feast that Jean Marie and the other guests had scrambled to assemble. It was a typical stunt for Roberto, who often took it upon himself to plan great big parties at other people's homes.

Jean Marie was able to laugh at his friend's foolish prank, but he was aware that many people found Roberto's strange sense of humor more than hard to take. On several occasions, he'd heard stories of how Roberto had brought grown men to fits of rage. But he also knew that most of the time, the angry targets of Roberto's jokes would calm down and, after several days, even shake his hand.

For Susan, Roberto's quirky comments seemed harmless and easy to ignore. Like the stable boys who swarmed around him, she found it exhilarating just to be in the company of the dashing polo star.

* * *

As the 1995 polo season wore on, Jean Marie received a
phone call from Christy, his friend at the Alta Mera Polo
School.

Chatting from the desk phone of his small back office at
Willow Run, Jean Marie listened as she told him that she
planned to take a short vacation, and then asked if he
wouldn't mind watching the school while she was out of
town. Not only would he be responsible for the lessons, but
he would also need to take over the accounting duties until
she returned from her three-day trip.

Jean Marie agreed. On the final day of Jean Marie's work
as manager at Alta Mera, he collected the checks. One by
one, each of the students had handed him a check for fifty-
five dollars—thirty dollars of which would go to him for his
instruction.

Reaching out to take the check that Susan Cummings was
giving him, Jean Marie looked down at the green paper and
saw that she had made it out in the amount of twenty-five
dollars.

"What's this?" Jean Marie asked her. He was puzzled by
the payment.

"Well," Susan began, "since we are coming together and
using my truck, I am only paying for the use of the horses."

Jean Marie could feel himself growing red. The muscles
in his arms tightened, his teeth clenched, as he pulled a cigarette from the pack that he kept in his rear pocket. He could
not believe what he was hearing. For much of the season, he
had put up with Susan following him around like a puppy
dog.

"That brat, that wealthy brat," the irate instructor mum-
bled under his breath. "How can she be so cheap? Does she
really have such little respect for my work that she feels
entitled to deny me the thirty dollars I charge for my instruction?"

Jean Marie could barely hide his anger. After all, he was
traveling with her on her invitation. And hadn't he offered
to pay for the gas?

The instructor remained silent during the thirty-minute

ride back to the Willow Run Polo School. He did not feel it was the right time to confront Susan.

The school's owner, Christy, meanwhile, had no idea what was going on between Jean Marie and the genteel horsewoman who had accompanied him to Alta Mera for most of the season. She knew that Susan was fond of the handsome polo instructor, and like many of the female students, probably had a crush on him. But she was also convinced that Susan's affection for Jean Marie was prompted in part by the fact that he had introduced her to a sport— and a way of life—that was bringing her intense pleasure.

It was clear to Christy that this naïve, gentle-hearted newcomer longed to be part of the polo community at Alta Mera. She appeared to have had few friends or hobbies and seemed anxious to be accepted by the close-knit group of polo enthusiasts at the school.

She believed that Susan found the atmosphere at Alta Mera to be friendly and much more open than it was at Great Meadow. There, everyone welcomed her. Nobody knew who she was, and nobody cared.

Even Christy had grown fond of the shy brunette woman from Warrenton. It seemed that whenever she looked around, she noticed Susan caressing her Labrador puppy or bathing one of her horses.

On the nights that Christy stayed late at the barn, Susan would wait and help her walk the horses up to the field. It was apparent to Christy, that Susan's feelings about animals was paramount to human beings. It was obvious that she would lay her life down to protect them.

In fact, she thought nothing of it when, at the end of each lesson, Susan presented her with a check that covered only the cost of the horses. And while most of the students paid for both the lesson and the horses in a single check, she assumed that Jean Marie and his companion had worked out an arrangement for the lessons. Besides, she was paying the Argentine instructor a flat fee of $100 per day, regardless of whether or not there were students attending the day's lesson.

Even so, Jean Marie was furious. Storming over to Susan's white Toyota, the infuriated trainer shouted at her: "You owe me six hundred dollars!"

His announcement was met with a cool, icy stare. She continued to wear the same enigmatic look as he accused her of swindling him out of six hundred dollars over a period of ten weeks.

Jean Marie was astonished at the way Susan avoided his gaze. He grew even more agitated when she refused to acknowledge that she had done anything wrong. He observed that her face remained expressionless, her eyes vacant, as he shouted at her, telling her that he was angry that she had not been paying for the lessons.

After a long pause, Jean Marie quieted down, waiting for Susan to apologize for her indiscretion. Instead, she told him that she had no intention of paying her debt.

"When I feel like I owe, I pay." Strands of her wavy auburn hair blew around Susan's bony face as she calmly explained her policy. "But I don't feel like I owe you."

"Well, then, Susan," the seething instructor began, "congratulations. You've just earned enough points to graduate from polo school."

That afternoon, when he returned to Willow Run, Jean Marie typed up Susan's polo certificate, handed it to her, and told her not to come back. It wouldn't be the last time Susan would antagonize the polo instructor to that degree. But she didn't care. Susan didn't need Jean Marie anymore. She had found another, more interesting possibility in Roberto Villegas.

CHAPTER 8

Susan Cummings could hardly believe that she was actually being courted by Great Meadow's star polo player.

Jean Marie couldn't believe it either. He was astonished as, during the weeks following his casual introduction, he saw his polo buddy making subtle advances toward Susan at the local polo functions and barbecues. And he found it even more remarkable when he observed the two of them at Great Meadow, walking together and holding hands. From what he could see, Roberto was smitten with the Cummings woman.

"Don't go out with her, Roberto." Jean Marie tried to persuade his friend to find somebody else. "She's so weird."

His advice went unheeded. Jean Marie could do nothing but smile when Roberto told him that he found Susan attractive and that her interest in horses was a welcome change. He knew that Roberto's previous relationship had ended, in part, because of his obsession with the game of polo. And although he had liked his pal's last girlfriend, Kimberly Quinn, he was aware that she had broken off their four-year affair because of Roberto's inability to give up the transient life the game of polo demanded.

It had often seemed to Jean Marie that Roberto spent more time in the barn tending to his ponies than he did in the house with Kimberly, who went by the nickname Kelli. And while she did nothing to hide her interest in settling down and starting a family with a man who had a steady job and a steady income, her longing became greater as the years passed.

Roberto had first spotted the curvy, dark-haired woman as she stood on the sidelines of a polo match at the Cheval Polo and Tennis Club, just north of Tampa, Florida.

Kelli, a college-educated woman from a wealthy family, kept a hunter/jumper horse at the grassy field. When Roberto first approached her, she was instantly charmed. It wasn't long before she invited him to move into the house she and her sisters owned in the working-class town of Bradenton, near Sarasota.

Although Kelli had no interest in learning to play the game of polo, she accompanied Roberto to the matches. She even traveled with him in the summers to Virginia, where the couple lived on the properties of the patrons who hired Roberto to compete on their teams.

The first year they were together, Roberto was invited to play for American League football star King Corcoran in Fredericksburg, Virginia. It was an honor to be asked to compete on the team of such a talented man, competing in a series of small tournaments in the Washington, D.C., area. He enjoyed living in Fredericksburg, where he and Kelli rented a house in the countrified town that is known for its Civil War battlefields.

All that changed in the middle of July. Members of the Rappahannock polo team approached him and explained that its patron, Bill Fannon, owner of Fannon Petroleum, and his teammates, were looking for a pro to help them qualify for the United States Polo Association's President's Cup competition. They had heard about Roberto, and were anxious to see if they could persuade him to join them in their quest to win the prestigious athletic event.

For Roberto, the invitation was not only flattering, it was one he could not turn down. That week, he and Kelli loaded his five horses onto his enormous trailer—big enough to accommodate sixteen ponies—and jumped into the cab of his Ford F350 pickup to head for Laurel Hill Farm in Rappahannock County, a rural, sleepy, gracious part of the South, sixty-five miles west of Washington, D.C.

It is not uncommon for wealthy landowners who are less skilled at the sport of polo to buy their way into the game by hiring professional players and supplying them with horses and accommodations. More often than not, the athletes come from a small group of young men from Argentina known as "Argies."

Because Roberto was an outstanding player, his housing was deluxe by polo players' standards. His cottage was amid the handful of polo accommodations clustered at the base of the Blue Ridge Mountains. Not only was the interior of his cottage impressive; the lodging also offered sweeping views of the expansive emerald-green pastures of Bill Fannon's rural estate.

When Roberto arrived, he was introduced to Juan Salinas Bentley, who was among the three players on the Rappahannock team. Practicing on Fannon's very own regulation-size polo field at his gorgeous hunt country estate was energizing for the skilled Argentine. On his days off, Roberto and his girlfriend enjoyed leisurely drives along the quaint country lanes, and would often stop to browse the town's craft and antique shops.

As the polo season progressed, the winning combination of Roberto, Juan, Bill Fannon, and Phillip Staple easily defeated the other seven teams in the Washington area to qualify for the national competition in Lexington, Kentucky. Roberto had not been back to the Midwest for nearly six years. He had been fired from the last job he held there in 1985; he'd gotten into a scuffle with the owner of the polo team on which he played. The tall, heavy-set patron accused Roberto of losing his temper when he learned of his termination, and said the young polo hopeful, who was nearly six inches shorter and fifty pounds lighter than the Indiana landscape contractor, pulled a knife on him in the parking lot of the Stardust Motel after he was asked to leave the premise. The team had been playing in a tournament in Napperville, Illinois.

Around the same time, Roberto's then-girlfriend, Margaret Bonnell of West Palm Beach, Florida, also complained of her lover's fiery temper. The dark-haired woman told a friend to summon the police to the small one-bedroom apartment the couple was renting in Napperville, after Roberto reportedly threatened her in an uncontrollable fit of rage. The two were in Napperville to buy polo ponies, and were leasing the tiny flat on a month-to-month basis. They intended to stay there only a short time; just long enough to purchase the horses and ship them to Florida, where they would train and then sell them for a profit.

When officers rang the doorbell on September 12, 1987, they were greeted by a sweating and shirtless Roberto. In a breathless voice, he told police that the two were only playing and assured them that there was nothing going on.

His girlfriend told the officers an entirely different story. She said an argument had erupted after two young women showed up at the front door looking for Roberto.

Deputies noticed scratches on Margaret's wrists, and scrapes on Roberto's chest. They listened as Margaret explained that her boyfriend had "hit me with the flat part of his hand very hard on the head" and "put a blanket over me so I would not be able to scream."

In a statement to police, Margaret accused Roberto of yanking the telephone receiver out of the wall after he learned that she was talking to a male friend. She reported that he then dragged her across the floor before throwing her on the bed and covering her up with blankets to muffle her screams.

"Would you for God's sake do something?" Roberto reportedly pleaded with his girlfriend as police clamped handcuffs around his thick wrists. "They are taking me to jail."

Margaret just smiled and said nothing.

Years later, she told a reporter that she—and not Roberto—had instigated the incident, and said that she was the one who had used physical force. Margaret explained that they had both gotten scratched because she had flown into a jealous rage at the sight of the two women looking for Roberto. She began punching him and he had grabbed her wrists to stop her.

She went on to say that she had allowed police to arrest her lover as a way of getting back at him for his hurtful indiscretions. According to Margaret, Roberto "loved women." She reported that he constantly flirted and sought the attention of women, even in casual interactions at the supermarket.

Margaret had one more reason for being jealous. She told reporters that Roberto was the father of her only child, a boy with what she referred to as "Roberto's smile."*

While living in Florida, Roberto's ability to excel on the grassy polo fields afforded him greater opportunities to earn a living doing what he loved. Off the polo field, he seemed to be in better control of his emotions.

But on the polo field, he was fiercely competitive.

The very nature of the game—and the payment schedule—demand a high level of aggression. Polo is an extremely physical sport, so much so that it is labeled a "blood sport." The grass version of the game requires two teams to chase a ball across a large field. But the stakes are even higher than in football or other contact sports because the four players on each team are all on horseback.

In order to succeed as a polo player, enormous strength is only the first basic requirement. In addition, the player must possess the coordination to both swing a mallet and ride a galloping pony. He must also be an accomplished enough horseman to control the spirited animal and successfully maneuver it to stop and to turn, even at high speeds.

Even though the horses are agile and well-trained, their massive size and weight, combined with the demanding moves that the game requires, necessitate that the rider put the horses' welfare above his own. A collision at such a high speed would be even more disastrous for the horse than for its rider.

But the physical aspects are only the beginning. More

---

*After the trial, commonwealth's attorney Kevin Casey received a phone call from an Alabama-based attorney who said he had been retained by Margaret Bonnell. He told the prosecutor that she had called upon him to inquire about the possibility of bringing a civil action against Susan Cummings on behalf of her son. Phone calls by the author to the attorney were not returned. At the time of this writing, no further information was available.

important is the mental attitude of the rider. The only way to successfully make a living as a polo player is to continuously win. Players are compensated based on the number of goals they score during a game. There are two ways that they can typically be paid. One way is to be retained by a patron for the entire polo season—spring and summer in the Northeast and winter in the South. Riders are paid based on their handicap at a rate of $1,000 per goal. In other words, a player like Roberto Villegas, who had a handicap of three in grass polo, would be paid $3,000 a month, plus room and board for himself and his horses. The handicap is calculated based on a formula developed by the United States Polo Association. The other method of payment is a set fee per game. A player might earn nine hundred dollars and up for each game he plays.

In either case, being good isn't enough. The tremendous pressure to score goals creates a nearly overwhelming level of competitiveness among players who are already physical and aggressive sportsmen.

In the midst of this highly cut-throat milieu, Roberto Villegas was a small fish in Florida's large and intimidating pond. The Sunshine State was a popular spot for polo players from Argentina. Even Argentines who were considered mediocre players at home, quickly became shining stars in a country that produced few good players of its own. Because many of them came from extremely poor backgrounds with few prospects for a better life, coming to America offered them the chance to make a good living—and do it by engaging in a sport they loved.

As for the Americans, they were more than happy to employ the South American imports. Amateur polo players in the United States could easily afford to pay the relatively low salaries of the "cheap goals"—the term used to describe players who are invited to emigrate from rural Argentina. Even a rider who was rated as a zero handicap in his native land might play as well as most three-goal players in the United States.

Roberto Villegas was one such player. While he was hardly a star in Argentina—and in fact had no real experience except for the casual games he played in his poverty-stricken rural community—the considerably more modest standards of the Florida polo scene enabled him to work regularly.

In the United States the young immigrant found something even more rewarding than polo. In 1991, he met and fell in love with Kimberly Quinn. The attractive, twenty-seven-year-old brunette worked at the Sarasota Polo Club, where Roberto was also employed. For a while, Roberto's future seemed bright. He enjoyed a solid relationship with Kelli, as well as triumph after triumph on the polo fields of Western Florida.

This year marked the high point in Roberto's career. He summered in Virginia, and traveled to Kentucky to compete in the grand USPA tournament as a member of the Rappahannock team. The fact that his team took home the prestigious President's Cup was the highlight of his polo career—a day he would never forget. In addition to his great win, Roberto was also recognized as "Most Valuable Player" and his black mare was named "Most Valuable Horse."

For a poor young man from Argentina, life had never been sweeter.

Something new was brewing on the polo scene in Virginia, something that was to markedly affect Roberto's life. For the first time, arena polo was introduced at Great Meadow equestrian center in The Plains in 1992, creating an exciting new venue for polo in Fauquier County and drawing many new athletes into the area. One of them was Roberto Villegas.

After his stunning win in Lexington, Kentucky, the year before, the Argentine sportsman was invited back to hunt country for the 1992 summer polo season, this time to play for Travis and Suzanne Worsham's Heart in Hand team. He had met the couple the previous summer at Bill Fannon's farm in Rappahannock County. It was there that he and Kelli had struck up a friendship with Travis and his wife.

Fannon's world was a hard one for someone of limited means to penetrate. But Roberto, with his warm and easygoing temperament, was readily accepted, and almost overnight, he found himself invited to numerous social functions.

His years amid the prominent members of Florida's polo circuit had given him a polish that allowed him to move with ease among members of the wealthy social set. But he never forgot where he came from and felt equally comfortable with the grooms, stable boys, and his fellow Argentine polo players.

When Roberto returned to Virginia for a second season, his affable personality, coupled with his skill in the newly-established sport of arena polo, made him an instant local celebrity. His technique also proved well-suited to arena polo; his handicap rose from a three on Florida's traditional grass playing fields to a four at Great Meadow's newly-constructed polo arena. The higher handicap earned him the rank of top player at Great Meadow, made him an instant local hero, and gave him both acceptance and respect from the area's socialites. Adding to his stature was his win of the President's Cup in Lexington, Kentucky.

His credentials earned him a spot on Suzi and Travis Worsham's polo team. The couple named their Heart in Hand team after the successful restaurant and catering business they operated in Clifton, Virginia, an affluent suburban town located thirty miles west of Washington, D.C.

Travis, a handsome, fortyish entrepreneur, had been playing polo since 1978. But he had met with a string of disappointments after both of the teams he founded with his brother fell prey to developers interested in building on the land they had leased for the polo fields.

In 1992, Heart in Hand found a permanent home at Great Meadow. Not only did the center provide his team with a place to play; it also increased his catering clientele to include members of the horsy polo set.

Roberto and Kelli instantly hit it off with the Worshams. They lived in an authentic log cabin at the family's Clifton estate, and enjoyed many of their meals with the family in the gracious main house. The couples attended dinners and parties together, and over time, Travis and Roberto became the best of friends. What started out as a simple career move for the sportsman turned into something much more as he fell in love with his new surroundings in Virginia, and even started telling his friends that, when the day came, he would like to be buried in hunt country.

Roberto returned to play on Travis Worsham's team the following season, and again, he and Kelli took up residence on the couple's estate. Ironically, while the foursome enjoyed countless good times, behind closed doors Roberto and Kelli were watching their relationship fall apart.

After celebrating her thirtieth birthday, Kelli's vague desire to settle down and start a family began to grow stronger. She realized that Roberto's profession as a polo pro would never ensure the couple a steady income, or a bank account for their future. Perhaps even more significant, however, was Roberto's nomadic lifestyle. Kelli was growing tired of their constant moves to follow the polo circuit. After four years of traveling back and forth between Florida and Virginia, she expressed her desire to put down roots and make one place her home.

One more factor in Kelli's decision was Roberto's fiery nature. She had all but decided to leave when his temper reared its head and forced her to file a restraining order against her boyfriend of four years.

While Kelli knew the breakup was for the best, Roberto refused to accept her decision. In spite of her repeated requests that he move out, he continued to drag his heels, telling his girlfriend that he needed more time to find a place to live.

Unable to convince the 160-pound polo player that it was time to move out, Kelli gave him a deadline.

"You have two weeks to find a place to live, Roberto," she told him.

But her ultimatum did not produce any results. On Saturday, February 11, 1995, the couple began sparring. Their fight escalated, with Kelli finally calling the police to intervene.

In an incident report filed with the Manatee County Sheriff's Office, Kelli detailed the events that led up to Roberto's outburst:

He began fighting and he became very angry and said that he had men coming down from Chicago that would hurt me or anyone that tried to mess with him. He was also angry with people at work and said that it didn't cost very much money to have someone hurt (He did not name any names). I was very frightened when he arrived at my home and I told him that he needed to leave. He calmed down and said that he wanted to work things out but I told him no that I needed some time and space to myself for a while & that he must find somewhere else to live. He said that he would leave Sun. or Mon.

Things were relatively calm on Sunday but I borrowed a car from one of my sisters because I did not want to be with him. After work on Sunday I was taking a friend home (who is a man) and Roberto was parked on the north side of University Pkwy with the hood of his truck up. I waved to him as we passed and he got in his truck and began to follow us. He asked me to pull over and I told him that I was taking Craig home and that I would talk to him later. He fell back behind us and then pulled up again and told me to pull over and, again, I told him no. He then swerved his truck in front of me and nearly hit me, but I reacted quickly and had to drive up on the median to avoid crashing. He chased us a bit further up Univ. Pkwy. but I made a U turn and lost him in some back roads. I am now genuinely afraid of Roberto. I am fearful that he will attempt to hurt me or my animals. I am also afraid that he would vandalize my home.

We both work at the same polo complex in Sarasota. I believe that I will be very safe and protected there. It is a very large complex and I don't have to be in close proximity to him.

Sunday evening two Sheriff's Deputies escorted me to my home and they asked Roberto to leave the residence and he did so voluntarily. I agreed to take the rest of his possessions to the polo club on Tuesday at 3:00 where I will be escorted by several other people. I do, however, want to make sure that he is not allowed to return to my home.*

*Incident report filed by Kimberly J. Quinn with the Manatee County Sheriff's Office on February 12, 1995.

In her report to the Manatee sheriff's office, Kelli wrote that Roberto had access to two rifles, and that he "becomes more verbally abusive when drinking."

Sheriff's deputies distributed domestic violence packets to both Roberto and Kelli, and then waited at Kelli's home while Roberto voluntarily removed his belongings.

After his difficult breakup with Kelli, Roberto returned to Virginia in 1995 to play for the Worshams. This time he came alone.

Only six months had passed since his breakup with Kelli, yet already he was interested in someone else. The gentle young woman had instantly captivated him.

For Susan Cummings, the polo player's attention was more than flattering. She knew that everyone at Great Meadow admired Roberto Villegas. It was no secret that he was considered "the prize" by the polo groupies who attended the matches on Friday evenings dressed in stylish mini-skirts and spiked high-heels.

Yet, the shy brunette was not an active participant in the flirtatious sideline games. Instead, she watched the olive-skinned sportsman from the safety of one of the horse trailers that were stationed along the grassy parking field. Peering through the truck's open window, she joked with the other women standing nearby, telling them that Roberto was hers, and no one else's.

It was easy for Susan to spot the dashing Argentine in the dusty polo arena. He always wore a red helmet trimmed with a stripe of white tape along the front. It was his way of distinguishing himself from the rest of the players on the field.

When Roberto finally approached her in late September, she happily accepted his invitations to dinner and the movies. Romances between pros like Roberto and wealthy horsewomen like Susan Cummings were common and generally short-lived, usually ending when the polo season was over. But the two had grown inseparable during their brief time together and Susan was convinced she had found a treasure in Roberto Villegas.

He was everything that she was not: confident, self-assured, and well-liked by his peers. His name could be found on everyone's social roster, and in spite of his humble beginnings, he was asked to attend the parties of the powerful and the super-rich. Although Susan was the one with the proper background, Roberto seemed to hold the ticket to the social events.

The son of a poor farmhand, Roberto had come to the United States at the age of twenty-one with dreams of earning a place in the international polo circuit. He was born on October 22, 1959, and raised in Chaján, Argentina, a small ranching village in the northwest part of the province of Cordoba.

The agrarian town was seventy kilometers from the city of Rio Cuarto and a twelve-hour bus ride from the rows of tidy high-rise apartments and impressive nineteenth-century houses of the country's sprawling megalopolis of Buenos Aires. The capital city—with its wide boulevards, palatial mansions, corner kiosks filled with bouquets of fresh-cut flowers, and bakeries and cafes on every block—is more reminiscent of Paris than the Spanish-style cities of its South American neighbors.

Roberto grew up far from the cosmopolitan, me-first society of Buenos Aires. Life was considerably simpler in the Pampas (the Plains) of rural Argentina. There, in the dry, windswept region, dotted with rugged, colorful mountain ranges and flat treeless plains, his family lived among the gauchos who herd the cattle that provide Argentina with the beef it consumes in mass quantity.

Like many of his neighbors, Roberto's father was a cattle rancher's helper and worked long hours for little pay. His stipend was barely enough to provide for his wife and their children—Roberto, his older brother, and younger sister, Patricia.

The family lived in a cramped bungalow that had no running water, electricity, or telephone service. To use the toilet, the children walked to the outhouse in the rear of the small, one-story dwelling. Chickens and goats roamed the dusty yards of the town's seven hundred residents.

It didn't matter to the Villegas family that they could not

afford a car. After all, there was little use for a vehicle on the village's three paved roads. Horseback was the preferred mode of transportation, and a means that Roberto mastered in his youth.

The gregarious, slightly overweight child with the thick black hair and a smile characterized by a mouthful of crooked, stained teeth, attended elementary school in the village. But he quit his studies after the seventh grade to work alongside his father, tending to the cattle on their employer's farm.

He enjoyed afternoon soccer games with the kids in the neighborhood, but his real dream was of becoming a polo star. After soccer, polo was a national pastime in the South American country, and young children idolized its ten-goal heroes. But Roberto's aspirations were far greater than his family's means.

Even at a tender age, Roberto understood that the sport was expensive. It required a large tract of flat, grassy land, and players needed to have access to at least six or seven ponies. The closest Roberto ever came to the gentleman's game were the afternoons when he borrowed his neighbor's horse and indulged in amateur matches with the other teens who lived in the area. At fifteen, he started competing with the local boys and, like his companions, secretly dreamed of turning the exciting afternoon activity into a real career.

When he reached his twenty-first birthday, the chubby, uneducated man got his chance. He was invited to come to the United States to work as a groom in sunny Florida for a high-goal polo player from Argentina. The professional sportsman promised to pay Roberto a small salary and provide him with a place to live in exchange for his services as a stablehand. It was an offer he could not refuse.

Approaching his mother, Roberto explained the exciting news, and watched as she courageously fought back tears.

"Mama," Roberto reportedly addressed the matriarch of his poor, tightly-knit family, "I don't want you to die in poverty."

In Argentina, it was not unsual for children to leave home, but it was rare for them to travel far from their families. Yet

Roberto's mother understood her son's reasons for wanting to leave. She knew in her heart that the stablehand job could ultimately offer her son a future in the United States.

As he stood in the doorway of the family's tiny house, Roberto watched as his mother broke down in tears and then waved him a sorrowful goodbye.

"This is a chance for you to make something of your life!" she reportedly yelled after him as he walked toward the bus stop, turning to flash her one last smile.

Toting the small piece of luggage that contained his worldly possessions—several pairs of jeans and a pair of work boots—Roberto landed in the United States. He spoke no English, and was barely literate even in his native language of Spanish.

When he arrived at the barn for his first day of work, he was out of shape and unrefined. Even worse, he soon became the butt of ugly jokes directed at the unappetizing green stains that coated his teeth. He knew they were tarnished from his repeated exposure to the caustic chemicals used to treat the drinking water in his tiny farming village. But he hadn't had the money to fix them and, as a result, his smile caused him great embarrassment.

In fact, Roberto's smile earned him the cruel moniker, "Green Teeth." But his easy-going nature allowed the taunts to roll off his back, and he even managed to laugh along as his fellow workers chided him about his unflattering dental condition.

He was in America now, and was being offered the chance to earn decent money for work that he enjoyed. His position exposed him to the local polo patrons, and provided him with an opportunity to get his feet wet using other people's horses. Soon, he was attracting the respect of other players, and found himself on the receiving end of invitations to represent teams in the resort areas of Tampa and Sarasota. He was even asked to play for a patron in Fort Worth, Texas.

A turning point in Roberto's career came when a local dentist in Sarasota gifted him with a full set of pearly white caps. The gleaming white teeth enhanced his appearance and

improved his looks and immediately earned him more respect among the members of the polo circuit.

Life among the palm trees and pristine white beaches of
the posh vacation towns of Florida's west coast suited the
young, ambitious player. Roberto found the members of the
high-society polo circuit a welcoming bunch. His talents on
the grassy polo field earned him invitations to the social
functions and barbecues held on the lawns of their impressive
summer estates—and steamy romances with wealthy patrons
who found excitement in the brief and lusty encounters.

But the game was competitive and it wasn't easy to make
a living as a polo player. Winning and scoring were what
earned players jobs, and there was no room for failure. The
simple rule of the game was no win, no pay.

On the playing field, Roberto blossomed into a well-
respected sportsman. He was skillful, aggressive, and determined to score goals. Because the sport is so ego-driven and
macho it sometimes escalates into fierce confrontations in the
arena. Players frequently shout obscenities at each other and,
in some instances, use physical force to show their displeasure with the maneuvers of opposing players.

On several occasions, Roberto was reprimanded for his
aggressive behavior on the field. He once infuriated an opponent when he struck the man in the face with his mallet
after the player scored a goal off him.

But from the start Roberto was someone special to Susan
Cummings. After their first season of dating, she knew she
had to visit him in Oxford, Florida, where he was engaged
by a wealthy patron to play polo for the winter season.

That October, Susan excitedly boarded a plane for Florida's west coast. Her relationship with the gallant sportsman
was going quite well. The two enjoyed sun-filled days and
shared intimate evenings at the local pubs and restaurants.
While there, she accompanied Roberto to the polo match he
was scheduled to play that week.

She was proud to be recognized as his girlfriend, and
watched from the sidelines as he scored goal after goal. But
an incident occurred on the playing field and Roberto was
ejected from the game.

Unsure how to respond, Susan waited by Roberto's trailer for him to come galloping over. She was surprised at how angry he was at what had occurred on the playing field. Apparently, one of his opponents had knocked into him during a point. The referee had called the maneuver a foul.

Susan watched from the trailer as her boyfriend jumped from his horse, the dust rising from underneath his boots as he strutted deliberately past her and into the stable. She looked on as he grabbed a long knife from his knapsack and stuck it down the front of his tight white riding pants. As she observed him march toward the trailer of the opposing player, she was not quite sure what he intended to do.

As he strode the grassy parking area, one of the game's referees, Steve Lane, appeared. He had been sent over by the other player to remove Roberto from the property.

"Take it easy, this was just a foul," the stocky, balding referee tried to calm Roberto.

"I want to talk to that S.O.B.," Roberto shot back.

Placing his arm around Roberto's shoulder, the stout referee tried to quiet him down. As the two walked toward the other player's trailer, the referee reached down to pat Roberto's stomach. He could feel the outline of what appeared to be a knife hidden beneath his polo shirt.

"You don't want to do this," the referee pleaded with Roberto, steering him away from his opponent's trailer and back toward his own. Lane was surprised by the Argentine's outburst. He had been refereeing the polo matches for several years, and not once had he seen Roberto lose his temper on the playing field.

Yet Roberto's burst of temper was short-lived. The referee's calming words served their purpose and after a few minutes, the Argentine retreated to his trailer.

As for Susan, she chalked Roberto's flare-up to nothing more than a momentary outburst that rose out of the heat of the match. For her, he was still "the prize"—and for once in her life she had won.

After her visit to Florida, Susan returned to Ashland Farm, where she spent the rest of the winter caring for her animals and dreaming of Roberto's return.

Over the months, the heiress kept in close touch with her Argentine lover, phoning him often and penning him letters filled with promises of a long-term commitment.

The cards she sent were carefully hand-picked, and featured pictures of rabbits, birds, and other small animals. And while she signed her notes, "your friend Suzanne," the messages she wrote to Roberto made it clear that there was far more to their relationship than just friendship.

On October 19, Susan mailed Roberto a birthday greeting telling him how she badly she felt that she could not be with him to celebrate. She thanked him for his frequent phone calls and told him she looked forward to seeing him soon.

In December, Susan wrote a second card telling Roberto how wonderful it had been to share the experience of polo with him that past summer and how she was looking forward to riding the horses together that coming spring. She acknowledged Roberto's love for her and professed her love for him.

In another note, Susan presented Roberto with ideas for their future together. She proposed that they remain in Virginia and play polo during the spring and summer months. At the end of the season, she suggested that Roberto travel south to follow the polo circuit while she remain at Ashland Farm to nurse the sick and injured ponies. She even looked ahead to the time when they tired of polo, suggesting that they move west, where they could work as rangers, tending to the animals and putting a stop to poachers.

CHAPTER 9

Susan could hardly wait for Roberto to return from Florida and for the 1996 polo season to get underway. The two had been separated for nearly six months and she missed him desperately. When her lover finally arrived in late April, the relationship was immediately rekindled. The two were like college kids on spring break, spending countless hours in each other's arms. Under Susan's care, Roberto shed his extra weight and cut down on the amount of alcohol he consumed.

At Montrose Farm in The Plains, where Roberto rented a field on which his seven horses grazed, stablehands whispered about the couple's public displays of affection. They watched as the two exchanged intimate kisses and shared romantic picnic lunches behind the old, red barn. On many afternoons, they took the horses for long, leisurely rides through the gentle rolling hills of the Virginia countryside.

For Roberto, Montrose Farm was centrally located, less than one mile from Great Meadow, and only a stone's throw from Cotswold Farm, the country estate that was home to the Cotswold Farm polo team for which he had signed on to play that season.

The team's owner, Bill Ylvisaker, was among the nation's most well-respected polo players. In the '70s, *Polo* magazine had named him "one of the two most influential people in the sport of polo over the last twenty years," and it was widely known in polo circles that his long list of credentials included a stint as chairman of the United States Polo Association. He also founded the Polo Training Foundation, the World Cup, and the Palm Beach Polo and Country Club in Palm Beach, Florida.

Being affiliated with such a powerful man gave Roberto access to many key figures in the sport and allowed him to meet and socialize with members of all the hunt country teams. It was a heady time for Roberto. The combination of his career success and his newfound sense of contentment with Susan made him feel he had finally attained everything he ever wanted.

But his involvement with Susan had an unwanted side effect: it was causing him to lose the focus and sense of drive that had made him one of the best on the circuit. He began making decisions that would ultimately wound him both professionally and personally. Determined to be with Susan, he opted not to return to Florida for the winter polo season and, instead, took a menial job picking apples at a local orchard for minimum wage.

Intoxicated by their growing closeness, Roberto volunteered his services for the countless tasks around Ashland Farm. When he wasn't picking apples, he filled his free hours fixing fences, mowing the grass, clearing land, and gathering hay for horse feed.

While most horse-farm owners had a full-time staff on hand to perform the backbreaking chores that Roberto was doing, Susan's obsession with frugality—no doubt learned at her father's knee—kept her from maintaining a staff or even hiring workers on a regular basis. Instead, she employed help only occasionally, bringing them in on a *per diem* basis, and carrying much of the load herself, with her sister's help.

Susan allowed her lover to take over the strenuous day-to-day maintenance of the 350-acre property, even though it meant that he would have little time to practice the sport of polo. Roberto even took on additional tasks at Le Baron Farm, the eight-hundred-acre estate Susan and her sister owned in nearby Culpeper County.

Roberto benefited little monetarily from his efforts, despite the countless hours he worked on the Cummingses two properties. Susan never paid him for any of his time, nor did she even offer him housing at the sprawling Ashland Farm. Instead, he lived like a migrant laborer, staying in a small room he was given at Sunnyside Farm, the apple orchard in nearby Rappahannock County where he was employed.

Eventually, Roberto's endless chores around the estate began to take a toll on their relationship. The two also began to disagree over the treatment and training of the polo ponies, the very animals that had brought the two of them together so many months before.

Susan willingly took on the responsibility of caring for the beloved ponies, but she had never learned to accept the rigorous workouts that Roberto routinely put them through. It was difficult for her to sit by and watch his methods, which she viewed as bordering on the abusive. And, she could never accept Roberto's arguments that the polo ponies needed a different diet and more strenuous exercise than horses used for dressage and other competitions.

Although neither of them really wanted to admit it, the simple fact was that Susan and Roberto had fundamentally different ideas about how the horses should be treated. In Argentina, where Roberto was born, polo ponies are viewed no differently from any other kind of work horse. In contrast, Susan saw the polo ponies as pets to be treated with kindness and affection.

As far as Roberto was concerned, Susan's soft treatment of the ponies left them inadequately trained to compete on the field. Not only was she feeding them far too much, she was also giving them only a partial workout. With too much food and too little exercise, the ponies were putting on too much weight. Besides, Roberto knew that overweight ponies tended to develop crippling arthritis.

Roberto's overt frustration grew. Sometimes he would joke in front of Jean Marie about the odd jobs that he was performing at the farm. But the dreamy cloud of romance he enjoyed with the heiress kept him from confronting her directly.

Susan's reluctance to allow Roberto to move in with her may have been colored by her mother's reaction to the Argentine playboy.

In August 1996, Sam and Irmgard came for an extended visit with their twin daughters. It was not unusual for the couple to make several trips a year, but with Sam Cummings' failing health, this visit would turn out to be his last. During the week the Cummingses stayed at their lavish apartment in Old Town Alexandria. Its location, a block away from Interarms, allowed Sam to keep up with his business affairs.

On weekends, they traveled by car to the farm where they relaxed and socialized with their daughters. They stayed in the main house, which was once their own, and received a steady stream of visitors in one of the mansion's few decorated rooms.

The trip provided the first opportunity for Susan's parents and Roberto to meet. Roberto later told his friend Jean Marie that Sam Cummings took to him immediately. He said that Sam had asked him to watch over his little girl.

Irmgard, on the other hand, was not at all taken with the handsome interloper. She made it clear to Susan and the rest of her family that she did not approve of her daughter's relationship with Roberto.

Nevertheless, her mother's open distrust of her lover did not deter Susan in the least. In fact, shortly after Sam and Irmgard left, the bond between Susan and Roberto was so strong that he made a fateful decision: to remain in Virginia rather than return to Florida for the winter polo season. For the first time in seventeen years, he wouldn't be following the circuit.

At the same time, Roberto moved his horses—some of them were lame, but others were worth upwards of $20,000 apiece—to Ashland Farm. Susan's offer to allow him to board his ponies at her estate initially struck him as a good deal. Because he was working as an apple picker, rather than as a $4,000-a-month polo pro, saving money on the horses' monthly board at Montrose Farm helped ease the strain on his finances. His arrangement with Susan allowed him to keep the horses at the 350-acre estate and use them for competitions without the added financial worry of feed, shoes, and medication.

He told several friends—perhaps to save face—that Susan

had paid him $20,000 for the seven horses, but records of the transaction have never been recovered. Susan would later testify at her trial that she did not buy Roberto's horses from him, and believes that he sold them back to the people he had purchased them from. But friends' of the polo player insist that the ponies were kept by Susan at Ashland Farm.

In any event, one can only wonder if Roberto was struck by the fact that, while his horses were permitted to live at Ashland Farm, he was only allowed to visit.

For whatever reason, Susan never invited him to stay the night.

Just days before Roberto's thirty-seventh birthday, he received the devastating news that his father had died.

Before he departed Virginia to attend the funeral, Susan presented him with a birthday present. Without him knowing, she had had his favorite saddle repaired for four hundred dollars, a sum that Roberto simply didn't have. With the gift, Susan enclosed a birthday card that she dated October 19, 1996.

In the note, she told Roberto that he should not fret about getting older, explaining that she was content in her older age. She wished him a safe trip to Argentina, and signed off with much love.

In late October Roberto boarded a plane for his homeland. It would be only the second visit he'd made since leaving his tiny village seventeen years earlier. News that his father had passed away came on the heels of his brother's death. The loss of Roberto's father left his mother and sister in poverty, and Roberto was suddenly thrust into the position of having to provide for his family in Argentina, which he was now unequipped to do.

Roberto took another fateful step away from his beloved sport of polo when, after returning to Virginia, he suggested to Susan that she form her own polo team. The Argentine horseman offered to play on the team, agreeing to forfeit his standard compensation package if Susan paid for his apartment and his meals—an odd mix of dinners in local bistros and steakhouses and simple spaghetti suppers she prepared for him at home.

Meanwhile, Roberto continued spending much of his days at Ashland Farm doing menial tasks, such as fixing fences, that he had done as a boy in Argentina. In some ways, he was not much different from the handful of people who did work at the farm, one of whom was Susan's housekeeper.

Roberto confided to Jean Marie Turon that one fall afternoon, he noticed the housekeeper sweeping away the avalanche of leaves that had fallen along the driveway with an old wooden broom. The chore seemed too much for the woman to handle, so he climbed into his big blue Ford and headed for the hardware store. There, he plunked down $125 for a leaf-blower and, returning to Ashland Farm, handed it to the maid.

What happened next stunned Jean Marie. He listened as Roberto told him that when Susan heard the racket coming from the driveway, she quickly ran outside to see what was going on. Her eyes grew round as she spotted the housekeeper using the bulky piece of machinery to blow the leaves to the end of the driveway.

Pulling Roberto aside, she confronted him about his purchase, agitated as she listened to him explain that the leaf-blower would make the woman's job easier. She would have none of it and told Roberto that she saw no reason why the woman needed the $125 lawn tool when the broom would suffice.

Susan's reluctance to spend money on what many others viewed as routine purchases was apparent to everyone. When Jean Marie offered to give her the extra answering machine he had lying around the Willow Run Polo School, she turned him down cold. The instructor explained that he did not want money for the machine, that he simply wanted to make it easier for members of the polo community to get in touch with Roberto. He told Susan that on numerous occasions, he and other polo players had tried in vain to reach the horseman at Ashland Farm—which was listed as the address for Roberto on the Great Meadow phone list. Jean Marie was stunned when Susan refused, telling him that she did not want the machine because she'd have no choice but to return the calls at her own cost.

In April of 1997, Susan and Roberto decided that he should move closer to Ashland Farm. His job at the apple orchard was coming to an end and the polo season was about to begin.

Checking the local newspaper, he spotted an advertisement for a room in Warrenton. He responded to the ad and set up an appointment to visit the house to view the available accommodations, a single room with a private bath.

The landlady, Virginia Kuhn, was taken aback by the seeming inability of this grown man to make a decision about where he would live without first getting his girlfriend's permission.

When the two returned later that day to survey the quarters, Virginia watched curiously as the couple held hands and giggled. She led them down the hall and waited in the doorway of the room as Susan inspected it closely before giving her okay.

With Susan's permission, Roberto agreed to pay four hundred dollars a month to rent the master bedroom and adjoining private bath, which was located on the main floor of the colonial ranch, directly across the hall from his landlady's smaller quarters.

Virginia took an instant liking to her Argentine boarder. She looked forward to chatting with him each morning in the brightly-lit kitchen, where he would pour himself a cup of her freshly-brewed coffee. Roberto was always fully dressed in jeans and work boots when he popped his head into the living room to say a few words, and although Virginia had other tenants, he soon became her favorite.

Every morning he greeted her with, "Good morning, Mrs. Kuhn, and how are you today?" And whenever he left the room, he took a dramatic bow and flashed her a hearty smile.

Virginia was enthralled by more than her Latin tenant's charm. She was also fascinated by his love affair with an actual billionairess. It puzzled her that Susan Cummings was interested in a man from a background unlike her own, and she couldn't help wondering how the affair would ultimately play out.

Roberto also expressed a sincere curiosity in his eighty-year-old widowed landlady. Being retired from her job as a bookkeeper for the IRS, and without her husband to keep her company, she had a lot of time on her hands. She rose early and spent many mornings walking the hilly farm-lined roads around Bear Wallow Drive.

She had lived in the one-story corner house for much of her life, a home she and her husband had purchased from her parents years before. Often, the petite, gray-haired woman covered one to two miles before returning for a shower and a rest. In the afternoons, she drove her big, four-door Cadillac Sedan deVille to the supermarket or to the adjacent mall for lunch at her favorite Italian restaurant.

In spite of her full schedule and remarkably good health, Virginia was lonely and longed for companionship. Her only son lived in Alaska and she saw him just once a year. She was fascinated with Roberto's ongoing relationship with the heiress, who visited her home once every month, her visits invariably coinciding with the rent payment.

Virginia was amused at the way Susan and Roberto spent hours in the living room, where she kept a large-screen TV and VCR. She watched from the kitchen as the two nuzzled on the couch, giggling and smooching as they watched videos of the polo matches they had played in during the previous month. When the movies were over, the lovebirds always headed for Roberto's bedroom, where they closed the door behind them and spent hours together before Susan departed for her own home.

Virginia was never able to stay up late enough to wave Susan goodnight, but she noticed that Roberto was always alone in the mornings. When she met him in the kitchen, he would inevitably announce: "I'll have the rent for you tomorrow."

Like clockwork, a smiling Roberto appeared with Susan's check the following morning, made out in the amount of four hundred dollars. The money was always drawn on her personal account, and signed and dated by the billionairess.

Roberto Villegas and Susan Cummings playing polo at Great Meadow. (*Sarah Libbey Greenhalgh*)

"No Trespassing" signs were posted outside Ashland Farm after the murder. (*Douglas Lees*)

Ashland Farm, the home of Susan Cummings. (*Douglas Love*)

Susan Cummings's dresser drawer showing knife and two empty plastic bags. (*Fauquier County Sheriff's Dept.*)

Susan Cummings's wounded arm in police photo taken at Ashland Farm prior to the time it was treated by authorities. (*Fauquier County Sheriff's Department*)

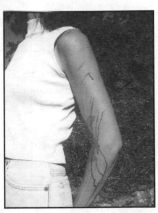

The desk in Susan Cummings's home, where police found a single unspent cartridge in the center of a white pad. (*Fauquier County Sheriff's Dept.*)

The kitchen table at which Roberto was eating breakfast. Rossi Firearms placemats covered the table. (*Fauquier County Sheriff's Department*)

The Walther pistol used by Susan Cummings and a single spent 9mm round on the floor just outside the kitchen where police found the items.
(*Fauquier County Sheriff's Department*)

Photograph of crime scene taken by first officers on the scene showing Roberto's body in the corner of the kitchen. (*Fauquier County Sheriff's Dept.*)

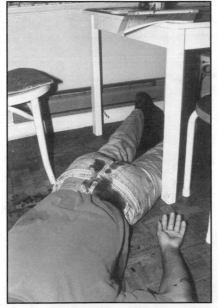

The body of Roberto Villegas partially beneath the kitchen table. (*Fauquier County Sheriff's Department*)

Roberto lay facedown in a pool of blood. (*Fauquier County Sheriff's Department*)

Police close-up of Roberto's body, showing the knife in the crux of his armpit.
(*Fauquier County Sheriff's Department*)

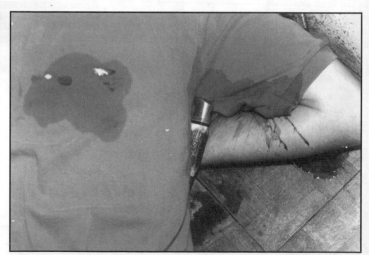

The home of Virginia Kuhn where Roberto Villegas rented a room. (*Douglas Love*)

Virginia Kuhn in the room she rented to Roberto. (*Lisa Pulitzer*)

Jean Marie Turon outside Willow Run Polo School. (*Douglas Love*)

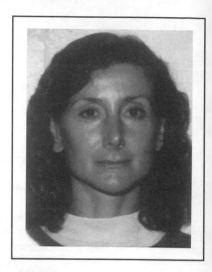

Mug shot of Susan Cummings taken hours after her arrest on September 7, 1997. (*Fauquier County Sheriff's Department*)

Susan Cummings, after being allowed to leave the country for fourteen days to visit her dying father. (*Sarah Libbey Greenhalgh*)

* * *

The formation of Susan's own polo team gave a stronger focus to the times she and Roberto spent together. In addition to Roberto playing without being paid, the team was using his horses.

His arrangement with Susan was in stark contrast to the typical agreement between polo pro and patron. If Roberto had been compensated according to custom and practice in the industry, he would have been receiving a compensation package worth close to $20,000. In addition to a monthly stipend, Susan would have been responsible for his housing, and for the board, feed, shoeing, and veterinary care of his seven polo ponies.

Roberto's previous arrangement with the Worshams afforded him $1,800 a month, plus a lovely private cottage on the family's Clifton estate. He was also provided with three square meals a day, and housing and veterinary care for his string of polo ponies.

While working for the Worshams, Roberto played for other local patrons and earned a *per diem* rate of anywhere from two hundred to nine hundred dollars per game. He also pursued his secondary business of training and selling polo ponies, a venture that earned him the bulk of his income. Like many pros, Roberto purchased young ponies for a modest price. He exercised and trained the animals, and then sold them for a profit.

But it was Roberto who had offered his services to the heiress free of charge, asking only that she pay his rent, and foot the bill for his food, clothes and the maintenance of his truck and trailer. She would also be responsible for the care of his seven horses and the equipment needed for the team.

The only other expense that Susan incurred was the salary of a third player for the team. Roberto explained that she needed to hire one player for arena polo and pay him the going rate. He suggested that she consider his friend, Jean Marie Turon.

That spring, Susan, Roberto, and Jean Marie debuted the Ashland Farm team at Great Meadow. Dressed in the team's white riding pants and navy-blue shirts, the words Ashland

Farm written across the front in crisp white letters, the three players enjoyed afternoons of "lo-goal" polo, a game that is played by members of amateur teams.

But the arrangement Susan had made with Roberto began to cause friction between the couple. Suddenly, Susan found herself in the uncomfortable position of paying for all of her lover's expenses.

With no real source of income, Roberto had to rely on Susan for just about everything. Often, he would joke in front of other people about the menial labor Susan had him doing at Ashland Farm, laughing about the fact that he was receiving no compensation for all his efforts.

To Roberto, money was not important. He was happy playing polo, he felt comfortable working around the farm, and he enjoyed being Susan's protector. Susan had also convinced him that "what's mine is yours." After he had moved his horses to Ashland Farm, she began telling him that "they are our horses. Everything is ours."

Friends of Roberto were skeptical when he talked about promises made by Susan. For example, when she decided to buy a new white Ford truck, she promised her old black one to Roberto. But when it came time to transfer the title to his name, he agreed when she told him that it would be easier for the insurance company if he left it in hers. By the end of their relationship, even Roberto's truck remained in her possession. After his funeral, she had it shipped to his family in Argentina.

But Roberto didn't seem to care. In his mind, he had everything a man could dream of. He was the star polo player at Great Meadow, and now he was a key member of what he perceived to be his very own team.

In the months that followed, tensions between the two began to build. Susan didn't want Roberto to ride the horses because she felt he made them "too hot."

And fellow polo players overheard Roberto complaining that his ponies were under-exercised and overfed. But even his frustration with Susan's pampering of the ponies did not sour him on their relationship. He continued to turn down invitations to play polo for sponsors who offered to pay him on a *per diem* rate. He was busy teaching Susan the fine points of the game, and with the constant list of repairs at Ashland Farm, he had little extra time.

Roberto remained enamored with Susan. He slept with her picture next to his bed and saved all of the notes and cards she wrote him in his top dresser drawer. When they were out in public, the two were never far apart, and Roberto would tell anyone who would listen about Susan's sweet nature and expertise in the kitchen. He was impressed by her spaghetti dinners and the cakes she baked especially for him.

When they dined out at Mosby's Tavern in nearby Middleburg, or Napoleon's restaurant in downtown Warrenton, Susan and Roberto snuggled close together and held each other's hands.

But friends who visited the couple at Ashland Farm found it odd that during dinner—always served in the tiny maid's galley—Susan would drift from the conversation, turning her attention to the tiny television in the corner of the room. She kept the set tuned to the Animal Planet, and liked to keep it on nearly twenty-four-hours a day.

By late June, Susan began objecting to Roberto's desire to return to the polo circuit on Sundays to earn extra money. She was irritated that he routinely used his ponies to play for the three sponsors who paid him up to nine hundred dollars per game and was fearful the extra day's workout would be too much for the horses.

For Susan, Sunday was the busiest day at the farm, and she wanted Roberto there to tend to the chores. And besides, it bothered her that he wasn't content to play solely on her team and felt the need to compete at a higher level.

With Roberto now using his ponies for the Sunday-afternoon matches, Susan decided that it would be a good idea to buy a few polo horses of her own. Enlisting Roberto's help, she spent several weeks visiting horse farms in search of just the right animals.

When Roberto told Jean Marie that Susan was interested in purchasing polo ponies, he suggested that she look at the horses owned by a long-time friend and business associate.

The transaction was yet another bone of contention between Susan and Jean Marie, who had one of his business associates bring his horses to Willow Run Polo School for Susan to inspect. After looking over the horses, Susan inquired as to their price. When the seller offered them at a price of $7,000 apiece, Susan made a face. Polo ponies are routinely sold for as much as fifty to sixty thousand dollars, so the $7,000 was a modest price.

Noticing her expression, Jean Marie asked what was wrong. He listened as she hemmed and hawed over the cost of the horses. Overhearing her concerns, the seller offered her a $1,000 discount, citing her friendship with Jean Marie as a reason. Again, Susan made a face.

"What's wrong?" Jean Marie inquired. "Do you have a problem with the price? Do you want to name a price?"

"Can I?" she asked.

"Certainly, go ahead," the instructor coaxed.

"How about five hundred dollars?" Susan offered.

"Five hundred dollars?" The seller grew infuriated, shooting an angry look at Jean Marie.

"Okay, if you want more money, I'll give you fifteen hundred dollars for three."

Jean Marie cringed as he watched the horse trader turn and storm out of the barn in a huff. Turning to Susan, he demanded to know what had prompted her to make such an outrageously low offer.

"My dad taught me this when I was a kid, and that's how I do business," she answered matter-of-factly.

Susan's father was notorious for his pursuit of a bargain and she knew by heart all of his techniques for haggling. Sam Cummings always looked for yard-sale prices, no matter where he shopped, whether it be in an upscale London art gallery or a boutique selling hand-woven oriental rugs.

Time after time, Susan had watched as her father negotiated with shopkeepers as if he were in a Turkish market. It was not at all unusual for Sam Cummings to leave a store empty handed and return time and time again, relentlessly continuing his negotiations until the weary merchant broke down and sold him the desired item at a wholesale price.

But what worked for the self-made billionaire arms dealer did not always work for his daughter. Often exasperated by Susan's endless haggling to save a dollar, Roberto demanded that she pay the asking price.

"Why do you go out with her, Roberto?" Jean Marie repeatedly asked his friend.

"She had a hard childhood," Roberto always responded. "Her family was cold, and she was sent away to school when she was only twelve years old."

Susan didn't always get her way when she was trying to be frugal. One day, Jean Marie listened as Roberto described how he had upgraded Susan's farm tractor without her permission, ultimately bringing the heiress to tears over the size of the bill.

Roberto told his friend that Susan had ordered the piece of farming equipment from a local dealer and had charged the $80,000 purchase on her credit card. He grew animated as he recalled the day the dealership called to say that the tractor had finally arrived from the factory. He said that Susan had asked him to pick it up.

Jean Marie puffed on a cigarette, paying close attention as Roberto explained that when he saw the tractor, he decided that the standard model that Susan had ordered was not to his liking. Instead, he told the salesman that he wanted to upgrade to a much more elaborate tractor, complete with an enclosed, air-conditioned cab and a stereo with a CD player.

Returning to Ashland Farm later in the day, he advised Susan that the tractor was not ready and that he would have to make a return trip to the dealership. When he went back the following week with Susan to pick up the fancy model, the clerk handed the heiress the credit-card receipt.

Stamping out his Marlboro, Jean Marie smiled. Brushing strands of his thick brown hair from his brow, he listened as Roberto recounted how Susan broke into tears when she saw the additional $10,000 for the custom options he had ordered.

Roberto went on to detail how he further infuriated the socialite by disappearing on the tractor for hours at a time.

Upset that she couldn't get in touch with him, Susan installed a cellular phone in the cab. But her efforts were for naught. Roberto simply shut off the phone, parking the tractor in a shady spot, turning on the stereo and the air-conditioner, and taking a nap.

Jean Marie was not surprised by the story. He had recently dined out with Susan and Roberto after a polo match. The three had gone to Napoleon's bistro to celebrate a game well-played. When the dinner bill arrived at the table, he overheard Roberto whisper to Susan that she should pick up the tab. He explained that Jean Marie was a player on the Ashland Farm team and told her that it was appropriate for the patron to spring for the meal.

Overhearing Susan's objections, Jean Marie was struck by the fact that she voiced concern about putting the forty dollar tab on her credit card.

As the summer progressed, tension between Susan and Roberto over the treatment of the ponies continued to grow. It seemed that Susan had grown tired of the polo circuit and was now talking about retiring the horses and keeping them at Ashland Farm as pets. She also began to discuss the possibility that she and Roberto retire to Montana, where they could purchase a large tract of land and work as rangers. Voicing a desire to rescue endangered wildlife from the poachers, she began to look into plane fare and accommodations for early fall.

Meanwhile, in the polo arena, players continued to overhear Roberto mumbling about his lackluster performance and the declining condition of the polo ponies.

"I'm not playing well today," he muttered to himself, loud enough for others to hear. "These horses are not properly exercised."

In July, Susan announced that she planned to travel to Europe to visit with her parents. Her father had fallen seriously ill and she wanted to spend ten days in Monte Carlo by his bedside. Inviting Roberto to tag along, Susan was disappointed when he told her that he preferred to remain in Virginia and continue to play polo.

Roberto's landlady was surprised when she saw her tenant packing a bag for an extended stay at Ashland Farm. In the five months he had lived in her home, never once had he stayed at the farm overnight. It always troubled her that Susan did not invite him to spend the evening and she found it even more bizarre that the heiress often called her house—sometimes as early as 6 a.m.—to ask that Roberto stop and pick up tools and other farm supplies on his way over to Ashland Farm.

When she had asked him about his long-range plans with Susan, Roberto raised his hands in the air and said, "One day we will get married, but it is many years down the road. All she wants to do is mother me!"

Virginia had never told her tenant about the nights that she'd seen Susan's big white truck roaring past the house. From the large bay window in the living room she'd watched the Ford pass and noted that Roberto was not yet home.

"He probably slipped away from her for a while," she would chuckle to herself.

Not long after Susan boarded the plane for Monaco, Roberto's friends observed a change in his behavior. They noticed that in her absence the polo player seemed relaxed and more like his old self. Members of the Great Meadow Polo Club had always wondered what it was about the heiress that had Roberto so in love. To them, she seemed awkward, aloof, and even a little bit odd. Many found it strange that, when they went to say a casual hello to the couple, Susan would drop her head, letting strands of her hair fall around her face, and mutter a hello in a soft, almost inaudible tone. When they asked her a question, sometimes she would not even answer them.

The way she carried on in public was not at all like Roberto. Unlike the heiress, he never turned down a chance to socialize, and loved spending evenings in the company of friends at the local pubs and restaurants. Roberto, like many of the players in the polo set, enjoyed the company of women and he never missed an opportunity to talk with a pretty girl.

Friends of Susan say they witnessed Roberto in the company of several women while she was overseas. But it is unclear whether they alerted her to his alleged escapades upon her return to Virginia.

On July 26, she and Roberto attended the annual polo party at the Seager residence. It was there that Susan confided in Jane Rowe that she was having trouble with Roberto and was afraid of what he might do.

According to a *Vanity Fair* piece, one afternoon, she had caught sight of a flirtatious moment between Roberto and Diana from the window of her mansion. She watched as her sister, clad in a skimpy bikini and sunning herself on a lounge chair in the yard where Roberto was mowing the lawn, blew the Argentine a kiss as he passed by her on the tractor. Infuriated, Susan ran down the stairs and out the front door. Racing up to Roberto, she scolded him and then ordered him into the house. Once inside, she chased him around the kitchen table and then locked him in the bathroom.

Both Susan and Diana deny that this "episode" ever took place.

By the middle of August, close friends of Susan and Roberto began to notice that their relationship had cooled. The two did not seem as enthralled with each other as they had in the past, and one polo photographer observed that Susan refused to stand next to Roberto when she was asked to pose for a picture of the Ashland Farm team. But to most, the couple exhibited a united front, kissing and holding hands when they were out on the town. Even Susan's sister, Diana, had no idea that there was anything wrong.

On August 30, Susan stopped by Virginia Kuhn's house on Bear Wallow Road. The landlady observed that there was nothing out of the ordinary about her visit. As always, she and Roberto snuggled in the living room, watching polo videos and holding hands. After a short while, they headed for the master bedroom, with Roberto telling his landlady that they planned to watch TV.

"Where will you sit?" Virginia could not help but yell after them.

Roberto smiled. "On my bed," he told her.

*   *   *

The following weekend, Susan and Roberto climbed into Susan's truck and headed for Pennsylvania. Earlier that week, she had telephoned polo player Gary Leonard in Pittsburgh to advise him that Roberto would not be attending the Saturday afternoon charity match. ·

"Can you find a substitute?" Susan knew it would be difficult, but she had made up her mind that she did not want to travel to Pennsylvania with Roberto and she certainly did not want him to take the ponies.

Leonard advised her that there was not enough time for him to find a replacement for Roberto, telling her that it would be nearly impossible for him to locate a player of Roberto's caliber.

"Well, if you don't hear from me again, that means we are coming," Susan sighed.   ·

The day before she placed the call to Gary Leonard, a woman claiming to be her friend had telephoned the Fauquier County Sheriff's Office. Identifying herself as Jane Rowe, the caller told police that the heiress wanted to schedule a second appointment to meet with an investigator the following Monday, September 8. The caller went on to say that Susan wanted to talk to Sergeant Gary Healy about obtaining an order of protection against Roberto Villegas.

The next afternoon Susan was on her way to Pennsylvania with the star of the Great Meadow Polo Club. She insisted on driving the truck and the large trailer that held the polo ponies. Her request did not bother Roberto, who sat in the passenger seat, as he usually did. He never seemed to mind that Susan wanted to control everything: the money, the horses, even the driving.

The couple checked into a motel late Friday afternoon. Immediately, there was a mixup at the front desk. Nicole Pusker, the clerk on duty, remembers that Susan was upset when she presented the heiress with a single room key. Telling the short, dark-haired Pusker that she had reserved two rooms—one for her, one for her polo pro—Susan insisted the situation be remedied. After all, this was the way that most patrons traveled, and the way she intended to travel on this trip.

Annoyed at the mistake, the usually-meek Susan announced her dissatisfaction loudly enough for Roberto's fellow teammates to overhear.

Her outburst embarrassed Roberto, who tried to step in and smooth things over. Flashing a wide, toothy grin, he assured the now-curious desk clerk that one room would be fine. But Susan was irate and demanded that the motel employee come up with a second room, as she had reserved.

Later in the weekend, Susan caught up with Gary Leonard, who was in his horse trailer tending to some business when she knocked. She had come there to advise the veteran polo player that she had not wanted to make the three-hour trip to Pittsburgh and the only reason she had come at all was for him and the horses. Leonard was surprised by her admission. He barely knew the woman and was not sure how to respond.

On the ride back to Warrenton, Roberto and Susan argued, reportedly over the horses. The heiress informed her lover that she would not permit him or the horses to participate in "The Taste of Argentina" the following day. They had had a long journey and a difficult workout at the Pittsburgh match and she did not want them playing in another event without proper rest.

The international polo match was scheduled for 2 p.m. at Gone Away Farm, the polo field across the street from the stately home of Baltimore attorney Joe Muldoon. The illustrious competition pitted the U.S. polo team against the unconquerable Argentina, and the Ambassador to Argentina was scheduled to attend.

Roberto was committed to play for Argentina and was looking forward to the chance to show the Ambassador and his countrymen that a poor boy from Cordoba had made something of himself in the United States.

CHAPTER 10

ROBERTO ROSE FROM HIS BED AROUND 7 A.M. THE LARGE framed photograph he kept on his nightstand of Susan mounted on top of an elegant brown horse caught his eye as he walked to the blue-tiled bathroom to grab a shower.

To him, it was a day like any other day and as far as his landlady could tell, the darkly-handsome polo player carried on in his usual manner. Virginia Kuhn remembers that she had brewed a pot of fresh Maxwell House earlier that morning. When Roberto appeared in the kitchen sometime before 7:30 a.m., he helped himself, as he always did, to a cup of coffee.

"Good morning, Mrs. Kuhn," he called out, poking his head into the living room where she was stretched out on the couch, watching television.

She looked up when she heard his voice and turned to see him flash her one of his broad, infectious grins. Waving his hand in the air, he called, "And how are you today?"

"Oh, fine, Roberto." She smiled.

Returning to the cheery yellow kitchen where a large picture window provided a panoramic view of the century-old trees and neatly-mowed lawn of the large, sloping back yard, Virginia poured herself another cup of coffee. She could hear Roberto moving about in the laundry room, just down the hall from the kitchen. She watched as he pulled several items of clothing from the dryer, folding them neatly on top of the washing machine.

Roberto smiled as he walked past her, carrying the basket

of freshly cleaned laundry that he had washed the night before. As he brushed by her, the handsome horseman bowed his head politely, then disappeared down the dimly-lit hallway to his bedroom at the far end of the first floor.

Virginia could hear the creaking of the wooden dresser drawers opening and closing in Roberto's room as she ambled back to the couch to catch the end of her program. She knew it was an important day for her tenant, because he had told her all about the prestigious polo match he was scheduled to play in that afternoon in Maryland. In fact, it was all he had talked about for weeks.

The elderly woman had been surprised when Roberto had told her that Susan did not want him to participate in the banner competition, which pitted Argentina against the United States. She had also found it strange when he said that Susan, similarly, had been opposed to their trip to Pittsburgh that weekend. She couldn't understand why the young woman wouldn't jump at the chance to spend some time away with him. Still, she didn't give it a second thought, especially after he explained that he'd finally convinced Susan to go by describing all the fun they would have at the gala party that preceded the annual event.

Virginia remembers vividly that Roberto acted just like he always did when he left the modest ranch house that morning. Nor was there anything strange about the time he departed for Ashland Farm. It was about 7:45 a.m.—the hour he usually headed for the door—when he called out to her. "Now you have a wonderful day today." The screen door slammed shut behind him. "I'll see you this evening."

The petite, gray-haired woman remained in the living room with her morning program. Pushing aside the lace curtain on the expansive bay window, she watched from her purple velvet couch as Roberto climbed into the cab of his black truck. She took special notice of the brimming cup of black coffee that he held firmly in his right hand.

Virginia had grown accustomed to Roberto taking her coffee cups along with him on the five-mile ride to Ashland Farm. She hoped he would return this one because it was part of her favorite dish set.

Unbeknownst to her, this would be the last time she would see her smiling tenant alive. In less than one hour, police would be summoned to the home of his demure French lover, where they would find Roberto lying face down on the kitchen floor in a pool of blood.

CHAPTER 11

CAPTAIN FRED PFEIFF HAD JUST RETURNED HOME FROM Sunday-morning mass and was about to indulge in a leisurely breakfast with his wife when the emergency call came in.

Communications officers stationed at the sheriff's office informed the veteran law enforcement officer that there had been a shooting at Ashland Farm, just off Route 211 in Warrenton.

Swallowing hard, he downed a mouthful of coffee and jumped up from the table. He was not at all pleased to leave the house that morning because his daughter was scheduled to visit with his new grandbaby, Madison.

The past several weeks had been busy ones for the sheriff's department. A murder every one to two years is average for Fauquier County. But it was only the beginning of September and the 1997 count was already at two. The Cummings case would make three.

The first murder of 1997 came in March when Cornelius "Jack" Furr allegedly killed his wife, Benita Kay, in the bedroom of their home in the nearby town of Orleans. The forty-four-year-old ceramics artist was found dead with a single gunshot wound to her head. There was no sign of a struggle, but her businessman husband was charged with the crime.

Five months later, a second killing played out on a stretch of Main Street in the neighboring town of Marshall. The Civil War was still very much alive in the upscale country town and a group of local citizens was fighting to maintain the town's rich history by identifying important sites with historic markers and preserving the road beds by keeping them the same width as they were in the 1860s. Several historic events had occurred within the town limits including a few noteworthy skirmishes and the march of General John Mosby with his Confederate troops.

But those interested in recapturing the town's former glory still had a long way to go. The main downtown strip was a well-known hangout for drug dealers and boozers. Police knew the area was ripe for disaster and predicted it was only a matter of time before one more bloody event put Marshall in the news again.

On August 12, their fears came true. A verbal dispute over fifty dollars ended in murder when burly, mustached James Martin Wyne, a forty-two-year-old carpenter, drew a gun on another local, Rodney Lynn ''Gator'' Fewell, blowing him away in the doorway to the local delicatessen.

Wyne was convicted of voluntary manslaughter, and sentenced to one year in jail on the felony charge.

Before those two murders, there hadn't been a homicide in Fauquier County for two years when, in September of 1995, police had found the sexually-abused and naked body of twelve-year-old Aleasha Jaye Jones handcuffed to a tree in a remote wooded area near her grandfather's 122-acre farm. Officers were horrified when they discovered that the young girl had been shot in the mouth with a .38-caliber revolver.

Her mother had left her chubby, bespectacled pre-teen in the care of her cousin, David Douglas Matthews, Jr., never imagining the horrible fate that would befall her. After an extensive investigation, deputies arrested the balding, round-faced Matthews and charged him with the heinous crime.

The shooting at Ashland Farm came less than one week after Captain Pfeiff and other members of the sheriff's department completed their testimony in the grisly Jones murder trial. The trial, which began on August 18, lasted sixteen days.

It took less than three hours for jurors to find Matthews guilty of abduction and murder. His prosecution cost the county $395,472.01 in expenses for court reporters, the jury, and witnesses—as well as fees and expenses for Matthews' court-appointed attorneys, Jud Fischel and Alex Levay, who accrued the largest portion of the bill.

Members of the sheriff's department were stunned when the twelve-member panel failed to impose the death penalty on the child-killer. Virginia was a conservative state and the death penalty was generally regarded as the appropriate punishment for murder. Instead, the jury broke with tradition and elected to send Matthews to prison for the rest of his life.

Now, three days after the surprise sentence in the two-year-old murder case, Captain Pfeiff was being summoned to what appeared to be the third homicide of 1997.

Pfeiff had worked countless murder investigations during his lengthy law-enforcement career. When he retired from his tour of duty as an investigator for the suburban Fairfax police force—which served residents of Alexandria, Virginia, and the surrounding bedroom communities of Washington, D.C.—the seasoned investigator had almost three decades of crime-solving experience. He'd spent twenty-one of his twenty-six years investigating homicides in Fairfax before becoming chief investigator of the Criminal Investigations Division of the more countrified Fauquier County Sheriff's Office.

The rangy, black-haired investigator had turned in his Fairfax police badge three and a half years before. But he was still young, and did not feel ready to end his career as a law-enforcement officer. At forty-eight, the idea of retirement from police work seemed premature. He decided to inquire about a position with the Fauquier County Sheriff's Office in Warrenton, where he lived with his wife. Three years before, the captain had relocated to the rural community at the edge of the county, which spreads over 651 square miles.

The decision turned out to be the right one. Both Fred and his wife liked the combination of the easy, rural life, among the sprawling horse farms and the excitement of being at the center of two internationally-known equestrian events.

Every spring since 1922, on the first Sunday in May, the

Virginia Gold Cup Steeplechase Race has been held in the region. The event, which takes place at Great Meadows in The Plains, adjacent to Warrenton, occurs on the same day as the Kentucky Derby. The demanding race consists of four miles over four-foot post-and-rail fences. The second equestrian event is the International Gold Cup Steeplechase Races, which take place every October. More low-key than the Virginia Gold Cup, the International Gold Cup competition attracts crowds of twenty-five thousand and draws riders and horses from across the United States and Europe.

While neither Pfeiff nor his wife participated in horse-racing, dressage, or any of the other activities of the horse culture, they enjoyed the gentle ambiance of Fauquier County.

To his delight, Pfeiff learned that a handful of his former colleagues—all fellow Fairfax detectives—were also donning the county's tan-and-brown police uniforms and weighty ten-gallon hats. The rural surroundings and slower pace provided a perfect venue for retired detectives who weren't yet ready to give up the chase.

Pfeiff's good friend, Gary Healy, had served twenty-two years on the Fairfax force before retiring as a major crimes investigator in 1993. He had joined the Fauquier County Sheriff's Office the following year, and was quickly elevated to Sergeant in Charge of Major Crime.

More astonishing was Pfeiff's discovery that his old pal Joe Higgs, a captain in Fairfax, had been elected sheriff of Fauquier County. When the Cummings case came in, Sheriff Higgs was in the middle of his second term as top law-enforcement officer to the hundred-man force. He was responsible for overseeing forty officers on active police duty, a surprisingly modest number given the county's population of 53,000. An additional sixty men and women performed support roles such as running the county jail and the courthouse. His first term had been filled with accomplishments, and his ability to get things done, combined with his affable personality, made him well-liked by his constituents and members of the force alike. He prided himself on his appearance, routinely dressing in stylish Italian designer suits, trendy leather shoes, and black-rimmed aviator glasses—not what one would normally expect of a country sheriff.

When the telephone rang at his private residence, Sheriff Higgs was upstairs changing into his gardening clothes. He had just returned home from a morning of prayer and was about to head into the yard to get started on the fall cleanup when his wife shouted to him to pick up the phone. Grabbing the receiver, the chief law-enforcement officer listened in amazement as the dispatcher on the other end of the line told him about the Sunday-morning shooting. Reaching for a pen, he jotted down the details. After hanging up, he paused momentarily in front of the mirror to check the part in his hair.

The sheriff returned to the bedroom to change his clothes once again, shoved his gun into its holster, and raced back down the staircase. He paused at the foot of the steps only long enough to blow a kiss to his wife, then flung open the front door and headed for the driveway.

As he steered his car onto the main roadway, his men were gathering at Ashland Farm. Higgs knew the property well. He made a point of being knowledgeable about the citizens whom he had been charged with protecting. He'd immediately recognized the address as the home of billionaire and international arms dealer Sam Cummings. Although he'd never met the firearms mogul personally, he was aware that the savvy businessman was once a CIA agent, and knew of his grand reputation. He had also seen Cummings' firm's headquarters, a block-long, red-brick storage facility on the banks of the Potomac River in the recently-revitalized waterfront district of Old Town Alexandria. It was here that arms imported from all over the world were temporarily stored before shipment.

Among members of Sheriff Higgs' police department, Cummings was rumored to be one of the richest men in the world. A handful of the sheriff's deputies had been on the force in 1984 when Cummings first took title to Ashland Farm, along with an even larger tract in neighboring Culpeper County that he had purchased for his twin daughters.

Unlike so many of the county's other wealthy residents, the Cummings family had never contacted Higgs to request extra security. As far as he knew, they were a very private bunch.

As the sheriff drove toward the Cummings estate, winding along the curving back roads of the county's north end, he paid special attention to the remarkable number of affluent and internationally-known celebrities and policy-makers whose mansions dotted the landscape. Movie stars, senators, and former CIA agents all owned large spreads in the posh quarter, which was also sprinkled with rambling horse farms and vast vineyards. Perhaps the most opulent estate was that of banking mogul Paul Mellon, with an air strip long enough to accommodate 737s.

The north end wasn't the only part of the county that served as a backdrop to the moneyed set. Higgs knew that an heir to the Arm & Hammer Baking Soda fortune owned a gracious spread among the cattle and dairy farms in the county's less pretentious, but equally pricey, southern section.

Higgs and his men were rarely summoned to the rambling estates of either the extreme northern or southern quarters of the rural county. Most of the calls they responded to were in the rapidly-expanding central southern district, where numerous subsidized-housing complexes and apartment buildings abutted mobile-home parks. The majority of these calls involved robberies, domestic disputes, and petty crimes.

The fact that a call had come in from Ashland Farm was clearly unusual. For the sheriff to be told that it involved a shooting was nothing short of extraordinary.

CHAPTER 12

"I WANT TO BRUSH MY TEETH." SUSAN RAISED HER EYES and spoke almost inaudibly to Deputy Jim Jones.

The officer was standing with the heiress on the driveway outside the mansion where he and his colleagues awaited the arrival of their superiors. Jones had already photographed Susan's wounds and she was now asking him to take her inside the house so she could freshen up.

He could barely hear her over the frantic bark of Diana's dogs. He could see the animals jumping around in the rear yard of the modest guest cottage she inhabited, just down the path from Susan's residence. He was unaware, however, that Diana had returned there to contact a lawyer for her twin sister.

Jones hesitated for a moment, glancing obliquely at Susan and wondering if he might have misunderstood her because of her accent. His eyes darted past her to Deputy Jim Tulley who was standing nearby when she made the request.

Tulley shrugged his shoulders and flashed the officer a puzzled look.

"Okay, let's go." Jones turned to escort the heiress toward the side door of the house.

Wrapping his right hand firmly around the brass handle of the outer glass door that led to the small porch area, Jones came face-to-face with Deputy Walters.

The diligent young officer was still in the foyer, clutching the lined notepad he was using for the crime-scene log. He nodded to Jones, as he documented the time of his colleague's re-entrance into the house.

"She wants to brush her teeth," Jones leaned forward and whispered to the deputy.

Walters raised an eyebrow, but said nothing as he looked at Susan and then back at his fellow officer. Placing his notebook on a small table, the deputy agreed to follow the two as they climbed the uncarpeted stairs to the master bedroom.

Jones ran his fingers through his thick mustache as they strode the upstairs hallway to the master bedroom and then stopped abruptly when they reached the entrance to the large suite. He positioned himself just outside the doorway so he could keep a close eye on the Cummings woman and still watch for any activity in the hallway.

Walters continued into the master bedroom, following Susan. They stepped over and around clothing that was strewn across the floor. Susan's handcuffs jangled as the deputy unlatched them from her wrists and posted himself at the door of the master bath, where he remained while Susan began brushing her teeth. He could hear gurgling sounds coming from behind the partially-closed door as he glanced around the messy chamber. As he stood waiting, his gaze moved across the room to the queen-size bed. It was covered with frilly lace bed linens and cluttered with a collection of colorful stuffed animals. It struck him as odd that the pillows were arranged at the base of the bed.

As Walters took it all in, Jones also checked out the bedroom. With one foot inside the room, he glanced around and was struck by the piles of women's garments that were spread about the floor and by the over-packed, open gym bag that revealed articles of disarrayed clothing. Looking up, he scanned the walls, which were trimmed in forest-green paint. He paused at the closet door, which was open just enough for him to see thin wooden shelves piled high with unfolded clothes. The officer shifted his glance beyond the closet to a wooden dresser. He noticed that the middle drawer had been pulled open and a handful of assorted garments was hanging out of it as if someone had rummaged through in a frantic search.

From inside the bathroom, Walters heard water running and the sounds of hands being rubbed together. It sounded as if Susan were lathering up her fingers, perhaps to scrub her face and neck. The stocky deputy did nothing to stop her from washing and thus the soap and water washed away any gunpowder residue that may have remained on her skin.

The deputy backed away from the door as his ward emerged from the bathroom.

"I want to change my shoes." The soft tone of Susan's voice, combined with her thick foreign accent, made her statement nearly incomprehensible to the deputies who watched as the jean-clad socialite ambled over to the black gym bag on the floor.

Kneeling down beside it, she reached into the satchel and rummaged around, pulling out a pair of shoes and an aqua-blue sweatshirt from the jumble of clothing that was stuffed inside the glossy nylon tote. Pulling off her white sneakers, she slid her feet into the second pair of footwear and flung the sweatshirt over her shoulders.

Deputy Jones bent over and picked up the Keds, holding them carefully between two fingers as he followed Susan back down the stairs to a small sitting room on the first floor.

He planned to place the sneakers in a sealed plastic bag for evidence. What they would ultimately reveal would help the prosecution's case.

Captain Fred Pfeiff noted the way the rays of morning sun danced off the murky gray waters of the large man-made pond that was off to his right as he steered his car up the driveway of Ashland Farm.

As he rounded the tree-lined path, he lifted his gold-rimmed sunglasses away from his eyes and glanced out his car window at the majestic stone manor house that stood to his left.

He saw that three of his deputies were out in front of the mansion unfurling bright-yellow police tape around the perimeter of the large house. The streamer-like strip was emboldened with the words "Crime Scene Do Not Cross." The tape flapped gently in the breeze as the men worked to secure it to the perfectly-trimmed hedges that lined the main entrance area.

The captain hoisted his lean, lanky body out of the car. He was pleased that his men were already cordoning off the property and knew the thick, plastic barrier would serve as a reminder to pedestrian traffic and curious onlookers that this was now an official crime scene and that only authorized personnel would be permitted to pass.

Glancing down at his wristwatch, he noted that it was just after 10 o'clock.

Inside the mansion, his two deputies, Andersen and Jones, had already strung the police tape across the doorway of the kitchen. The officers had also isolated the long breezeway and the home's small office in order to keep unauthorized personnel from entering the rooms. They wanted to prevent any contamination or destruction of important evidence.

It was about 10:05 a.m. when Captain Pfeiff called a meeting of the deputies on the scene. Towering over the group at six-foot-four, he listened attentively as they took turns apprising him of what they had found. He was told of the condition of the victim, as well as the peculiar scratches on the murder suspect's arm.

"She's already asked for a lawyer," Sergeant Healy jumped in.

Healy could tell from the captain's reaction that the information was helpful—but not welcome. In short, it meant that the suspect was "off limits" until her lawyer arrived, and that nothing could be done in the house until a search warrant was obtained from a judge.

Silently, the captain reviewed the information he had just heard and began to formulate a rough plan. He needed to determine if additional manpower would be necessary to secure the location and what resources would be required to carry out the investigation.

He decided that Sergeant Healy would be the one to return to the sheriff's office and fill out the forms needed to obtain a judge's signature for the warrant. Investigator Michael Lamper would accompany him.

As the men walked back down the driveway toward their

car, they spotted Sheriff Higgs pulling up alongside them. From behind dark sunglasses, he gestured a hello with his chin and waved his hand as he steered past them.

"How are you men doing?" he called through the open car window.

It was almost 10:30 a.m. when Captain Pfeiff took his first walk down the long hallway of the servants' wing to conduct a visual inspection of the kitchen. Officers pointed the way as the long-limbed investigator strode along the emerald-colored tiles of the second breezeway. Pfeiff shifted his glance from left to right as he surveyed the layout of the grand estate.

In addition to his supreme abilities as a detective, the captain was known around the stationhouse for his colorful neckties and his talent for woodworking. Sheriff Higgs liked to boast about how his second-in-command had saved the department a bundle each year by putting his hobby to official use—designing clocks, plaques, and trophies to honor the work of valued officers and department employees.

Sergeant Andersen greeted his superior at the entrance to the kitchen. He had roped off the doorway to the room and was leaning on the wall just outside the crime scene. Captain Pfeiff noticed that a second deputy had posted himself at the end of the hall to make sure that nobody entered or left the scene through the rear door of the house.

Peering into the kitchen, the captain was surprised at how small the room was, no bigger than the extra bedrooms in his own home. From where he was standing, he could see the body lying on the ground about six or seven feet from the doorway.

On the floor just a few feet from the refrigerator, he spotted two 9mm shell casings. On the wall, just below the telephone, he noticed a bullet strike mark. A second hole was visible on the closet door just above the kitchen table.

The captain remained in the doorway, returning his gaze to the dead body on the floor. He observed that the man lay prone with his feet tucked under the table and that the blood that had poured from the man's wounds had already begun to separate.

It seemed strange to him that there were no broken dishes or any other signs of a struggle. Instead, everything was in order and the TV was still on in the corner of the room.

On the dishwasher next to the double sink, the veteran officer spotted the knife sheath that Chief Grimsley had seen earlier that morning. On the floor below the sink, he saw small droplets of blood and made a mental note that the tiny stains were more heavily concentrated in the area of the dead body.

As he wandered back down the hallway, Pfeiff mentally pieced together what he had just seen. Entering the small sitting room where Susan Cummings was being detained, he peered down through the gold-rimmed glasses that were balanced on the tip of his nose at the wounds on her left arm. They were still bleeding, but it was clear to him that her injuries did not require a trip to the emergency room.

Sheriff Higgs had checked earlier on Miss Cummings. When he had noticed the cuts on her arms, he had immediately asked her if she was in need of some sort of medical assistance. Politely, she had declined.

Standing over the slight brunette heiress, Captain Pfeiff spoke briefly with her. She revealed little about the events of that morning and graciously asked that she be permitted to speak to her attorney.

After his visit to the kitchen, the captain decided that he would need three investigators to carry out the processing of the crime scene, which entailed photographing, diagramming, and documenting the evidence.

He was convinced that evidence collection should not be limited to the small maid's galley where Roberto's body was discovered. Instead, he declared that the exploration would encompass the entire mansion.

Ordering his men from the house, the captain gathered the deputies on the outside walkway to map out a strategy that would expedite the evidence collection and ensure that none of the clues were overlooked or, worse, contaminated.

First, he designated Investigator Erich Junger and Deputy Jim Jones to the daunting task of crime-scene processing, which would take nearly seven hours and yield more than three hundred photographs. The captain did not consider the day-long undertaking unusual; his experience had taught him that homicide investigations could sometimes take two to three days to complete.

Next, he assigned sheriff's deputies to fan out across the 350-acre Ashland Farm spread to locate any potential witnesses who might have seen or heard anything unusual that morning.

Three separate officers took statements from Susan's sister, Diana. One of them was Captain Pfeiff. When he found the pretty blonde, she was seated in the library next to her sister. Pulling a notepad from his rear pocket, the captain sat down on the couch beside the twins and asked Diana what she had done that morning.

"I went to the barn around seven, or seven-thirty," she answered. Her husky, almost masculine voice seemed an odd contrast to her elegant looks and continental accent. "I came back to my house, and I was in my yard puttering around with my dogs when I heard three gunshots. I suspected she [Susan] was in the main house. She was supposed to leave that day for a game. Because it was early, I suspected she was there.

"Since the gunshots were coming from the direction of the house, I decided to go and check," Diana went on with her story, her demeanor calm, her description dryly reportorial. "I walked toward the main house. I entered the laundry-room door where the garage doors are.

"I found my sister on the phone in the office," she recalled. "She was talking to police. She remained on the phone for about five minutes. Once she hung up, a police car showed up," Diana said without emotion. "I went to the front door of the main house and met the officer. As soon as I met him, my sister was behind me and he handcuffed her."

When the officers questioned the attractive blonde, she told them that she believed it was nearly 9 a.m. when she heard three gunshots coming from the direction of her sister's home. The officers noted that Susan had told Diana that she would be out of town that morning and that Diana said she had intended to go to the main house to feed the animals.

Deputies were surprised to learn that after hearing the gunshots, Diana waited nearly five minutes before walking down the path to her sister's home and entering through the laundry-room door, which, she said, was unlocked. Once inside, she told detectives that she found her sister in a small rear office speaking on the telephone. Diana recalled that Susan appeared upset.

"She told me she was on the phone with police," Diana recalled. "It seemed like only seconds passed when a police officer showed up at the mansion and handcuffed Susan."

The barn worker, Jane Gritz, also recounted hearing a series of loud popping sounds sometime between 8:15 and 8:30 a.m. She said she believed they were the sounds of a hammer that came from the direction of the mansion. The portly blonde told police that she did not wear a watch in the summertime and was basing the time on her usual morning routine.

She recalled that she was in the small barn tending to the horses when she suddenly heard several loud cracks. The noise, she said, startled her, and she looked up at the home, convinced that the loud banging was nothing more than a continuation of the construction that had been going on at the main house for the last six months. Police noted that Jane didn't stop what she was doing to check on the heiress, and it wasn't until they found her in the stable that she learned that the loud noises were gunshots.

As investigators took statements from witnesses in the barn, Captain Pfeiff returned to the driveway and continued to dole out assignments to the men on the scene. He designated Investigator Junger as the primary investigator, assigning him the duties of evidence collection and preservation.

For Junger, it was to be his second big murder case of the year. In August, he had been named lead investigator in the homicide case against James Martin Wyne, the man who shot another man to death on the steps of a delicatessen in nearby Marshall.

Captain Pfeiff was aware that Junger was overburdened. He knew that, like most of his men, the investigator was already handling between thirty and fifty cases a month. But he had great faith in Junger's work. He knew that his background included a Ph.D. in forensic science and work as a forensic scientist at the Bethesda Naval Hospital and was certain that he was the right man for this assignment.

Investigator Junger was ecstatic with the way his police career was going. During his stint as a forensic scientist, he had secretly longed to get out in the field and try his hand at detective work.

Since Captain Pfeiff decided that he wanted to be personally involved in evidence collection, he alerted the bushy-mustached Junger that he would be taking on the role of crime-scene artist, to prepare the sketches and diagrams.

The captain designated Deputy Jones as his assistant, telling the Dennis Weaver lookalike that he would be responsible for helping out with the measurements and any other duties that arose as the men forged ahead with their examination.

As the officers waited in the driveway, basking in the warm September sun, a fancy sports utility vehicle pulled onto the property. The deputies looked on as a slight, fair-haired man with an athletic build stepped out of the truck, attired in slacks and a sport shirt, and carrying a briefcase.

They watched as he ambled toward them, extending his hand to Captain Pfeiff and introducing himself as Blair Howard. In a thick Southern drawl, he explained to the superior officer that he had been called to act as Miss Cummings' attorney and wanted to speak with her.

Mr. Howard was well-known to the deputies of the Fauquier County Sheriff's Department. The courtly Southern barrister had a reputation for excellence in the Virginia legal community, where he did a fair amount of criminal work in Fauquier County and the surrounding area, and his services were held in the highest regard. His clever courtroom manner and his ability to captivate a jury with carefully-crafted words had earned him a number of stunning courtroom acquittals.

But he was best-known for his defense in the Lorena Bobbitt case. Most people in and around the Washington area instantly recognized him as the lawyer who defended the Manassas woman who pleaded self-defense after cutting off her husband John's penis, driving away with it in her car, and tossing it out the window into a grassy field.

Mr. Howard explained to the officers that Susan's sister Diana had contacted him at his residence in nearby Marshall. Unbeknownst to the officers, she had obtained his name and number from a mutual friend in the foxhunting circle.

Like Diana, Howard was a huntsman and enjoyed the great outdoors. His skin was eternally tanned, and he was not ashamed to admit that he participated in the sport of the hunt. The sport had come under scrutiny in recent months by members of animal rights organizations.

When Diana contacted the lawyer, he agreed to come right over, assuring her that Ashland Farm was less than fifteen minutes from his home.

As deputies escorted the criminal attorney to the area where Susan was being detained, Investigator Junger, eager to get a head start on the investigation, grabbed his camera. Slowly, he made his way around the exterior of the house, climbing behind the shrubs to check the home's doors and windows for any signs of forced entry.

He knew it would be several hours before Sergeant Healy returned with the official signed document that would allow him to begin his methodical exploration of the interior, including the grisly crime scene itself.

CHAPTER 13

IT WAS JUST BEFORE NOON WHEN SERGEANT HEALY returned to Ashland Farm with the signed warrant that would permit the team of officers to search the mansion at 8714 Holtzclaw Road. On the upper portion of the official document he had listed the offense: Murder-Virginia Code 18.2-32.

The official paperwork authorized police personnel to remove the body of Roberto Cerillio Villegas, and to seize items from the house such as the dark-colored semi-automatic pistol that lay at the top of the steps leading to the kitchen, ammunition for the weapon, photographs of the home, and blood and any other evidence of the crime.

Even though Susan had granted the officers permission to enter the house, police thought it prudent to first obtain a judge's signature. They didn't want to make any mistakes in what they knew was destined to be a high-profile case.

Steering up the winding blacktop driveway, Sergeant Healy, accompanied by his colleague Michael Lamper, slowed down to look at the crowd of people who had congregated on the walkway just outside the stone manor. He had no idea who they all were, but he assumed that at least some of them had to be members of the Cummings family.

Investigator Lamper had accompanied Healy to the judge's chambers where he had presented a second warrant to the magistrate, asking the court for permission to arrest Susan Cummings and take blood, hair, and fiber samples from her person.

As the men climbed out of the police car, they were greeted by a deputy with surprising news: Susan's attorney was on the scene. The officer went on to explain that the attorney had been summoned by Diana Cummings and that he had already spent several minutes with his client in the courtyard in the front of the mansion. Healy couldn't hide his irritation and shook his head in disappointment.

The deputy continued to bring his superior up to date as Investigator Lamper, his hair slicked back, scoured the property looking for Susan Cummings. Ambling over to the lawn, he found her standing next to a sheriff's deputy. Her attorney had been instructed to leave the scene and wait for his client at the sheriff's office in downtown Warrenton.

Pulling a pair of shiny silver handcuffs from his belt loop, the investigator clasped them shut around Susan's bony wrists. It was 11:55 a.m. when he placed her under arrest for the murder of Roberto Villegas.

Lamper nodded to his colleagues as he led the shackled woman down the pathway toward his police car. Opening the back door, he motioned Susan to get in, placing his free hand between the car's doorframe and her head to make sure she didn't injure herself while in police custody.

Starting up the car, he waited, watching in his rear view mirror as Sergeant Healy ran down the driveway and jumped into the passenger seat. He glanced over and noticed that the sergeant held a sealed plastic bag containing a pair of white Keds sneakers in his left hand.

The heiress sat silently in the back of the police car as the threesome pulled onto Route 211 and headed east toward the sheriff's department. Susan had stopped in at the low-slung brick building just two weeks before and met with Sergeant Healy, who now sat in the passenger seat just in front of her. Whirling blue lights flashing from the top of the vehicle flickered in her eyes as she stared out the window, watching as the deputy steered past the stately colonial homes and ancient oaks, ashes, and silver maples that lined the winding road leading to the village center.

As they waited at the stop sign for a break in the Sunday traffic, Susan gazed at the Fauquier County Library on the corner. She had been told that there was a book about her father in the institution's collection, but had never bothered to check it out.

Susan could feel the car slowing as they turned into the concrete parking lot behind the sheriff's office on Keith Street. She watched through the rear window as Sergeant Lamper jumped out of the driver's seat and came around to open her door.

As the investigator helped Susan out of the vehicle, his eyes darted across the street to the rows of tombstones that lined the adjacent cemetery. He glanced at Sergeant Healy and then led the way inside the red-brick headquarters.

Climbing the staircase to the second floor, Susan was escorted to the Criminal Investigations Division for the purpose of being interviewed. But the interrogation would have to wait. As the three entered the second floor office complex, they were greeted by Blair Howard. The attorney extended his arm and politely introduced himself to Sergeant Healy.

"I would like a few minutes to speak with my client," he said, smiling.

Reluctantly, the sergeant led Susan and her attorney to the small interview room—the same room in which Healy had met with her two weeks earlier. Closing the door behind them, the sergeant ambled down the hallway and took a seat behind the industrial-style desk in his office. There, he waited for their meeting to end, still hoping he would get a chance to speak with Susan about what had happened that morning.

The jaunty lawyer arranged himself in the cramped interrogation room and studied his new client's fragile face as she introduced herself. She was attractive in a peaceful, serene sort of way, Howard thought as he jotted down some notes on a legal pad.

Susan perched delicately on the edge of one of the wooden chairs and in modulated tones explained to the attorney that she had been trying to end the affair with her former lover when he attacked her with a knife in the kitchen of her Warrenton home.

Howard listened attentively, recording his observations as Miss Cummings carefully reviewed the details of her two-year romance with the dead polo star. Between sips of hot coffee, she recounted a harrowing tale.

The delicate-boned woman appeared understandably upset to the attorney. He waited patiently as she took a few moments to compose herself before launching into the details of the morning's events.

Sitting on the edge of her chair, her hands folded neatly on the table in front of her, she began.

"I felt there was someone in my house." Susan spoke in a slow, steady voice. "I didn't see anybody. I called out his name.

"He acknowledged he was downstairs, but not immediately," she paused. "I did not go down right away; I waited for five or ten minutes.

"I found Roberto in the kitchen. He was sitting at the kitchen table. I noticed a bag of croissants on the table. I came into the room and sat at the kitchen table right across from him.

"I told Roberto, 'You know that you must take your belongings and leave. I had asked you this yesterday, so I am sure you are aware that you must leave as quickly as possible.'

"He responded by saying that he had a game planned for today in Potomac, Maryland, and that he was going to get ready to go and play at that game.

"I told Roberto in my calm way, 'Roberto, I know that you have a game. You can go to that game, but you cannot take . . . but you have to make different arrangements for the horses because I am . . . you cannot take my horses for the game.'

"Roberto became very angry. In a split second, he retrieved a knife, and in a . . . in a quick minute later, he reached from across the table, he took hold of my neck and put the knife at my face. I did not react. I was very fearful and I . . . I stayed motionless. He pressed the knife against my cheeks. I remember feeling pressure on both sides, and I remember him switching the blade from left to right or right to left. He insulted me once again.

" 'You f---ing piece of s---,' he shouted. 'No woman is

ever going to tell me what to do. I'm going to teach you a lesson.' "

The lawyer's wide green eyes remained fixed on his client's pale, thin lips as she continued with her story.

"And he . . . he started to apply more pressure on my cheeks, still holding me by the neck. And then he said, 'I'm going to go down and deeper.' He began to slash my arm slowly, laughing and commenting about the fear in my face.

" 'Oh, you look so scared with your big eyes,' he said to me. 'What's wrong?'

"My heart was beating. I felt that my blood was rushing down. I felt extremely scared. I felt that my life was in danger. afraid for my life. I felt . . . I thought to myself, this is it, this man is going to kill me."

The lawyer watched as Susan paused to reposition herself. The straight-backed chair squeaked as she adjusted her 130-pound frame.

"Was it the first time he'd drawn a weapon on you?" he asked her.

"Yes," she replied, pressing her hands on the seat of her chair, and crossing her skinny legs at the ankles. "When Roberto started slashing my arm, I . . . I . . . I thought to myself, I've got to say . . . I've got to tell him . . . I've got to calm this man down. So I was telling him, 'Okay, Roberto, no one is going to die today. You can ride the horses. You can use the horses. Please, Roberto, you are hurting me, please stop.'

"I reached for Roberto's hand, the one that was holding the knife, and I directed it downward. Roberto managed to calm down somewhat, and he got out of the chair and stood in front of the sink and ran some water from the faucet. I was still seated in the chair, and I did not make any attempt to run at this point. I was motionless. I was afraid. Here was a man who is very strong, very quick, very unpredictable. I . . . I knew that . . . I was cornered. I was in the part of the kitchen where in order to run out, I would have had to come in close contact with him to exit. There was no way for me to do that without him grabbing me or killing me.

"At some point in time, Roberto had returned from the

sink area to sit down back to the table. I felt very uncomfortable having Roberto seated across from me. So, I told Roberto, 'I'm going to get . . . to make some coffee.' I headed toward the sink area and I . . . at this point, I was facing the sink area and running some water. And at the same time, I was telling Roberto, 'I'm going to wipe my arm and we are going to forget about this incident.'

"I stopped the water, and then walked slightly to the right where the coffee was. . . . I thought about calling Sergeant Healy. I thought about calling my sister. . . . I also thought about the pistol in the kitchen cabinet which was right below the coffee area.

"And I thought, maybe if I could get to my pistol I could control the situation.

"I bent down and I retrieved the pistol. As I took the pistol out of the kitchen cabinet, I heard what I thought was a scraping of a chair. As soon as I heard that scraping, I took a few steps back. I turned in the direction of Roberto, and I saw, and I fired.''

Blair Howard exhaled. Staring directly at Suzanne, he waited to see if there was any more.

"What I saw was a very angry Roberto,'' Susan continued. "His face was red. His eyes were threatening. He had a very tense look in his face. He was coming out of the chair, and he was looking at me directly and with a locked jaw.''

Blair Howard looked up from his notepad. "Then what did you do?'' he asked.

"I took the pistol and I ran out of the kitchen and threw the gun on the floor. Then I ran to the office and made the 911 call.''

Susan's attorney studied her expression but remained silent. Turning his attention to the long vertical scratches on his client's left arm, he ran his fingers along them and asked her what had happened.

She told him that she had sustained the cuts when Roberto pulled out his knife and attacked her.

Blair Howard added the information to his notes. Leaning forward in his chair, he squinted his eyes and focused on what he believed to be two scrapes on her right cheek.

''What about those?'' he asked, pointing to the thin scratches with the tip of his pen.

Again, Susan told him that she had sustained those injuries at the hand of Roberto.

Marking down her answers on his lined writing tablet, the attorney continued his questions. He focused on the material that he would be incorporating into a plea of self-defense. The plea would be presented to a judge the following afternoon.

As Susan and her lawyer sat for the next three hours discussing their legal strategy, members of the Fauquier County Sheriff's Department's investigative crime team were methodically piecing together their own version of the morning's events, one that bore little resemblance to the one that Susan Cummings had just related to her lawyer.

CHAPTER 14

"THERE'S A KNIFE HERE!" INVESTIGATOR JUNGER YELLED out to the officers who stood pulling on their latex gloves in the doorway of the maid's galley.

Captain Pfeiff and Deputy Jones climbed down the creaky wooden steps, and then slowly walked over to the dead body to get a glimpse of their colleague's finding.

Looking down at Roberto Villegas' lifeless frame, the two men's eyes followed Junger's finger to the man's arm. Along the right side of his body, nestled in the crook of his elbow, the deputies spotted the knife. It was a Bertram Cutlery knife with a six-inch blade and a bone handle.

The captain had not seen the weapon when he looked into the room nearly three hours earlier, and its absence had been the topic of discussion among Deputies Andersen, Walters, and Tulley as early as 9:15 a.m. that morning.

Investigator Junger stared down at the weapon and contemplated its position. The location was troubling, and from the frowns on the other officers' faces, it appeared that they, too, were suspicious.

To Junger, the weapon looked as though it did not belong there. From the angle at which the knife was resting, it did not seem plausible that it could have fallen from the man's hand and landed blade first with the knife tip touching the blood-soaked floor. The investigator noticed that there appeared to be something engraved on the fancy black-and-white handgrip. He would later learn that the knife was one of Roberto's most prized possessions; he had won it in a polo competition in Sarasota, Florida, several years earlier, and used it for everything from eating his meals to cutting his horses free when they became tangled in their ropes.

The bright flash of Junger's Nikon recorded the position of the knife against Roberto's body, as Captain Pfeiff sketched out what he saw on a bulky drawing tablet. The officers had been alerted to the fact that the pool of blood that encircled the victim's body had already begun to gel and separate when Sergeant Andersen tried to find a pulse nearly four hours earlier. They knew that the separation of blood meant that the man had to have been dead for at least half an hour. The information would prove valuable to the investigators as they plotted out their theory.

Only minutes before, Investigator Junger had collected the single spent 9mm casing that he had found on the floor in the hallway, and the Walther P-1 pistol that was lying beside the bullet near the entrance to the kitchen. When he had picked up the gun, he noticed that there was an empty magazine inside it. It looked to him as though the gun could hold up to eight rounds.

The forensics expert was intrigued by the heavy German pistol in his gloved hands, and studied it for a while. He admired its superior design and long, thin muzzle before dropping it into a plastic bag and sealing it tightly as evidence. The gun was one of the best-selling items in Sam Cummings' arms catalog. Everyone who'd ever seen a James Bond movie knew the Walther name. Bond always carried a Walther PPK.

Junger was about to enter the kitchen when he spied a second shell casing in the hallway, partially hidden at the threshold just beneath the door. Pointing his camera down and refocusing the lens, he snapped a photo of the empty casing and then advanced the film as he stepped over the threshold down the steps into the maid's galley. He was struck by how cramped the room was, no bigger than a walk-in closet. The space was so tight that there was barely enough room for the three investigators to work comfortably.

Following the plan they had made earlier in the day, the

three plainclothes officers assumed their roles, with Junger collecting the evidence, Pfeiff recording it on his sketch pad, and Jones assisting the captain with the measurements.

As the men glanced around, Junger noticed two more spent shell casings lying side-by-side in front of the built-in refrigerator. Knowing that the Walther ejected the empty shell casing each time it was fired, the investigator paused momentarily, trying to visualize where the shooter had been standing when the gun went off. With two of the spent casings inside the kitchen and two outside in the hallway, he was faced with a puzzle: where was Susan when she fired the first shots?

Raising his camera to record the position of the second two spent shells, Junger realized that he would have to do extensive forensics work before he could answer that question. Looking up at Pfeiff and Jones, he nodded his head to indicate that the deputies should begin taking measurements of the casings.

As the men inched closer to document the location of the spent rounds, Junger continued his investigation. Shifting his attention to the opposite side of the room, he took a slow and cautious step toward the kitchen counter. Lying on top of the stainless-steel countertop and next to the double sink, he spotted the empty leather knife sheath.

Gingerly, he strode around the tiny droplets of blood that stained the floor in front of the sink, pausing momentarily to capture the sheath's location on film. His hands were sweating inside the tight latex gloves and there was no hint of a breeze from the partially-opened window on the opposite side of the room.

Using the back of his arm, the compactly-built investigator wiped the tiny beads of sweat that were collecting along his brow and in his thick mustache.

Digging around in his evidence-collection kit, he pulled out a sterile cotton swab, and then knelt down to wipe the tip along one of the blood droplets that stained the floor immediately in front of the sink. He smeared the red liquid as he collected his sample and then placed the skinny wooden handle on the edge of the sink to allow the swab to air dry.

He could hear the scratching of Captain Pfeiff's pencil on the sketch pad as he collected his paraphernalia and moved toward the opposite end of the kitchen, taking just two strides to cross the tiny room. The investigator had been to numerous crime scenes during his career as a forensics expert. But the bloody aftermath of gunshot wounds still made him shudder. His eyes scanned the corner where Roberto's body lay at a forty-five-degree angle—head and right shoulder immediately next to the wall, left arm outstretched by his side, right arm tucked underneath his body, legs partially hidden beneath the small kitchen table that jutted out from the wall and was under the room's only window.

The investigator noted the tremendous amount of blood that was splashed on the floor, walls and open pantry door next to the victim's body. It looked as though someone had thrown a bucket of blood with great force up onto the door's top right panel. There was more blood on the base of the door and on the floor nearby.

Junger moved in closer to examine the chair on which the victim had been sitting and enjoying breakfast only hours earlier. His eyes were drawn to the edge of the tan and blue chair cushion, which was stained with blood, and he noticed that more blood had spilled off the chair and onto the floor below. Oddly, the rest of the diamond-patterned cushion was clean and free of blood-stains, prompting the investigator to wonder if the victim was, indeed, seated when the first slugs ripped through his body.

Careful to avoid the pool of blood around the victim, Junger backed a few feet away and found a clean spot on the floor where he could put his evidence kit down. He moved closer to examine each inch of the walls, door, window. He was looking for slugs. He began with the bullet he'd spotted earlier that day in the wall beside the open window. Tightly closing one eye, the deputy leaned against the pale-yellow wall and peered into the finger-sized hole. He quickly spotted the glint of the copper jacket, lodged in the wall next to the window. Prying the molding loose, he used two cotton-tipped applicators to extract the slug.

Taking a closer look at the bloody white chair, he spotted another splintered bullet hole that he'd missed during his initial inspection. Judging by the position of the hole, he decided that the slug must have passed through Roberto's back, punched through the door, and gone into the pantry.

The slug had to be in there somewhere, he thought to himself. He began rummaging around, moving canned goods and other foodstuffs as he went along hoping to find something out of place. After some time, he found the slug embedded in the pantry door.

Motioning to his colleagues, he indicated that he intended to take both the chair and blood-soaked cushion as evidence. As he collected the items, Captain Pfeiff and Deputy Jones made their last few measurements.

Finishing up in the pantry, Jones let the measuring tape spool back into its chrome case and followed Junger and Pfeiff down the hall, checking inside each room they passed as they made their way through the breezeway and past the line of floor-to-ceiling windows.

Junger mused that, despite all of the Cummingses wealth, they hadn't spent much money on renovations. Unlike many of the old estates in the area, the main house at Ashland Farm was still largely in its original condition of disrepair. Because of the decades-old hardware and the warped wood panels, the men found themselves struggling with each door along the way. Every few steps, they'd reach for an old knob and find it stuck. A simple push usually didn't produce any results either. Instead, the officers had no choice but to throw a shoulder against each door or give it a swift kick.

As they continued down the corridor, the thick-set Junger noticed some movement at the far end of the hallway, breathing a sigh of relief when he realized that the commotion was one of the cats scurrying from one room to another. The animals seemed to be everywhere, and though the investigator hadn't bothered to keep count, he was certain there were at least a dozen of the furry creatures roaming the house.

Climbing the three steps to a landing area, the officers continued for several feet before reaching a small, neatly-kept office. Junger's eyes were immediately drawn to the one item that was starkly out of place: a live, 9mm round, sitting in the middle of a white, lined pad on the heavy wooden desk. He waited for Captain Pfeiff to record its location on his sketch pad before picking up the bullet with his gloved hand.

Earlier, Diana had told Captain Pfeiff that her sister had placed the 911 call to the sheriff's department from the phone in this room which had once been used by the family as a second bedroom. Junger, Captain Pfeiff, and the others didn't know that the girl's father had converted the downstairs sleeping area into an office to use whenever he was visiting the farm.

Sealing the single piece of ammunition in the evidence bag and adding it to his growing collection, Investigator Junger joined his colleagues as they scoured the desk, the floor around the desk, the chair, and a small bathroom nearby. They were looking for any sign of blood that might have dripped from the numerous cuts on Susan's arm when she placed the call.

Junger was struck by the fact that there was no blood anywhere, not on the desk, the phone Susan had used to call the police, the towels in the bathroom, or the bathroom sink. In fact, he observed that there was no indication of anything unusual, except for the bullet. On the wall just in front of the desk, he noted a color-photo calendar that featured a picture of a handgun for the month of September.

Wrapping up their search of the mansion's first floor, the deputies made their way back through the maze of hallways to the main part of the residence. Junger chuckled after Captain Pfeiff complained about the home's strange layout, with all its different levels. It seemed that every few feet there were several steps leading up, and then down, the home's long, narrow corridors.

The investigators lugged their equipment up the stairs to Susan's bedroom. As they entered the spacious room, Junger's eyes grew round. Everywhere he looked, clothes and other paraphernalia were strewn about. It was clear to him that this fabulously wealthy heiress had no maid to keep the house in order.

He walked to the oversized closet with its lime-green walls and stopped to stare at the untidy mess. Inhaling deeply, he plunged ahead, wondering what, if anything, he would find. He knew that Deputy Jones had already explored the room earlier that morning. He glanced over at the tall, dark-haired officer to acknowledge that he, too, was taken aback by the room's disheveled state.

Standing beside the closet door, Jones and Pfeiff watched as Junger began his methodical search. It wasn't long before the investigator raised his arm and pointed to a black leather holster on one of the closet's shelves.

The officers watched as he held up the holster for his captain to see. The holster was empty and its flap was open. Junger had a strong hunch that the semi-automatic Walther they had just found in the kitchen hallway would fit into the holster perfectly.

Wondering what his captain was thinking, the investigator stole a quick look at his superior. The hint of a smile on the captain's face told him what he wanted to know: the two men were thinking the same thing.

But why was the holster up here? he wondered.

Just beside the gun case and on top of some clothing, Junger found an open box of ammunition that, judging from its weight, appeared to be nearly full. He flipped the box over and saw that it was supposed to contain 50 rounds of 9mm ammunition.

As the captain observed, Junger counted the rounds that remained. "Forty-two rounds," he said as the superior officer scribbled some notes on his pad.

Holding the small cardboard carton between his fingers, the forensics expert pulled a plastic bag from his satchel and dropped the evidence inside. The clank of the metal bullets hitting against each other as they moved around in the box added to the drama of the discovery.

Captain Pfeiff moved in closer to watch as Junger pointed to a collection of ammunition boxes and a magazine holding eight 9mm rounds on the bottom shelf. The rest of the boxes, he noted, were unopened.

Rummaging through the piles of clothes that filled the closet shelves, Junger fingered a bulky object inside a small black nylon bag and pulled it out to take a closer look. Unzipping the bag, he saw a semi-automatic .22-caliber pistol, a Walther TPH.

Other deputies were called to help as the investigators continued their search of the master suite. The collection of stuffed animals arranged on Susan's bed fell onto the floor as they lifted the mattress to reveal a loaded ROSSI .357 Magnum hidden between the box-spring and mattress. The weapon was found at the head of the bed, tucked a foot or two from the headboard. But from the way the pillows had been arranged, it appeared to the investigators that the person who slept in the bed had lain down with her head at the bed's base, facing away from the wall.

Rays of afternoon sunlight streamed through the windowpanes of the airy master bedroom as the investigators moved their attention to the dresser. A sweet-smelling breeze wafted in through the partially-opened window as Deputy Jones called the others' attention to something that he'd noticed earlier: one of the drawers had been opened a few inches and it appeared that the contents had been moved about.

Jones moved aside as Junger kneeled beside the drawer to have a better look inside. It looked to Junger as though someone had been rummaging through the drawer in search of something. Two clear plastic bags were lying incongruously on top of the clothing. He saw that one contained a Swiss Army knife; the other was empty. The empty bag was left open, as if someone had quickly extracted its contents and not bothered—or not had the time—to dispose of the bag.

Kneeling down next to the dresser, the officer poked around the bottom of the drawer to see what else might be stuffed in with the clothing. He smiled as his hand brushed across something hard and metallic. He could feel the outline of another gun. Pushing the clothes aside, he uncovered a small .22-caliber Walther P88.

The police found the holster for the P88 downstairs in the rifle room where Sam Cummings had proudly displayed a sample of his vast collection of antique muskets, rifles, and handguns; some were behind locked glass, others hung unprotected on the walls.

Officers listed the fourth weapon on the evidence sheet, along with other items they found in the bedroom, including Susan's address book and an envelope with Roberto's name written across the front.

As the deputies continued their methodical exploration of the mansion at Ashland Farm, its owner, Susan Cummings, was posing for pictures at the Fauquier County Sheriff's Department.

"Susan, step in front of the camera." Sergeant Lamper smiled. His boyish good looks were of no interest to the heiress, who was preoccupied with the idea of her "mug shot" being snapped for the official police record.

She stared straight ahead and kept her lips pursed firmly together as the officer clicked off one exposure after another using a camera mounted atop a tripod. After getting one shot with her looking toward the camera, the officer ordered her to turn ninety degrees to the right for the profile.

The frontal pose was most unflattering and documented her with a wavy mop of brown hair tucked tightly behind her ears to reveal a shiny scrubbed face and thin, uneven eyebrows. The color photo would be distributed to the media the following morning and by Tuesday it would be splashed across the front pages of newspapers around the world.

Susan was being formally charged with her crimes. Sergeant Lamper and Investigator Healy arrested her on felony charges and read her the Miranda Rights. Her official offenses were listed as Murder and Use of a Firearm in the Commission of a Felony, both of which carried jail time and substantial fines.

She had emerged from her meeting with Blair Howard unwilling to speak with police. Sergeant Healy, who had waited in his office for nearly three hours in the hopes of speaking to her, was disappointed. Her refusal to talk left police with no choice but to transport her to the Adult Detention Center just up the block on West Lee Street for booking. There, she would again be the subject of photographs, this time to record the numerous superficial cuts on her left arm.

Arriving at the center, the two deputies escorted Susan inside and then summoned Kimberly Slack to the booking area. They had called on Slack because it was police protocol to have a female officer conduct body searches of all women prisoners.

With a hearty grin, the pretty young deputy greeted Susan. She was about to be married and her excitement over her impending nuptials was written all over her face.

Susan returned the officer's kind smile, but was incredulous when the heavy-set woman asked her to remove her clothing. Handing her a folded orange prison suit, Deputy Slack pointed to a small dressing area where Susan was to change out of her street clothes.

Susan clutched the cloth outfit in her right hand as she turned and entered the enclosed area, emerging a few minutes later with her clothes flung over her arm. She surrendered her Levis 550 jeans, T-shirt and the aquamarine B.U.M. sweatshirt she had obtained from her upstairs bedroom to the deputy who held a "PERK Kit" in her hand. The Physical Evidence Recovery Kit contained the vials and plastic containers the officer needed to collect samples from her prisoner.

Susan watched as the thick-set deputy raised a pair of scissors between her long fingers and grasped a small clump of her wavy hair. She tried not to flinch as Slack trimmed several locks from just below her right shoulder and placed the clippings in a tiny Zip-lock casing. Out of the corner of her eye, Susan could see the small diamond engagement ring that was tightly secured on the officer's left ring finger, and the deep red polish that decorated her manicured nails.

Next, Slack stuck a needle into Susan's arm, withdrawing a vial of blood to be sent to the lab. Then she rubbed ink on the tip of the prisoner's right thumb to record her fingerprint and place it on file.

The final part of the physical evidence collection proved a challenge for the deputy. Instructing Susan to hold out her fingers, the deputy pulled out a thin wooden stick that she planned to use to scrape any particles under the heiress's short, stubby nails. As she lifted Susan's right hand, Deputy Slack noticed that there was something wrong with her fingers. Her nails did not protrude enough for the officer to be able to get a sample of what was underneath them.

Susan told the deputy that she suffered from an ailment—which she did not disclose—that prevented her nails from growing over the skin of her fingers. Her explanation excused her from the unpleasant test.

The items the officers seized were taken to the conference room in the rear of the Criminal Investigations Division, where they were photographed and packed for shipment to the lab. Articles of Susan's clothing were still moist from the blood that stained the back of her white T-shirt and the bottom of her sneaker when they pulled them from the plastic evidence bag, so the deputies laid them out on a table to let them air dry.

It was nearly dusk—just about 5 p.m.—when the shiny medical examiner's van whizzed up the driveway of 8714 Holtzclaw Road. The local medical examiner, Ralph Robinson, was there to make a cursory assessment of the dead body. The officers could not move Mr. Villegas without the M.E.'s permission.

Captain Pfeiff and Deputy Jones were in the room when the M.E. arrived. The commanding officer had briefed the doctor about the early-morning shooting and the scratches on Susan's arm when he telephoned him from the scene earlier in the day.

It is customary for the local medical examiner to perform an initial evaluation of the deceased at the crime scene, before the state examiner has a chance to conduct a more thorough probe. Authorities believe that the preliminary check provides the M.E. with an important frame of reference that can be referred to when the autopsy is performed later at the lab.

The doctor remained on the scene for less than twenty minutes. Before he left, shortly before 4 p.m., he granted the investigators permission to move Roberto Villegas' body so they could continue with their investigation.

Investigator Junger returned to the kitchen. Pulling on a fresh pair of rubber gloves, he approached Roberto's body and rolled it onto a clean portion of the floor, careful not to disturb the telltale blood patterns that were just above and to the left of the victim's head. Blood oozed out of the dead man's wounds as the investigator repositioned the body.

Raising his camera, the officer photographed the pool of blood that was under Roberto's body and the small, and moderate-sized blood droplets on the floor nearby. The photographs were later analyzed by an expert in blood-stain analysis.

Before the day was done, police confiscated a 9mm Walther semi-automatic, a ROSSI .357 Magnum, two .22-caliber Walther pistols, and hundreds of rounds of ammunition. They also snapped more than three hundred crime scene photographs, many of which would later be used in Susan Cummings' murder trial.

The police investigators' findings would punch some holes in the heiress's claims of what happened that day at Ashland Farm. Her attorneys would counter the inconsistencies by arguing that police had bungled the crime-scene investigation and misinterpreted the evidence.

CHAPTER 15

THE FOLLOWING AFTERNOON SHERIFF JOE HIGGS ARRIVED at the county jail to find a weary Susan Cummings uniformed in the institution's bright-orange jail suit.

The baggy two-piece garment resembled a surgeon's scrubs and hung almost comically on her rail-thin figure, but she was not much of a fashion plate and didn't give the shapeless outfit a second thought.

"It's time to go to the courthouse," the sheriff called to the slender brunette. She was escorted from her holding cell by a pair of jail guards, one of whom asked that she place her arms out in front of her. Reaching behind his back, he unsnapped the handcuffs from his thick leather belt, and closed them gently around her wrists.

Sheriff Higgs, dressed in a dark sport jacket, white shirt, and jazzy blue tie decorated with colorful flowers, remained on Susan's heels as the two exited the building and climbed into an awaiting patrol car. His hair neatly combed and his dark sunglasses concealing his brown eyes, the sheriff made a point not to smile at the multitude of TV cameras pointed in his direction.

Reporters from *The Washington Post*, the Associated Press, and the local print and broadcast media lined the sidewalk in front of the jail. Even reporters from Roberto's homeland were there to cover the hearing. The crowd of journalists was equally dense outside the Fauquier County General District Court where the bond hearing for Susan Cummings would momentarily get underway.

Court officials were stunned by the turnout. They found it unbelievable that attendance for the bond hearing of Susan Cummings was greater than it had been for the sentencing of David Matthews just one week before. It seemed unbelievable to them that the media was more interested in the crimes of an heiress than they were in the brutal assault and murder of a twelve-year-old girl.

But it wasn't the defendant that caught the media's attention. Word spread throughout the press corps that the alleged perpetrator of the Sunday-morning shooting was the daughter of billionaire arms dealer Samuel Cummings, and that the killing had occurred in the kitchen of her sprawling Virginia mansion. It appeared that the opulent setting, the vast fortune of the Cummings family, and the intrigue of a romance between a wealthy patron and her dashing Argentine polo pro were a magic combination to editors at the nation's top newspapers and television stations.

Inside the courthouse, Blair Howard was preparing to argue Susan Cummings' case before Judge Charles Foley. His decision to offer a plea was unusual for a bond hearing.

Observers wondered why the attorney was presenting the court with a defense when one was clearly not required for this legal proceeding. But that was this lawyer's style, the sort of tactic that had earned him a shining reputation as a defense counselor. It was also one of the many reasons Susan Cummings had been advised to hire him.

Blair Howard had all the right credentials. The old-style Virginia gentleman had attended the University of Virginia, where he earned a bachelor's degree before joining the United States Army to help pay the high cost of law school.

He deferred his time in the service while attending American University Washington College of Law in Washington D.C. Once he passed the bar, he enlisted in the armed forces and was stationed in Pirmasens, Germany, about thirty miles from Heidelberg. The overseas assignment was a wonderful opportunity for the curious adventurer to see Europe. It was also where he learned to ski.

When he returned to Alexandria, he joined up with his father, T. Brooke Howard, a criminal attorney who was well-known in legal circles. Blair admired his dad and hoped that joining his firm would help him glean the tricks of the trade from the elder pro.

He conducted his legal practice from a modest four-room office in Old Town Alexandria, just steps away from the fancy coffee shops and designer boutiques of the revitalized waterfront. It was also less than seven blocks away from the headquarters for Interarms in the United States, where Susan Cummings' father conducted much of his business. T. Brooke Howard had founded the small firm there decades earlier, when Sam Cummings was doing business from his offices on the banks of the Potomac.

"The Court calls the case of *Susan Cummings vs. the Commonwealth of Virginia,*" the bailiff said, announcing the opening of the bond hearing to the packed courtroom.

Attired in a conservative dark suit and patterned tie, Blair Howard jumped up from his seat behind the long wooden table in the center of the tiny courtroom when his client's name was called. He motioned Susan to stand beside him.

"Susan Cummings?" The bailiff addressed the slender brunette.

"It's Su-ZAHN," Susan corrected him in her soft, accented voice. Her remark was met with snickers from the spectators seated in the gallery. Diana sat among them.

As the proceeding got underway in the windowless courtroom, the commonwealth attorney called several police witnesses to the stand. One of them was Captain Fred Pfeiff.

The sheriff's investigator sauntered to the stand, adjusting his lean, lanky frame in the hard-backed chair. He looked directly at Tina Tisinger, the commonwealth's attorney, as she directed him to describe for the court what his men had found at the Ashland Farm crime scene the previous morning.

Blair Howard listened intently, his arms folded on the table in front of him. When it was his turn to cross examine the witness, he sprang from his chair. In a slow, deliberate voice, he asked the captain if he had observed any marks on his client's left arm.

"I observed superficial marks that were very long and thin," the superior officer testified.

Staring directly at Judge Foley, Mr. Howard pointed to his client, his bright blue eyes accented by the blue shirt he wore beneath his suit jacket. The lawyer described the series of lacerations that Susan had sustained to her left arm and then the scratch marks that she now wore on the side of her face.

"She had these things inflicted by the person whom she is charged with murdering," Mr. Howard explained to the court.

His remarks were met with curious stares from the spectators seated in the gallery. The onlookers continued to pay careful attention, many taking furious notes, as they shifted their focus to Miss Tisinger.

Silence fell over the room as the neatly-dressed assistant attorney rose from her chair and stood before the judge. Citing the severity of the charges pending against Miss Cummings and the defendant's dual citizenship, she asked that bond be denied. The attorney maintained that Susan's two-country status put her at great risk of flight to avoid prosecution and insisted that holding two passports was reason enough to reject her bond.

Although unusual, Judge Foley ruled that defense counselor Blair Howard could call to the stand two neighbors who had business relationships with the Cummings sisters. The lawyer wanted to establish that his client was reliable and accountable, and did not pose any real flight risk to the court.

Diana sat silently in the first row as the two men took the stand to paint a picture of her sister for the court.

Jock Queen told the judge that he rented two hundred acres of land from the Cummings sisters. He went on to describe the thirty-five-year-old heiress as gentle and kind, and said that Susan was a woman who loved animals and enjoyed the tranquillity of Ashland Farm.

"She wouldn't hurt anything," the clean-cut businessman told the court. "I have all the confidence and trust in the world in her."

Another business associate, John Pennington, the owner

of an excavating business, told a similar story.

"Susan is a very reliable girl," the contractor assured the judge.

At the end of the thirty-minute hearing, Judge Foley rendered his decision. Rejecting the Commonwealth Attorney's request that bond be denied to Miss Cummings, the long-limbed, dark-haired magistrate ordered that the heiress be held on $75,000 bail and that she surrender her passport and all of her firearms. He also ruled that she remain in Virginia, telling her that she would be permitted to travel beyond the state's borders only to tend to important business matters.

The judge's decision was met with mixed reaction. Friends of the heiress rejoiced at the news, believing that his decision to allow her to return to Ashland Farm was just.

Yet, members of the polo set were deeply mournful of Roberto's passing and were outraged at the court's apparent disregard of their friend's unexpected and violent death.

In light of the charges pending against her, many area residents were surprised at the modest figure the judge had chosen to set for bond.

"If the tables were turned and it was the other way around, Roberto would be in jail now and there would be no bail," one irate polo player huffed under his breath.

Outside the courthouse, reporters encircled Blair Howard. Writing furiously on their notepads, they called out questions to the well-prepared defense attorney.

"We will defend this case and defend it vigorously on the basis of self-defense." The fair-haired lawyer clutched the handle of his tasteful leather briefcase as he spoke. "My client feared for her life. I think she was scared to death."

When reporters contacted Commonwealth's Attorney Jonathan Lynn, he declined to comment on the self-defense claim.

"At this point, this case is very much under investigation," the county's top attorney told the journalists.

After filling out several pages of legal paperwork, Susan Cummings was free to return to her mansion.

That evening, on the advice of her attorney, she paid a

visit to a local Warrenton internist. Blair Howard had told her that Trice Gravatte had a reputation in and around Warrenton as a well-respected general practitioner, and although Susan had never been seen by the tall, soft-spoken doctor, his medical opinion would be important to her case.

When she arrived at his office in the heart of downtown Warrenton, she was escorted to a private examination room, where she waited for Dr. Gravatte to evaluate her wounds.

Extending her arm out for the physician to examine, Susan watched his face as he counted the slender slices that ran along her left bicep. She also alerted him to three scratches she had on her right cheek.

As Susan and her attorney were planning her defense, her victim's friends were mourning his death and planning his funeral.

CHAPTER 16

DRESSED IN A DARK SUIT AND TIE, HIS NUT-BROWN HAIR combed neatly to one side, his upper lip hidden beneath a thick mustache, a somber Jean Marie Turon climbed into his Saab 900. Glancing in the rear-view mirror, he checked to see that there was no one behind him as he backed his car out of the dirt driveway behind the Willow Run Polo School and pulled onto Route 17.

As he crossed the busy roadway and neared Great Meadow, a sinking feeling came over him. Tonight would be the final polo match of the season and Roberto wouldn't be there for it. It sickened him to think that it was there that he had introduced Roberto to Susan Cummings, never imagining that one day his friend would die so violently at her hand.

Passing the polo field, Jean Marie recalled talking to Roberto on the phone the previous Saturday afternoon. It had surprised him when his friend had asked to borrow several of his ponies for ''The Taste of Argentina'' competition at Joe Muldoon's place in Potomac, Maryland. Although he had found Roberto's last-minute request odd, he hadn't asked why he was not able to use his own horses—or the three ponies that Susan had bought earlier that summer for the Ashland Farm team. One of the ponies was his own mare, Tina. The other two were horses Susan had purchased from Roberto's long-time friend, Omar Cepeda.

As Jean Marie negotiated the sweeping turns of Old Tappan Road, the scenic two-lane roadway between Warrenton and Middleburg, he could feel his fury growing. He thought back to the day when Susan had embarrassed him in front of his friend, the horse trader, by brazenly offering him a meager five hundred dollars apiece for polo ponies worth at least ten times that much. It still irritated him that he had let Roberto talk him into selling Susan his own prized horse. The only reason he had agreed to the sale was because Roberto had asked him to do it as a favor.

Passing Montrose Farm, Jean Marie glanced out the car's window at the small green pasture where Roberto had kept his string of ponies. He reached into his suit pocket, pulled out a pack of Marlboros and lit one up. The gentle breeze from the open window drew the smoke from his lips as he exhaled.

The sight of horses grazing in the hilly pasture near the big red barn brought his thoughts back to Roberto's Saturday-afternoon phone call. He vividly remembered being caught off-guard when Roberto asked that he accompany him to the polo match that Sunday to help with the ponies. He'd wondered why Susan wasn't going along to the match, but didn't think it was his place to ask. Instead, he told Roberto that he had to teach a class that morning and would be willing to lend him a hand if they could leave after he finished his lesson.

He could still hear Roberto's final words ringing in his ears: "Okay, Jean Marie, I'll be by around noon to pick you up."

Jean Marie had waited, but Roberto never showed.

The wind from the car's open window tousled his thick hair as he drove along, passing the sharp corner that marked the halfway point between Warrenton and Middleburg. Shaking his head in disbelief, he thought back to a conversation he had had with his polo buddy several months before. The two had been discussing their futures, and Roberto had told him that he loved Virginia so much that he wanted to be buried in hunt country when he died. The discussion now seemed eerie to Jean Marie.

Did Roberto sense trouble with Susan even then? he wondered.

Pressing his foot on the clutch and shifting into first gear, Jean Marie waited at the stop sign for a break in the traffic. Route 50, the main thoroughfare through the town of Middleburg, seemed busy for a Thursday morning. As he passed the gray stone façade of the historic Red Fox Inn, Jean Marie slowed his car. The quaint and historic hotel was less than one minute from the church where Roberto's funeral would soon get underway.

Tightening his fingers around the leather steering wheel, he took a left onto Sam Fred Road and pulled into the parking lot of St. Stephen's Catholic Church. As he stepped out of the car, he turned to leave his sunglasses on the dashboard. The sun was so bright that it forced him to squint as he walked toward the double doors of the sparkling-white building.

The fact that Roberto's funeral was being held in Middleburg was telling in itself. The town was a stronghold of well-heeled, moneyed residents, and holding Roberto's funeral there served as a tribute to how well the charming young polo player had been accepted by the socially-conscious polo set.

Washington Redskins owner Jack Kent Cooke and banking mogul Paul Mellon both owned homes in Middleburg. Director Alfred Hitchcock had eaten there often, and actress Elizabeth Taylor had purchased groceries at the Safeway supermarket when she lived nearby. And there were even rumors that George Washington had slept there.

For a short time, President John F. Kennedy and his family weekended in Middleburg, which offered the President a quiet place to relax and unwind, and his wife Jackie the equestrian activities and local foxhunts she excelled at. They delighted in the area's proximity to Washington, D.C.

When the First Family discovered hunt country, St. Stephen's Catholic Church was still under construction. The Kennedys attended mass there only once, on October 7, 1963, just weeks before the President was assassinated in Dallas, Texas. Before St. Stephen's was completed in 1963, the town had no Catholic Church. Instead, Middleburg Catholics—including the Kennedys—attended mass in the small Community Center on Route 50.

In the thirty years since the President and his wife put Middleburg on the map, a handful of horsy boutiques, casual cafes, and charming bed-and-breakfasts have sprung up around the church.

Making his way up the flower-lined path of St. Stephen's, Jean Marie was encircled by a pack of reporters.

"Roberto could ride like the wind." Jean Marie overheard Richard Varge, the president of the Great Meadow Polo Club, telling reporter Betsy Branscome of the *Fauquier Times-Democrat* as he neared the door. "He was an incredible horseman."

Pausing momentarily to answer their questions, Jean Marie stepped inside the church to join the other mourners. As he strode down its narrow aisle, he could hardly believe the number of people who were already seated in the wooden pews that lined the airy, sunlit sanctuary. From what he could estimate, there were well over a hundred mourners in attendance.

Beams of light streamed through the windows of St. Stephen's as Jean Marie scoured the rows looking for a place to sit. Glancing around the room, he noticed one of Roberto's countrymen waving him over. Sliding his slender frame along the hard wooden bench, he settled in next to a group of Argentines. He felt melancholy as he scanned the pews, looking for familiar faces. Joe Muldoon and Great Meadow Polo Club founder Peter Arundel and his wife, Brady, had all found seats close to the altar. A few rows away, Jean Marie recognized Roberto's former polo patrons, Travis and Suzi Worsham.

With no family in the United States, the Worshams had assumed the role of executors for Roberto's estate. In Virginia, they were Roberto's closest friends. The couple had attended weddings with Roberto and Susan and on a number of occasions had been invited to dine with them at Ashland Farm. In spite of Roberto's assertion to Jean Marie that he'd sold Susan his string of polo ponies for $20,000—a quarter of their worth—Jean Marie and Travis could find no record of the business transaction.

In fact, they discovered that even Roberto's horse trailer no longer belonged to him. He had borrowed $3,500 from Travis to purchase the rig and had died owing the money to his former polo patron. Jean Marie and Travis were also unable to find a bank account or any other financial holdings in Roberto's name.

The only money they did find was the check for nine hundred dollars that Roberto had been paid for his participation in the polo benefit in Pittsburgh the week before. The men discovered the uncashed bank note in the polo player's briefcase along with Roberto's citizenship papers and a handful of photographs. There was a picture of Kelli, and one of Noland, the Jack Russell Terrier the Worshams had gifted him several years before. There was also a snapshot of his parents, and one of his sister, her husband, and their two young children.

With no money in Roberto's estate, the Worshams had assumed responsibility for the funeral. Richard Varge and his wife, Patrice, offered their home on Edgwood Farm Road to host the reception.

Jean Marie could hear the creak of the heavy wooden doors of the church closing behind him as Father James D. Muldowney took his place at the pulpit. His eyes were drawn past the priest to the shiny white coffin that contained Roberto's body. He and a couple of the other men had arranged Roberto's polo mallets and boots on top of the casket.

As friends of Roberto took the pulpit to read poems and tributes to the beloved horseman, Jean Marie felt a lump forming in the back of his throat. Although he had known Roberto for only seven years, the two had become very close. He had taken an instant liking to Roberto and enjoyed being in the company of such a gregarious person.

The sound of the organ playing a somber hymn filled the church as Jean Marie continued to look around. He noticed that many attractive young women—including at least one of Roberto's ex-girlfriends, Kelli Quinn—were present.

It pained him to think that Roberto's breakup with Kelli

may have been what led him into the arms of Susan Cummings. He knew that Kelli and Roberto had remained close friends after their tumultuous affair, and was not at all surprised when he learned that Roberto had been keeping in close touch with her, phoning her often and meeting her for coffee whenever she was in town.

He'd heard gossip among the polo crowd that Roberto had been trying to win her back, and that he had remained in town the previous winter and worked as an apple picker, not because he wanted to be near Susan Cummings, but because he wanted to prove to Kelli that he could indeed stay in one place.

Sadly, Roberto's plan had backfired, Jean Marie thought to himself as he watched Kelli slide into a seat next to the Worshams. The couple had stayed friendly with Roberto's ex even after she and the horseman had gone their separate ways. Yet, it was clear that she remained devotedly attached to Roberto and her intense loyalty would become even more apparent in the weeks to come.

How different things would have been if Kelli and Roberto had stayed together, Jean Marie thought as he watched her rise from her seat and make her way to the podium. It saddened him as he listened to her eulogize the man she had once loved.

"The time you won your town the race," Kelli began. She was reading from the poem, "Ode to an Athlete Dying Young."

When Roberto was with her, he seemed independent and in control of his life, Jean Marie thought. With Susan, he had become like a dependent child, constantly trying to please his patron. Jean Marie hated the fact that Susan had Roberto working on the farm and paid him nothing for his participation on her polo team. Even though Roberto was the one who volunteered to play for Ashland Farm, Jean Marie still believed that Susan had taken advantage of his generosity and good nature. He was not sure why Roberto had bought into her promise of a life together. And it annoyed him that Roberto made excuses for her odd behavior. Jean Marie was convinced that Roberto had fallen into a trap that

Susan had set, using her father's money to lure him in.

Perhaps, he mused, his carefree friend had fantasized that their ultimate marriage would make him financially secure—comfortable to ultimately pursue his own desires.

Yet it continually surprised him that Roberto put up with Susan. It wasn't like him to take directives from anyone. In fact, Jean Marie lost count of the number of times Roberto had promised to be somewhere, knowing full well that he had no intention of keeping his word.

Whether it was dinner plans or an afternoon of chores, Roberto had a difficult time saying no. To avoid a confrontation, he just nodded and agreed to whatever was being asked of him and then failed to show up or even to call. Even more frustrating was the way he turned up the following day, wearing a hearty smile and acting as if nothing was wrong.

He even did this to Susan. On a number of occasions, Jean Marie had been at Roberto's side as he chatted with the heiress on the telephone. He overheard his friend agreeing to join Susan at Ashland Farm for supper after he finished tending to his business at the barn. But, when an invitation for a card game or a night out with the boys suddenly arose, Roberto had no trouble ignoring Susan's plans. Sometimes he'd show up at Susan's place after his escapade, other times he'd wait until the next morning to make an appearance.

As Roberto's memorial service came to a close, Jean Marie and Travis led the procession of mourners to a private viewing room at Royston's funeral home, where well-wishers paid their final respects to the slain polo professional.

In his casket, the men ceremoniously placed his polo mallets, boots, and signature red polo helmet with the thin white stripe. They had asked police to release the helmet—one of the many items the investigators had collected as evidence—to their custody so they could send it back to Argentina with Roberto's body.

Members of the Fauquier County Sheriff's Office found it curious that prominent local residents went to such lengths for a hired professional from Argentina. The enormous turnout of businessmen, polo patrons, and distinguished members of the Virginia community planted even more doubt in the minds of investigators, who were already suspicious of Susan Cummings' claim of self-defense.

Despite Jean Marie Turon's assertion that Roberto had expressed a wish to be buried in Virginia, the polo player's body was shipped home to his family. Because the Villegases were too poor to pay the cost themselves, the Argentine Embassy took on the financial responsibility.

The return of Roberto Villegas' remains to his homeland was front page news there. Newspapers told the story of a poor farm hand from Cordoba who had found fame and social standing among Virginia's polo elite, only to die at the hands of his billionaire patron and lover.

In Virginia, when local reporters turned up at Ashland Farm that week to talk to Susan Cummings about the shooting, they found a "No Trespassing" sign posted on the post-and-rail fence outside the estate.

It struck many of the journalists as strange that she'd agreed to post the sign to protect herself from the onslaught of media descending on her home, but had chosen to forgo the protective signage when Sheriff's Investigator Gary Healy had advised her that it might save her life.

In the coming weeks, articles about the murder appeared in *The New York Times*, *The Washington Post*, *People*, and the tabloid magazine *Star*. In the stories, friends of the heiress defended her actions.

One of Susan's acquaintances, a skinny, fair-haired woman, alleged physical abuse, telling a reporter that in the weeks leading up to the murder, she'd observed several alarming incidents at the Cummings estate. She described Roberto as "possessive" and said that his relationship with the heiress was "turbulent."

Yet, another young woman who boarded a horse at Ashland Farm countered that claim. She told journalists that she'd never witnessed any trouble between the couple and in fact, she had observed Susan and Roberto riding together just days before the shooting.

After his death, Roberto's circle of friends remained loyal to the horseman, telling journalists that he was a kind and gentle person. They insisted that he never lost his temper, even during the most important and competitive polo matches.

In the weeks before the murder, Roberto had confided to several of his companions that he wanted to end his relationship with Susan. He told others that he and Susan were planning to travel to Montana in October to purchase some land for their future.

"Her friends say she was trying to break off the relationship, but his friends say he was trying to end it," one insider told Miss Branscome of the *Fauquier Times Democrat*. "Really, it all depends on who you talk to."

CHAPTER 17

WITH ONLY THREE PROSECUTORS IN THE COMMON-
wealth's attorney's office, and a full docket of cases on their
roster, the Cummings case fell into the lap of Assistant Commonwealth's Attorney Kevin Casey.

From his small office on the fourth floor of the circuit
court building on Lee Street in Old Town Warrenton, the
slight, forty-year-old prosecutor prepared for the first murder
trial of his career. He had been practicing law for almost
thirteen years when Commonwealth's Attorney Jonathan
Lynn assigned the high-profile Cummings case to him.

When he graduated from Virginia's Washington and Lee
Law School in 1984, he joined a small private practice in
Prince William County, not far from the Fauquier County
line. But, five years later, when he learned that a position
had opened up in the Fauquier County District Attorney's
Office, he immediately jumped at the opportunity.

A career as a county prosecutor was appealing to the ambitious young attorney. It was a job that he had always
wanted. Securing the spot meant that he and his wife, a successful prosecutor in Prince William County, would be com-
muting approximately the same distance from their home in
Manassas.

The son of a career naval officer, Casey was accustomed
to moving around. Born in Japan, his family briefly lived in
Paris, France, before returning to the United States to take
up residence in Rhode Island, where his father attended the
Naval War College.

After one year in the Northeast, the Caseys moved to Hawaii and then to Northern Virginia. Kevin spent much of his teen years in the leafy Southern state. But just before he entered his senior year of high school, his father announced that the family would return to Rhode Island where he had secured a teaching position at the Naval War College. The move was difficult for Kevin, who had to leave his childhood friends behind and conclude his final year of high school as the new kid in town.

After completing his undergraduate studies at Boston College in Massachusetts, Kevin returned to Virginia to attend law school at Washington and Lee University in Lexington. There, he met his future wife, who was already in her senior year. The two were about to celebrate their daughter's third birthday when the Cummings case was turned over to Kevin.

It was an unusual time for Fauquier County. A spate of murder cases had filled the court docket. In a town where one murder every two years was the norm, prosecutors were suddenly faced with three homicide cases at the same time.

Mr. Lynn and Deputy Commonwealth's Attorney Greg Ashwell were finishing up the capital murder trial of David Matthews, the man who sexually assaulted and murdered his twelve-year-old cousin and then left her dead body tied to a tree. That meant the three murder cases would be distributed equally among the three young lawyers.

Casey had never tried a murder case before, and spent much of his time in the commonwealth's attorney's office handling a potpourri of cases, including run-of-the-mill traffic violations, bad-check charges, shoplifting, and grand larceny. Still, Mr. Lynn was confident that the young prosecutor could handle the Cummings case.

The lean, impeccably-dressed attorney with the straight, brown hair and neatly-trimmed beard spent hours studying the evidence supplied to him by the sheriff's office. Every Monday and Thursday afternoon, he returned from general district court and waved a quick hello to his assistant, Wanda, before closing the door to his tiny office in the rear of the fourth-floor complex. Seated amid the college diplomas and photographs of his wife and daughter that decorated his six-foot-by-six-foot cubicle, Casey reviewed the pages of police notes and the three hundred crime scene photos that deputies had collected at Ashland Farm. Although the officers had uncovered many telling clues during their eight-hour search, he was convinced that the most important piece of evidence was the 911 tape. On it, Susan Cummings had confessed to Dispatcher Zeets that she had shot Roberto Villegas on the morning of September 7, 1997.

Casey believed that her admission would be the key to proving that she had murdered the Argentine polo professional. To make a case against the heiress, he had to demonstrate to a jury that Susan Cummings had killed the horseman with premeditation in her kitchen that morning.

Casey was determined to stick to the evidence he had been provided by the sheriff's office and not get off-track by speculating on what Cummings' motive might have been. In his mind, the whole question of motive was nothing more than a red herring.

"My position is it doesn't matter," Casey told *Citizen* reporter Mike Sluss. "He could have been the baddest man on the planet, but that doesn't give you the right to shoot him the way he was shot."

So far as Casey was concerned, the defense had the tougher job ahead of it. To get their client off, defense attorney Blair Howard and his associates would have to prove that Susan had acted in self defense when she fired four shots from her Walther 9mm because she was in imminent fear of her life.

"I think it will be relevant to her state of mind, which is very much an issue," Blair Howard told Sluss. "If she had expressed fear of the fella, it is very relevant."

Casey was certain that Mr. Howard's team would argue that Villegas had been abusive, and that their client had been forced to act because of the horseman's violent and unpredictable behavior. He speculated that the defense was planning to ignore the crime-scene evidence and mount a case that would support Susan's claim that Roberto had been threatening her. That meant putting witnesses on the stand to bolster what he believed to be Susan's implausible story.

To Casey, the scientific evidence was what really mattered.

On Thursday, October 9, 1997, Casey walked around the corner from his office on Culpeper Street to the grand old courthouse on Court Street where general district court was held. Under his arm, he clutched several of the files that sheriff's deputies had turned over to him the month before.

Across the way at Tailfeathers, a quaint bakery and gourmet cafe, customers watched from the store's big front window as the Assistant Commonwealth's Attorney climbed the wide, cement steps of the historic courthouse. The Civil War–era building was the centerpiece of the town. They marveled at the crowd of reporters, photographers, and television crews that had assembled outside the yellow federal-style building. The onlookers watched as Casey, dressed in a dark suit, bow tie, and matching suspenders, stopped to say a few words to the reporters before disappearing inside the courthouse.

Even though Warrenton was the County Seat of Fauquier County, it was rare to see such a showing of media. Even the capital murder trial of David Matthews the month before did not draw nearly as much attention.

The sheriff's deputies who were manning the metal detector in the courthouse's small foyer immediately recognized Casey. On the wall behind them, signs reminded visitors of the commonwealth's strict dress code. "Shirts and shoes required," the sign read. "Tank tops, short shorts, and beach apparel not permitted!"

"No packages or umbrellas allowed in the courtroom," read the sign that was posted on the double doors leading to the first-floor courtroom. "Overcoats and raincoats to be removed before entering."

Clutching his files under his arm, Casey swung open the heavy wooden doors and entered the century-old circular courtroom. He was struck by the number of spectators seated shoulder-to-shoulder in the three rows of mahogany benches. The natural light that streamed in from the large glass windows reflected off the crystals of the two ornate chandeliers hanging from the room's tall ceiling.

Seated at the defense table was Blair Howard. Casey knew of Howard's reputation. He'd followed the Lorena Bobbitt case in the press. Casey also knew that Howard had an ability to craft ingenious defenses and often won exoneration for clients in seemingly-hopeless murder cases.

Casey had faced off against Mr. Howard just once. The case involved a man who wanted to use dynamite to blow up a beaver dam on his property, and a local game warden who was trying to stop him. As the prosecutor sat in the courtroom looking at Mr. Howard and his co-counsel, Thomas Hill, he couldn't recall who had won.

As the proceeding got underway, his opponent's incessant questioning of the commonwealth's witnesses surprised Casey. Casey expected the preliminary hearing to be short and perfunctory as they always were. The function of the hearing was to introduce probable cause that a crime had been committed, and to identify the accused, in this case, Susan Cummings, as the one who committed the act.

Casey introduced the 911 tape and called three witnesses to the stand. He had Dispatcher Michael Zeets testify about Susan's call to police. Next, he called Captain Fred Pfeiff to describe the search of her stone mansion. And finally, he put Sergeant Gary Healy on the stand to explain how Susan Cummings had come to him seeking help, and then declined to follow his advice to obtain a restraining order against Roberto Villegas.

Returning to his seat at the wooden desk in the center of the room, Casey watched Judge Charles Foley's reaction as Blair Howard sprang to his feet and began probing each of the commonwealth's witnesses. Mr. Howard seemed to have his own game plan, using the proceeding as an opportunity to scrutinize the witnesses in what Casey figured was an attempt to learn as much as possible about his case.

Seemingly playing to the spectators and the press, Mr. Howard then stunned Casey when he detailed to the court the self-defense case he planned to present at trial. Casey knew that it was highly unusual for a defense counselor to reveal his case to the prosecution at this stage of the game. He was convinced that there could be only one explanation: Mr. Howard was trying to feed his story to the press.

Casey was pleased when Judge Foley rejected Mr. Howard's attempt to introduce the police statement that Susan had filled out for Sergeant Healy several weeks before, and ruled that the prosecution had provided sufficient evidence to send the case to a grand jury.

"At this stage of the proceeding, the Court views the evidence in a light most favorable to the Commonwealth," the judge said, banging his gavel on the bench. "I have no doubt that there will be self-defense arguments asserted, but the Circuit Court is the proper forum for that."

On November 24, Casey learned that the grand jury had returned a "true bill" against Susan Cummings for the murder of Roberto Villegas. The news came as no surprise to the prosecutor, who was already prepared to begin the trial.

Within a month of the shooting, the investigation by the sheriff's office was complete, and the deputies had provided Casey with copies of everything in their files, including transcripts of interviews with Roberto's friends, teammates, business associates, and former girlfriends. Casey learned that Sheriff's Investigators Lamper and Lucas had flown to New York to interview one of Roberto's ex-girlfriends. They had also traveled to the west coast of Florida to follow up on a lead that Roberto had been in trouble with the law there.

Upon their return from the Sunshine State, the officers told Casey that their meetings with friends and business associates of the polo player had turned up nothing to support that claim.

As the lab results came trickling in, Casey made certain to promptly send copies of everything he received to Blair Howard, fearful that any delay could result in an accusation that he was hiding something.

He had already prepared his case with the assistance of Sheriff's Investigator Michael Lamper. The two had been meeting on a weekly basis to construct a witness list and go over the exhibits they intended to use in court.

Casey was presented with a roster of 35 potential witnesses. For a while, the confident young lawyer toyed with the idea of putting some of them on the stand to defend Roberto's character. He knew that Blair Howard was planning to introduce witnesses who would paint a grim picture of Roberto, and he contemplated countering their testimony with witnesses of his own. But he ultimately decided to refrain from calling any character witnesses for the victim because he was afraid that the move could backfire under Virginia's sometimes-tricky legal system.

He knew that under Virginia law, Blair Howard would be allowed to present evidence about any bad acts that may have been committed by Roberto in the past—even if Susan knew nothing about them when she committed her crime. Casey didn't want to get into a court fight over whether Roberto was a good guy or a bad guy. He feared that putting a witness on the stand to testify on Susan's lover's behalf could leave the defense attorney with an opening to come back on cross-examination and try to undermine the witness's testimony. Under the law, Mr. Howard could question the witness about things he may—or may not—have been aware of in Roberto's past. The same law prevented Casey from introducing witnesses to speak about Susan's character or reputation unless they specifically pertained to the crime for which she was being tried.

Casey's analysis of the evidence, plus his knowledge of Virginia state law, allowed him to predict the course that the trial would take before he'd even gone to court. Based on what sheriff's investigators had learned from the crime-scene evidence, Casey believed that he had an airtight case against the heiress. He also knew that, in light of what the evidence showed, Blair Howard would focus his defense on anything but the crime scene itself.

That meant Mr. Howard would concentrate his efforts on discrediting the police investigation of the crime scene, and presenting Roberto in a bad light to the jury. Casey was convinced that, presented with the all the evidence, jurors would see through Mr. Howard's tactics and find the defendant guilty as charged.

CHAPTER 18

IN DECEMBER OF 1997, KEVIN CASEY FACED BLAIR HOW-
ard in court again. This time Susan and her attorney were
asking the judge to approve a motion to modify her bond so
that she could travel to Monaco for ten days to visit her ailing
father. She had surrendered her passport to the court during
her arraignment and had been ordered not to leave Virginia
until her felony case had been heard.

Seated at the prosecution's table in the windowless courtroom of the modern-style Fauquier County Circuit Court,
Kevin Casey listened as Diana Cummings, in a husky, accented voice, testified before Judge Carleton Penn. She described how she had seen her father bed-ridden after
suffering a series of debilitating strokes.

"My sister and our father, we share a very close relationship," the slender blonde said, glancing at her sister sitting
quietly with her hands folded in her lap. "He asked numerous times as to when she was coming. He's wondering why
she's not coming. He feels he might be abandoning him,
although I know she is not."

To help prove the point, Mr. Howard introduced letters
from Sam Cummings' personal physician, Ralph de Sigaldi,
and Cummings' wife attesting to the arms merchant's ailing
health.

Sam Cummings had not been told of the murder charge
against his daughter, and Susan had kept it a secret from him
during their weekly telephone conversations, Mr. Howard explained to elderly Judge Penn.

"Because of his fragile state of health," he stated, "he has not been advised of the situation for fear that it would aggravate his condition."

Casey opposed the defense's motion to let Susan travel abroad and told the court that, in light of the charges against her, Susan posed a flight risk. Springing from his seat, the assistant commonwealth's attorney argued that allowing her to travel overseas "was not a reasonable risk to take."

"Your Honor, having an extradition treaty with a country is no guarantee that you will get that person back," he declared in a clipped tone. "Having this defendant go to Monaco creates an unreasonable risk she will not return."

Casey insisted that Susan's phone conversations with her seventy-year-old father could allay any fears that the arms dealer might have that his daughter was abandoning him.

"Our concern would be, what if she got there and said, 'I like it here a whole lot more than I do in the Commonwealth of Virginia'?" Casey said, posing a hypothetical situation for the judge.

Addressing Casey's concern, Mr. Howard countered by informing the court that Susan and her sister were willing to put up the $2.3 million Ashland Farm property as collateral.

"If she had any inclination to leave," the defense attorney said, "she certainly could have done it by now. This is simply an appeal from a daughter who wants to see her father."

From his seat at the commonwealth's table, Casey listened as Judge Penn rendered his decision. He stared at Susan, dressed casually in dark jeans and a black cardigan, and noticed that her expression did not change when the judge announced that he would grant her request and allow her to leave the country for two weeks.

Casey was advised that on December 16, Susan picked up her American passport from the court and boarded a plane for Monaco. Thirteen days later, he learned that she had returned it to the clerk's office. He could not have known that her visit with her ailing father would be her last.

Two weeks before the murder trial was scheduled to begin, the commonwealth's attorney was informed that Sam Cummings had passed away. He was half-expecting the defense to ask that the trial date be postponed so that Susan would have time to grieve. But the felony proceedings got underway as scheduled on May 6, 1998, exactly eight months after the shooting at Ashland Farm.

Casey was well-prepared. He had spent countless hours in his tiny office with Investigator Lamper, surrounded by a collection of personal knick-knacks: a green plastic toy alligator, a miniature sheriff's police car, and a handful of pins with sayings such as "God is coming and is she pissed."

In the three weeks before the trial, Casey and the investigator met like clockwork every day at 3 p.m. to go over the last-minute details of the case. They even met on Saturdays, which was something new for Casey; he had never worked on weekends in the past. The men had put together a witness list that included various police personnel, forensic scientists, and Roberto's landlady, Virginia Kuhn.

Casey intended to call the elderly widow to testify as to the time that Roberto had left her home on the morning of the murder. He wanted to establish that the polo player had arrived at the estate earlier than Susan was alleging, and that she had shot him at least thirty minutes before she placed the 911 call to police.

Casey had no way of knowing, but his decision to call Virginia Kuhn as a witness was causing her great anxiety— so much so that she took a tranquilizer before going to the courthouse to testify. She seemed perfectly fine when he met with her in his office before the proceedings began. One of the reasons she was so anxious was that she had no idea when she would be called to testify. Casey had no way of determining for sure when she would have to take the stand; it all depended on how long jury selection would take. He figured that the process would not last too long but had no way of predicting what Mr. Howard might do.

Normally self-assured and outspoken, Virginia Kuhn had worked herself into a frenzy and feared that she would not be able to convey to the court her theories about the shooting or her feelings on what a wonderful person Roberto had been. She had also read about the press coverage the sheriff's office was expecting and was nervous about taking the stand in front of a bunch of reporters.

When Virginia arrived at the two-story, brick-and-glass building, she was immediately escorted past the extra security that Sheriff Higgs had posted at the entrance.

Sheriff's deputies, attired in the county's official tan-and-brown uniforms, were armed with hand-held metal detectors. The officers were not taking any chances. No one was allowed into the courtroom until all of his or her bags had been searched. Anyone who left the courtroom for a minute or two to use the washroom was forced to undergo the search again.

Seating in the courtroom's small, second-level gallery was available on a first-come, first-served basis. The no-nonsense judge who was presiding, Carleton Penn, made it clear that he intended to begin the proceedings promptly at 8:30 a.m. Those not in the courtroom at that time would not be permitted to enter until there was a break in the trial.

Sheriff Higgs, dressed breezily in a suit and tie, directed members of the media to arrive at 6:30 a.m.—two hours before the proceedings were set to begin—and place their names on a list for a seat. The top law-enforcement officer had set aside twenty seats in the courtroom for the media and reporters were forced to scramble to get themselves onto the list. There was not much the sheriff could do about the seating because the courtroom was so small and accommodated no more than forty people. He reserved the twenty seats that remained for friends and family of Susan and Roberto and interested members of the public.

As Casey had expected, jury selection proceeded without a hitch and took less than four hours to complete. The two attorneys were able to agree upon twelve jurors and two alternates from the pool of twenty-four prospective panelists who had been called to sit that week in the circuit court. Blair Howard made his selections with the aid of a co-counsel and a jury consultant who observed the proceedings from the front row of the upstairs gallery. Kevin Casey did not enjoy the same support because of the commonwealth's budgetary restrictions. Limited staff and an overabundance of cases forced him to go it alone.

During the course of the selection process, Mr. Howard and his team seemed to have a clear picture of the type of juror they wanted to sit on the case. The defense counsel appeared to want women who were born and raised in Warrenton and the surrounding area—women whom he might have believed would be sympathetic to his client's plight. Mr. Casey, meanwhile, seemed less concerned about who would be sitting on the jury, presumably confident that he had an open-and-shut case.

The clock hanging on the wall over the jury box read 11:45 a.m. when the assistant commonwealth's attorney began his opening remarks. Facing the ten women and four men seated in the jury box, Casey began to outline the case he intended to present.

The prosecutor asked the jurors to turn their attention to the defense table, where Susan Cummings sat dressed in a black jacket and straight-legged slacks. She was flanked by her defense counselors.

"She is charged with murder," Casey declared with aplomb as he pointed his finger at the heiress. "More specifically, she is charged with killing Roberto Villegas.

"You will hear the 911 tape. You will hear Ms. Cummings say Mr. Villegas tried to kill her. This is not a question of whether Mr. Villegas is dead and whether Ms. Cummings made him that way.

"There were two people in the kitchen that morning. Mr. Villegas is dead and there is one person left to tell us what happened and that is Ms. Cummings.

"What's left behind in the kitchen is a lot of evidence. The prosecution will show you that she shot Mr. Villegas not once, not twice, not three times, but four times while he was seated at the kitchen table having breakfast.

"We will ask you to find Ms. Cummings guilty of using a firearm to kill Mr. Villegas." The slender commonwealth attorney paused in front of the jury box and stared at the panelists. He then twirled around, returning to his seat at the long wooden defense table. He had delivered his opening remarks in less than three minutes.

Astonished at the brevity of his opponent's statement, Blair Howard glanced at his co-counsel, Thomas Hill, whose arm was supported by a canvas sling, before rising to address the jury.

"The things I'm going to tell you are not to be treated as evidence," the athletic and impeccably-dressed attorney began in a thick drawl.

Casey listened carefully, jotting down notes on his yellow pad as Mr. Howard launched into a forty-minute litany of the events leading up to the September 7 shooting. The prosecutor's face revealed no emotion as Mr. Howard outlined his case to the jury, detailing Susan's two-year relationship with Roberto and describing the many witnesses he would call to substantiate Susan's contention that her boyfriend was a violent man.

"He was a man with a violent temper," the defense attorney told the jury. "If you crossed him, he reacted. Not only did he react badly; he would try to intimidate you."

Casey eyed the clock on the wall as Mr. Howard continued to address the panel of twelve jurors and two alternates, spinning a story of a shy girl's ill-fated love affair with a dangerous man.

"Under subpoena, we have former girlfriends with restraining orders and former girlfriends who didn't make complaints, but were victimized by this man," the fair-haired defense counselor with the deep tan told the jurors.

"This case is not about cold photographs and scientific theory," Mr. Howard continued. "This case is about human emotion. The hand that held the dagger struck, and Susan Cummings acted within the law, in her own home, to protect herself in self-defense."

Rising from the bench, Judge Penn called a one-hour lunch break. Journalists closed their notepads and ran to call their editors from the one pay phone in the courthouse lobby. Some of them never did get to speak to their news desks because of the long line, and were forced to return to the courtroom at the end of the lunch break.

"Mr. Casey, please call your first witness," the distinguished judge declared, his green bow tie peeking out from under his black robe.

The elderly justice did not want to waste any time. His role as a traveling judge—bouncing between three counties—prompted him to want to complete the case in the three days he had allotted on his calendar.

"Virginia Kuhn." Kevin Casey stood confidently in the center of the courtroom and made his pronouncement.

Spectators seated in the stuffy and cramped upstairs gallery watched in silence as the bailiff opened the wooden door next to the judge's bench. Roberto's friends, Travis and Suzi Worsham, were seated in the last row, near several friends of Diana. It appeared that only one other friend, Jane Rowe, had turned out in support of Susan. The temperature outside was climbing into the eighties, and the room's air-conditioner was straining to cool the chamber.

Journalists scribbled feverishly in their notebooks as the short but solidly-built woman in the white cardigan made her way to the jury box. Many of the reporters had tried to speak with the eighty-year-old woman before the trial but had turned away when she asked for money for an interview.

Adjusting her frame in the hard-backed witness chair, Virginia glanced at Susan Cummings. Her gaze was quickly interrupted by the sound of Mr. Casey's voice. He began by asking her how Roberto had paid his rent.

"The first two months he paid in cash," Virginia answered, her voice cracking nervously. "He had the money folded up in his hand, and he bent over and handed it to me like that," she said, demonstrating Roberto's polite bow. "After that, it was paid by a check."

Casey paused for a moment before asking his next question. "Whose name was on the check?"

"Susan Cummings'," Virginia replied.

"Can you tell the court what time did Roberto leave the house that morning?" Casey took a few steps closer to the witness.

"A quarter to eight that morning," Mrs. Kuhn said without hesitation. ''I was eating my breakfast in the living room and watching TV.''

Next, the prosecutor called Jane Gritz to corroborate Virginia's recollection that Roberto had arrived at Ashland Farm earlier than Susan Cummings claimed.

The thick-set blonde told the jury that she kept two horses at Ashland Farm and explained that she worked as a groom to pay for the animals' board.

Gritz said that she arrived at the estate between 6 and 6:30 a.m. that fateful morning. She began her day by feeding the horses in the smaller of the two white barns on the property, the one that was farther away from the main house. Later that morning, she moved on to the larger white barn. It was there, she said, that she heard the gunshots.

''I was over there helping and heard a noise,'' she told the jurors. ''I thought it was somebody working on the roof. They were doing work on the main house for the last six months. It happened kind of quick. It sounded like banging.''

''What time was it when you heard the noise?'' Casey asked the young woman.

Jane responded, telling the court that she was not certain of the exact time. She said that, based on a typical work day, she estimated that it was sometime between 8 a.m. and 8:15 a.m. when she heard the noise.

''What did you do?'' Casey continued.

''I just kept on working,'' the young woman replied.

Rising to his feet, Blair Howard positioned himself directly in front of the witness box.

''Was there some activity that was unusual that morning?'' he asked.

''It was my birthday,'' Jane answered. ''We took a break to exchange presents.''

''What time did the exchange take place?'' Mr. Howard inquired. He was trying to establish that Miss Gritz may have been ten minutes behind her normal schedule that fateful morning.

''I never looked at a clock,'' the young woman responded. ''I get lost in the horses. I sometimes don't look up until noontime, until the work is done.''

Dispatcher Michael Zeets took the stand to confirm that he had answered the 911 call from Miss Cummings that morning. Wearing a dark suit, striped shirt, and tie, the tall, blond switchboard operator with the bushy mustache told the jury that when he asked the caller if she had shot Mr. Villegas, she replied: "I had a gun, yes."

Sheriff's Deputy Cuno Andersen confirmed that he was the first officer to arrive at Ashland Farm on the morning of September 7. Turning to face the judge, the uniformed policeman recalled how he met Susan Cummings and her sister Diana at the front door of the mansion.

Pointing to his arm, he described the scratches and "bright red blood" that he had observed on the defendant's left arm. In a deep, confident voice, Sergeant Andersen told the court that Susan hadn't responded when he questioned her, not once, but twice about her injuries.

Not certain what had happened, and not knowing what role, if any, Susan had played, the deputy said he twirled her around and clamped handcuffs on her wrists before entering the mansion to conduct a search for the victim.

Looking directly at Judge Penn, Andersen described how he had followed Susan Cummings and her sister through a maze of rooms before finding Roberto Villegas lying face down in a pool of blood. He told the jury the blood had already begun to separate when he went into the room to check the victim for a pulse.

"Things did not appear right to me," Andersen said. "Within minutes, Deputy Walters arrived. I instructed him to bring in his Instamatic camera to the scene. I wanted to make sure the crime scene was documented as I saw it."

Deputy Shawn Walters confirmed Sergeant Andersen's testimony, and then eagerly told the court that he had escorted Susan Cummings to an upstairs bedroom when she had asked to brush her teeth.

Deputy Jim Jones told the jury that he had accompanied Deputy Walters to the master suite that morning and had watched from the doorway as Susan Cummings changed her shoes and grabbed a blue sweatshirt from a gym bag that lay open on the bedroom floor.

Next, rescue volunteer Chance Kimbel stepped into the witness box. The young medic testified that he offered first aid to Susan Cummings at the scene. He told the court that he treated the scratches and lacerations on the heiress's left arm.

"No bandaging needed to be done," the baby-faced volunteer told the jury. "The bleeding had stopped. I asked if she had any other injuries or any other areas that needed to be treated. She said 'No.'"

With the time nearing 5 p.m., the judge announced that Sheriff's Deputy Kimberly Slack would be the last witness to testify that afternoon. The stocky brunette with the bounce in her step told the court that she was now going by the name Ellis after taking her marriage vows earlier in the year. In a loud, confident voice she addressed the jurors, explaining that she had collected clothing and blood and hair samples from Miss Cummings at the county jail.

CHAPTER 19

STICKING TO JUDGE PENN'S STRICT SCHEDULE, TUES-day's proceedings got underway promptly at 8:30 a.m. Journalists stood in the lobby of the Circuit Court building reading daily newspapers and comparing their articles with those written by their competitors.

The Washington Post focused its story on Blair Howard's opening arguments. The defense attorney told jurors that Roberto was ''an abusive brute who once put a noose around her neck, had assaulted previous girlfriends, and had threatened men with knives,'' reported Brooke Masters and Jennifer Ordonez.

The second day of the proceedings got underway with the Commonwealth's attorney calling Captain Fred Pfeiff to the stand. The light from the chandelier overhead reflected off the officer's gold-rimmed glasses as he explained to the packed courtroom that he supervised the investigation at Ashland Farm that tragic morning. He said that he entered the small maid's galley at 10:30 a.m. and observed two 9mm shell casings on the floor in front of the refrigerator and two bullet holes in the wall above Mr. Villegas' body.

Captain Pfeiff's underling, Sheriff's Investigator Michael Lamper, testified that he placed Miss Cummings under arrest at the scene at 11:55 a.m. on September 7.

Lamper's colleague, Mack Halley, told the court that he took photographs of the victim's body at the Fauquier Hospital morgue. The middle-aged investigator with the wavy gray hair said that he conducted a gunshot residue test on

Mr. Villegas' hands, which had been covered in plastic bags at the crime scene to preserve evidence, and that he collected fingerprint samples from Roberto's body.

After a short recess, Sheriff's Investigator Erich Junger strode to the witness stand, his thick dark hair slicked to one side. The investigator watched as Kevin Casey rose from his seat and approached him with a number of sealed plastic bags containing items that had been removed during the search of Susan's mansion.

One by one, Junger identified the objects as those that he had marked as evidence months earlier. The Walther 9mm, the spent shell casings, the knife sheath, the Bertram Cutlery knife, the Q-Tips with the blood samples, and the Swiss Army knife that was found in the pocket of Roberto's jeans were among the items the investigator said he removed from the first floor of the Cummings home.

Continuing to I.D. the evidence, Junger turned to face the jury. In a clear, succinct voice, he confirmed that the three guns, the open box of ammunition, and the holster that fit the Walther 9mm were among the items he had taken during the search of Susan's upstairs bedroom.

Investigator Junger's testimony was followed by that of state medical examiner, Frances Field. The tall, dark-haired woman told the court that she had performed the autopsy on Mr. Villegas hours after the county's own medical examiner, Ralph Robinson, had taken a preliminary look at the victim's body at the crime scene. Her findings suggested that Roberto had suffered fatal wounds to the neck and chest, and wounds to his right arm and back.

Responding to Mr. Casey's inquiries, the medical examiner said that three of the slugs struck Roberto's face and upper torso and traveled downward and to the left after they entered his body, lending credence to the prosecutor's contention that he was sitting down at the time he was shot. The fourth bullet, she said, caused a superficial wound, entering and exiting the skin and fatty tissue of Roberto's back. Dr. Field testified that, like the other bullets, the path of the fourth bullet traveled in a downward and leftward direction.

Readjusting her lanky frame in the witness seat, the medical examiner with the short-cropped hair and oversized round eyeglasses made it clear to the jury that although she had numbered the wounds for the purposes of her examination, she had been unable to determine the order in which the bullets were fired. Kevin Casey was contending that the first bullet had struck Roberto in the neck, and then, as his body was slumping over the table, the other bullets entered his body.

After lunch, the medical examiner returned to face questions from the defense counsel. During the cross-examination, Blair Howard sought to establish that Roberto could have been standing when the first bullet struck him and that it was the impact of that slug that forced him backward into his seat.

Asked if it was possible that the force of the slugs would have been enough to spin Roberto around, Dr. Field answered, "Yes."

Some jury members appeared dazed, if not bored, after hearing hours of scientific testimony, some of it highly technical, from Dr. Field and others. Jurors seemed more attentive when forensic pathologist Jack Daniel, a former assistant chief medical examiner for the state in Richmond, was called to testify about the wounds on Susan Cummings' arm.

In March, Mr. Casey had retained Daniel, a private consultant, to review photos of Miss Cummings' arm taken at the crime scene, and determine if her injuries were inflicted by an assailant or not. On the stand, Dr. Daniel testified that the photos showed twelve to fourteen "superficial" scratches, all similar in length and depth.

"None of them were life-threatening in any way," was his response to a question from Mr. Casey.

The youthful pathologist went on to say that the "small clusters of two or three" scratches "are certainly typical of the type of wound that an individual might inflict on themselves."

On cross-examination, Mr. Howard asked the doctor if the wounds might have been inflicted by someone trying to frighten or torture Miss Cummings.

"It seems unlikely," Dr. Daniel replied.

The doctor's response prompted whispers from journalists seated in the gallery. The following morning, a headline in *The Washington Post* would lead with a quote from the pathologist's testimony.

Next, the prosecutor called state forensic scientist Douglas DeGaetano to the stand to offer his opinion on how close Miss Cummings was standing to Roberto when she opened fire. The scientist, who had conducted tests on gunshot residue removed from Mr. Villegas and Miss Cummings, said that he found no traces of "primer residue" in Mr. Villegas' sample, suggesting that he had not been shot at close range.

Another witness, state firearm examiner Gary Arntsen, told the court that he had tested Miss Cummings' 9mm Walther in a laboratory, shooting it at targets from various distances. Noting that he had not found any gunpowder residue on Mr. Villegas' clothing, Mr. Arntsen said that it was his belief that Miss Cummings was more than four feet away from Mr. Villegas when the shots were fired.

Raising his left arm in the air to mimic the pistol's action, Arntsen demonstrated how the Walther that Miss Cummings used to kill Mr. Villegas operated. He told the court that in order to fire the German-made pistol, the user must pull back on the slide and flick the safety lever off. He said that the slide action automatically ejects any unfired round that may be in the chamber.

Mr. Casey believed that the Walther's operation helped answer one of the little mysteries in the case: how an unfired round wound up on the desk in the office at Ashland Farm. It was the prosecution's contention that Miss Cummings had retrieved the gun from her upstairs bedroom, and cocked it when she entered the kitchen, not realizing that there was already a bullet in the chamber. An unspent round fell onto the floor when she pulled back the slide in preparation for firing. Mr. Casey was convinced that Susan later picked up the round and carried it into the office where she made the 911 call.

With the gun theory planted in the minds of the jurors, the testimony of Mr. Casey's next witness, Karolyn Tontarski, was designed to further discredit Susan Cummings' claim of self-defense. The state forensic scientist was an expert in DNA testing, and had analyzed blood samples taken from the crime scene and from Mr. Villegas and Miss Cummings. She had also conducted DNA tests on articles of clothing taken from Miss Cummings, including a pair of sneakers that she had been wearing when she shot Roberto, and a sweatshirt that she had changed into after police had arrived.

Using an overhead projector to illustrate blood typing, Miss Tontarski told the court that there was no trace of Miss Cummings' blood in the corner of the kitchen where Roberto had collapsed and died. She said, though, that she had found traces of blood matching Roberto's on the bottom of Miss Cummings' right sneaker, as well as under the sneaker's toe, or ball, area.

Continuing her testimony, Miss Tontarski told the jury that she had also found traces of Mr. Villegas' blood on the back right sleeve of the blue sweatshirt police had seized from Susan at the county jail. The significance of this testimony would become clear only later when Mr. Casey would present the jury with the Commonwealth's theory on the shooting.

The most compelling element of her testimony pertained to the tiny speck of blood she found on the tip of the knife that Roberto was allegedly holding when he was shot.

Although the defense was contending that Roberto had attacked Susan with the bone-handled knife, using it to slice her left arm more than a dozen times, Miss Tontarski told the court that she had found only a small quantity of blood at the very tip of the weapon.

Tests revealed that the sample contained a mixture of Susan's and Roberto's blood. But there were no traces of blood anywhere else on the blade. She also explained that she could find no evidence of blood or fingerprints on the knife's heavy bone handle.

After a short recess, Mr. Casey recalled Erich Junger to the stand. He asked the investigator to demonstrate how the bullets had struck, and in some cases passed through Roberto

Villegas' body. Using a life-size foam mannequin and red wooden dowels as props, the investigator showed the court how the bullets had struck Roberto from above and traveled down through, his body.

"It was pretty clear early on that Mr. Villegas was seated when he was shot," Junger told the jury.

The following day, Junger was back on the stand for a third time. Once again, he displayed the foam mannequin and dowels used in his "trajectory analysis." Taking his testimony one step further, the forensic scientist said that the trajectory of the two slugs that entered and exited Mr. Villegas' body matched the bullet holes in the kitchen wall behind the table where Roberto had been eating breakfast. The blood spatter on the wall behind the table, which was some forty-two to forty-six inches above the floor, led Investigator Junger to determine that Roberto had been seated when Susan fired on him.

The final prosecution witness was Robert C. Zinn, a Prince William County investigator and expert in blood-stain analysis. Mr. Zinn, who examined crime-scene photos and other evidence, told the court that the height of the blood droplets on the kitchen wall, the blood on the cushion of the chair, and the "impact spatter" on Roberto's jeans led him to conclude that the victim had been seated at the time he was shot. The absence of blood on the lower portions of Roberto's jeans was further proof to the investigator that the victim could not have been standing, as the defense had claimed.

"The only way to get blood on his thighs is if he was standing," Zinn stated for the official court record. "Blood would be predominantly on the floor. The lower part of his legs would be shielded."

Jurors perked up as Sergeant Zinn explained that he found little blood on the bone-handled knife that police had found in the crux of the victim's arm. He told the court that his finding showed that it was unlikely that Mr. Villegas was holding the weapon in his hand when he was shot.

"We have all of this wet blood and none of it on the knife. That would not happen," he said.

Mr. Howard's attempts to shake Mr. Zinn's testimony proved less than successful. When asked by the defense counselor whether Roberto could have been standing when the first shot was fired, the unflappable witness said "it was really not plausible."

Sergeant Zinn capped off two days of expert witnesses, and a confident Kevin Casey rested the commonwealth's case.

After learning that the trial would run longer than the scheduled three days, and concerned that the case would interfere with other cases on the court calendar, Judge Penn directed the defense team to begin presenting their case.

CHAPTER 20

SPRINGING TO HIS FEET, DEFENSE ATTORNEY BLAIR HOW-
ard called his first witness, rescue volunteer William G.
Grimsley, to the stand.

The veteran emergency medical worker was there to be
questioned as to why a diagram he'd drawn several days after
the shooting differed from those prepared by sheriff's deputies on the scene.

Mr. Howard asked the medic why his sketches showed
four shell casings on the floor in the kitchen while police
sketches showed two casings in the kitchen and two in the
hallway. The defense counselor also questioned a written
statement that strongly implied that Grimsley had entered the
kitchen, checked for a pulse on the victim, and took special
care to avoid stepping on shell casings and blood as he
backed out of the tiny room.

In examining the witness, Mr. Howard asked whether Mr.
Grimsley recalled that he had spoken to him two months
before the trial, and that the volunteer had not disputed the
validity of the report and the accompanying sketch he had
made days after the murder.

Only one week before the trial, he faxed a letter to the
defense counselor's Alexandria office stating that he had just
realized the sketch and memo were "inaccurate" in key respects. Learning of Grimsley's decision prompted Mr. Howard to ask the court to declare him a "hostile witness."

On the stand, the volunteer rescue worker reiterated that
his report was inaccurate. He further testified that he had met

with the state's Investigator Lamper on April 30, and that the session had "refreshed" his memory. He told the court that he had been mistaken in his recollections and that after speaking with members of his staff, and seeing a statement he had given at the scene of the crime, he recalled that he had never entered the kitchen, but stood at the threshold of the room and said he had declared the victim dead because Sergeant Andersen told him he had tried—to no avail—to find a pulse on the victim.

Warrenton physician Trice Gravatte was called to testify about the wounds he had treated on Susan's arm the day after the shooting. In a soft, almost inaudible tone, the doctor told the judge that he had counted thirteen lacerations on her upper left arm, five on her shoulder, and three "superficial" scratches on her cheek.

The general practitioner, who had an office in downtown Warrenton, said that during his career he had treated ten to twenty patients for self-inflicted wounds—almost all of them on patients with psychiatric problems—and believed that Susan's injuries had been inflicted by someone other than herself.

"I have never seen someone self-inflict wounds on themselves who were not psychotic," Dr. Gravatte stated.

Springing from his chair, Mr. Casey asked the doctor if any of the patients he had seen with self-inflicted wounds were facing criminal charges.

"No," the doctor replied.

Diana Cummings took the stand next. Raising her right hand, she swore to tell the truth. She told the court that she resided in a small cottage three or four minutes from the main house where her sister lived. She said it was about 8:45 a.m. and she was out in the yard with her dogs when she heard three gunshots coming from the direction of the mansion.

"Since I live in the country, it is not unusual to hear gunshots. So, I stood around for about five minutes," the slender blonde testified.

It was only then, she said, that she walked the short distance to her sister's home and found Susan on the telephone with a police dispatcher. Diana told the jury that her sister seemed shaken up.

Following Diana's brief testimony, Blair Howard surprised the court by calling the defendant to the stand.

The jurors stared at the heiress as she slowly ambled to the witness box.

CHAPTER 21

SUSAN'S MOTHER, DRESSED CASUALLY IN BLACK JEANS and a designer sport jacket, her dark, shoulder-length hair streaked with silver, looked on from the first row of the upstairs gallery as her daughter settled into the wooden witness chair. She had arrived in town the previous evening from Monte Carlo, where she had been taking care of her late husband's affairs.

"Would you speak up and give the members of the jury your full name?" Blair Howard directed his client.

"Susan Cummings," the heiress responded in a soft, accented voice.

"And tell the members of the jury, Ms. Cummings, where you live and reside."

"I live in Fauquier County, outside Warrenton, approximately two miles at Ashland Farm."

"Now, Susan, tell the members of the jury, when you were growing up, were there ever any guns in your home, as a child?"

"Yes, sir." Susan sat with the posture of a ballerina, her hands folded squarely in her lap, and responded in soft, measured tones to her attorney's questions.

"Excuse me. Why was that?" Blair Howard asked as several members of the jury leaned forward in their seats.

"Due to the nature of my dad's business, who he is in the gun business, it wasn't unusual for us to see his guns in the house."

"What sort of guns were in the house?" Mr. Howard

continued, shifting his gaze from his client, to the jury box, and then back to Susan.

"They were mostly sporting guns and also antiques, shot-guns and rifles," the heiress replied.

"Where did you keep those pistols in your home?"

"I kept the pistols and one revolver in my bedroom for three of them, and one of them in the kitchen cabinet down-stairs."

"Now, tell the members of the jury, what was your pur-pose in having the pistols in the house?"

"Being a single woman and living by myself, I just find it more comfortable to have pistols in my house. And since it is also legal in the state of Virginia, I thought there is nothing . . . it's . . . let me . . . I'm sorry. I need to rephrase this. Can you ask me the question again?"

Susan sat back in the chair, seemingly comforted by the supportive half-smile on her attorney's face. Her eyes re-mained fixed on him as he asked the question once again. "These pistols that you kept in your house, why were those pistols kept there?"

"They were kept there . . . again, they were presents from my father, and since I lived alone, I felt safer having, you know, at least a few guns in my house."

"Ma'am, has there ever been any time that anything has occurred out there on the farm that caused you concern? And I'm talking about where you've noticed intruders or people around the farm in the evening?"

"Yes," Susan responded. "On a few occasions, and only on one occasion that I called the police that that happened. In 1996, right before Thanksgiving. I had heard my dogs barking, and I knew there was something unusual.

"So, I stepped outside my house. . . . I'm sorry. I forgot to mention that it was late at night, around eleven o'clock. I went outside with my flashlight, and I found a man hidden in the bushes near by the house, and I only saw him from his shoes up to the waist . . ."

Susan told the jury that she had called 911, and it had taken police nearly thirty minutes to respond.

A journalist seated in the gallery wondered if Susan was

referring to an incident that Roberto had told Jean Marie about. He said he had come to Ashland Farm one evening and found the front door locked—surprising him, since Susan rarely locked the doors to her home. After ringing the doorbell and pounding on the door, he told Jean Marie that he resorted to throwing pebbles at the window of the room where Susan and Diana were watching TV.

To his astonishment, he watched from the bushes as the two women appeared in the doorway. According to his account, both were armed with rifles, and both opened fire. Susan was never asked about this version of events from the witness stand.

Susan had been on the witness stand for nearly ninety minutes when her attorney moved on to the subject of Roberto Villegas.

"Would you tell the members of the jury, if you would, please? Did you have any occasion to meet Mr. Villegas in the summer of nineteen-ninety-five?" Blair Howard asked his star witness.

"Yes, I did," Susan responded in a soft voice.

"How did this occur, please?"

"I met Roberto in the spring of nineteen-ninety-five through the polo instructor who was teaching at Great Meadow during that summer."

"Could you tell the members of the jury, after the initial meeting, did you start dating right away, or did you see him often that summer?" Howard posed the question in a calm, deliberate tone.

"No," Susan answered, as members of the jury stared directly at her. "I met Roberto in the spring of nineteen-ninety-five, and I would see him on occasion at different polo functions, barbecues and games. But we did not start dating until the end of September of that year."

"At the end of September when you started dating, can you just give the members of the jury what your intial impressions were of Roberto Villegas when you first met him?"

Susan paused. Raising her brown eyes to meet those of her attorney, she began. "When I first met Roberto, he was very polite and very, very nice to me. He always had a smile, and he was very attentive, and seemed to like to talk to me. He enjoyed talking to me.''

''From a lady's standpoint, could you tell the members of the jury how you perceived him as someone that perhaps you would like to date in terms of . . . ?''

''Yes.''

''Any attraction?''

''He was a handsome man, muscular, aggressive. He played good polo, and he was just a generally attractive man.''

Later, Susan recounted for the jury several occasions on which Roberto had been abusive. At one point, she described an incident that ended in physical violence.

''I met Roberto at the barn one afternoon, and he . . . he was using a hole-puncher. He was inserting holes in one part of the saddle. And I had asked him to not do this because these were new saddles and this would damage them.

''And he got very angry. And he said, 'No woman is ever going to tell him what to do,' that I should just shut-up. I insisted he not use the hole-puncher. And he got very, very angry. His face became red, and he had a very tense look about himself.

''He lifted his hand holding the hole-puncher, and made the gesture as if he was going to throw the hole-puncher in my face. And I . . . I made a motion downward, and instead he kicked me in the crotch, and I fell backwards.''

Susan also described for the jury how Roberto had threatened to harm her if she attempted to leave him.

''He wanted children,'' Susan recalled, her vacant eyes staring straight ahead. ''He wanted to get married. I said I had no intention of having his children. He said if I didn't agree, he would kill me.''

Susan's porcelain face remained impassive as she described for the rapt jury the details of the September 7th shooting.

''I found Roberto in the kitchen,'' she began in her soft, French-accented voice. ''He was sitting at the kitchen table.

I came into the room and sat at the kitchen table right across from him.

" 'You know you must take your belongings and leave? I told you yesterday.' He responded that he had a game in Potomac, Maryland, and he was going to get ready for that game."

"Do you recall what your response was to that ma'am?" Howard asked.

"Yes. I told Roberto in my calm way . . . I said, 'Roberto, I know you have a game. And if you may, you can go to the game, but you cannot take . . . you have to make different arrangements for the horses because I am . . . you cannot take the horses to the game.' "

"What, if anything, was his reaction to that, ma'am?"

"Roberto became very angry. He . . . in a split second, he retrieved the knife, and in a . . . in a quick minute later, he reached across the table, he took hold of my neck and put the knife at my face."

"Now, let me just ask you this ma'am, when you say he took hold of your neck, tell the members of the jury, what was your reaction to that?"

"I did not react. I was very fearful, and I . . . I stayed completely motionless. He pressed the knife against my cheek, switching the blade from left to right.

"He insulted me. . . . He began to scratch my arm, slowly laughing about the fear on my face. I didn't want to say 'scratch,' I wanted to say 'slash,' " Susan corrected herself.

"My heart was beating. I felt my blood rushing down. I felt extremely scared. I felt that my life was in danger. I felt . . . I thought to myself, this is . . . this man is going to kill me."

"Why is it that you didn't try to run?" Blair Howard asked his client.

"I was afraid. Here was a man who was very strong, very quick, very unpredictable. I knew that I was cornered," Susan explained. She told members of the jury that she felt trapped in the small maid's galley, and said that she feared that if she tried to run, Roberto would grab her.

Even if she made it out of the kitchen, she said, she'd still have to thread her way through a series of rooms and hall-ways before she could get out of the house. Answering her lawyer's question, Susan described for the jury the twists and turns she would have needed to make in order to get from the kitchen to the front door of her home.

"Would you tell us please, what happened next?" Blair Howard inquired, reminding Susan that Roberto was at the sink, and she was still seated at the breakfast table when he led her off on a description of the layout of her mansion.

"At some point in time, Roberto had returned to the sink area to sit back down to the table. I felt very uncomfortable having Roberto seated across from me. So I told Roberto, 'I'm going to get' . . . 'make some coffee.'

"And so I headed towards the sink area, and I . . . at this point, I was facing the sink area, and running some water. And at the same time, I was telling Roberto, 'I'm going to wipe my arm, and we are going to forget about this incident.' And I stopped the water . . . stopped the running water, and then walked slightly to the right where the coffee was."

Susan hesitated, seeming as if she had suddenly lost her place. Unsure what to do, the heiress asked her attorney if she could speak to him for a moment.

"And pardon me for asking," she paused. "Can I ask you a question?"

Telling her that that was not possible, Mr. Howard asked his client a question that seemed to cue her in to what she was to say next. Nodding her head as if to say that she had recalled her lines, Susan continued her testimony.

"Let me ask you this," Howard suggested. "What were your thoughts when you were there at the sink?"

"Okay," Susan seemed relieved. "A million things were going through my mind. I was . . . I felt my life was in great danger. I thought about calling Sergeant Healy. I thought about calling my sister. I . . . I was feeling . . . I . . . I was very scared.

"But I also thought about the pistol that I had in the kitchen cabinet which was right below the coffee area. And I thought, 'maybe if I can get to my pistol, I could control the situation.' "

". . . Do you recall what happened to him as you fired the gun?" Mr. Howard asked Susan.

"All I recall seeing is a man that was jolted slightly backwards, and then he tilted forward, and he fell.

"Once he was down on the ground, I stood at . . . in the area where I had fired. I stood there for a few seconds, and then looked at his left hand, which shocked me because it had turned almost white.

"What did you do then?"

"I walked towards Roberto to check him, and I just looked at him and backed up.

"I recall walking out of the room, making a left turn, and then returning shortly after and putting my pistol on the kitchen cabinet next to the sink.

"All right. Where there any shells in the pistol?"

"No shells, but there was still one bullet in the chamber. I took . . . I extracted the last bullet out of the chamber and released the magazine."

". . . Ma'am, that night you had seen . . . I think it's Exhibit Number Seven?" Blair Howard requested that the Court provide him with Exhibit Seven, the bone-handled knife.

"Had you seen this knife before this particular day?

"Yes I have," Susan responded, telling the court that she recalled seeing the weapon in her truck sometime in the spring of nineteen-ninety-seven.

Displaying the bone-handled knife in his left hand, Mr. Howard asked Susan about a conversation that she had had with Roberto about the knife.

"I had indicated to Roberto that I did not want him to carry a knife in my truck. He was actually leaving this knife underneath the seat of my truck. And I explained to him that it is against the law in the State of Virginia to carry concealed weapons."

"And?" the defense attorney motioned for his client to elaborate on her response.

". . . and my concern was, I did not want to be responsible for this knife being hidden in my truck."

Susan told the jury that she had indicated to Roberto that

she did not like him keeping the knife in her truck, and had removed it from its location underneath the seat without him knowing. She said she kept the weapon at her house for a period of time, but returned it to Roberto when he discovered its absence at Dr. Seager's party on July 26.

Bounding to his feet, the neatly-combed prosecutor opened his cross-examination with a question about the knife.

"When was that, that you took the knife and hid it?" he asked Susan.

"I recall taking the knife sometime prior to the middle of July," the heiress answered in a cool, relaxed tone.

"And where had you kept it after you had it in your possession?" Kevin Casey ambled closer to the witness box.

"I kept it in the . . . downstairs in the kitchen, the first kitchen in one of the closets."

"The same kitchen in which you killed Mr. Villegas?"

"No, sir." Susan's gaze traveled down toward the floor as she readjusted her delicate frame in the witness seat.

"Different kitchen," Casey responded in clipped tone. "When did you give the knife back to him?"

The prosecutor already knew Susan's answer. He would address the issue of the knife again, during his closing remarks to the court. What he really wanted to hear from Susan was her admission to the jury that she killed Roberto Villegas. After all, her acknowlegement was the basis of his case.

Pacing the small carpeted area in front of the witness box, Casey continued his inquiry, moving his focus to the morning of September 7th.

"I shot him," Susan pronounced in response to one of Casey's questions. "I started shooting and I don't know at what point I stopped. I acted in a moment of desperation. I never intended for Roberto to get shot. . . . I needed to get this man out of my life."

On Monday, May 11, Blair Howard called four character witnesses to testify about Susan's reputation in the community.

A neighbor, John Pennington, said that she had an excellent reputation for honesty. Victoria McDonald, a biology professor who said that she met Susan in 1993 when she volunteered to assist in a study of birds, stated that the heiress was "poised, calm, and non-combative." Louisa Woodville, a young woman who boarded her horse at Ashland Farm, told the court that Susan had a reputation for "truth and veracity." And veterinarian Lewis Springer described Susan as a "nice lady," telling the court that in the thirteen years she'd been bringing her animals to him for veterinary care, he'd never heard anyone speak badly of her in public.

Next, the defense called Gary Leonard, the polo player from nearby Stafford who had organized the September 1997 charity match in Pittsburgh. Leonard testified that Susan and Roberto had agreed to participate in the event earlier that summer, but several weeks before the competition, Susan had tried to renege.

"I received a message from Susan that they would not be able to make the match," the polo player recounted. "I called her back and said that I needed to talk to her. I told her this is not a polo game but a charity game to raise money."

Leonard recalled that Susan and Roberto had parked their trailer directly next to his. After the match, he said, Susan came over to him.

"She said, 'Gary, the only reason I came to this polo game was for you and the horses,' " Leonard testified. "Then she said, 'I can't talk about it anymore now.' "

The polo player with the salt-and-pepper hair and thick mustache told the court that Miss Cummings had also promised to play in another game in Maryland the following day, but told him that she was worried that playing in two matches over the same weekend might put the ponies at risk.

"I explained to her that with polo ponies you can ride them three times a week and they get along fine," he said. "The game is broken down into seven-minute increments with the horse and it is not constant running. It is not a hardship for the horses to go back-to-back . . ."

Under cross-examination, Leonard said that he saw no fighting between Roberto and Susan. "There were no angry words, no acts of aggression," Leonard replied to one of Mr. Casey's questions. "We sat with Roberto and Susan that Friday night and had dinner with them."

In a stunning blow to the defense, the judge ruled to disallow the testimony of forensic scientist Tom Bevel, an expert in blood-stain analysis. Mr. Howard had hoped that Bevel's analysis of photos depicting blood spatter would counter the testimony from Sergeant Zinn. But Mr. Bevel, a former captain of the Oklahoma City Police Department, was never allowed to discuss what he had found.

After learning that Mr. Howard had provided this witness with a copy of Sergeant Zinn's testimony to study over the weekend, Judge Penn determined that the defense counsel had violated the court's rule that prevented one witness from knowing about the testimony of earlier witnesses prior to giving their own testimony.

Hoping to get the case back on track after his setback, Mr. Howard called forensic consultant Jack Dillon, a self-employed consultant and former FBI agent, who had used lasers to conduct a trajectory analysis on the bullet holes in the maid's kitchen at Ashland Farm. After a long-winded explanation of why the laser is more accurate than the wooden dowels used by Investigator Lamper in determining trajectory, the round-faced expert told the court that his analysis showed that one of the bullets that passed through Mr. Villegas' body was fired from inside the kitchen.

Upon hearing Dillon testify that his fee was $2,000 a day, spectators in the upstairs gallery began to contemplate the amount of money Susan Cummings was spending on her defense.

While it was not unusual for an expert witness to charge in excess of $1,000 for his time and testimony, the pronouncement of his fee sparked speculation among journalists who wondered about Susan's legal bills. They contemplated that the number of hours Blair Howard must have clocked, and the amount of money that his team of investigators must have spent tracking down potential witnesses, probably put Susan's bill into the six figures.

Polo umpire Steve Lane had been flown in from Florida

to tell the court about an incident that occurred in October of 1995. Answering Blair Howard's questions, the portly referee with the curly brown hair detailed for the jury the day that Roberto was ejected from a match.

Mr. Lane, a professional umpire for the U.S. Polo Association, described an incident involving vulgar language on the field. He testified that Roberto had cursed at one of the other umpires and was suspended from the game. Telling the court that the first confrontation between Roberto and himself occurred in the fourth chukka, Lane described how the polo player had been warned. But when, in the sixth chukka Roberto again spoke to Mr. Lane in a vulgar manner, the umpire ousted him from the game.

Lane described for the jury a problem between Roberto and another polo player, Rodrigo Salinas (no relation to Juan Salinas Bentley), and said that in order to defuse the situation he went to Roberto's trailer.

"Roberto, what are you doing?" he said he asked the polo professional.

Patting the Argentine on the shoulder, and then the stomach, he said he felt "what was my one-hundred-percent belief to be a knife."

"I want to talk to the son of a bitch," he said Roberto told him.

"He looked at me directly in the eye, I looked back at him and said, 'Come on, let's go back to your truck and trailer.' "

Under cross-examination, Lane told the court that in spite of the fact that polo is a rough, physical game, and it is not unusual to have heated disputes, this was the first time he'd ever seen Roberto lose his temper.

"It was out of character for him," Lane said.

To further support the defense's claim that Roberto had a wild temper, Mr. Howard called Miriam South to testify.

The farm manager described for the jury an incident in which Roberto allegedly threatened her. Miss South said that in the summer of 1994 Roberto moved in to a small cottage on the farm that she managed in Madison County, Virginia. She told the court that he was receiving room and board and pasture for his horses in return for playing polo on the owner's team.

"He was always very friendly, very polite," the tousled, unfashionable woman told the court.

The woman's face contorted as she described the afternoon that Roberto learned that the owner of the farm had permitted another polo club member to put his horses in Roberto's pasture.

"Around mid-day, I had just stepped off my front porch when I heard Mr. Villegas' truck coming out quickly. When he got to my yard, he swerved a sharp right, drove across my lawn, and stopped twelve feet short of me.

"I assumed it was some sort of emergency," she continued for the court. "He threw open the door of his truck. It appeared he was angry. He started yelling in a mix of English and Spanish. He was furious, spitting saliva when he spoke and gesturing wildly. He stomped close up to me, turned his back, and walked toward his truck.

"He was considering it my fault that he was being imposed upon by the horses," Miss South recalled, telling the court how he frightened her when he began using vulgar language.

" 'You're so f---ing stupid,' he said to me. By the time he was finished, he had saliva dripping from his mouth. I just froze in place."

"Did he touch you?" Kevin Casey inquired under cross-examination of Miss South.

"He was in a rage, he was gesturing very wildly. He was coming up very close to me and stomping back to his truck," the witness responded. "He got close enough to me that saliva hit me on my face."

"You didn't shoot him?" Mr. Casey continued.

"I didn't have a weapon at the time," Miss South said. "If I did, I would have drawn it, but I don't know if I would have pulled the trigger."

As the heavy-set woman stepped down from the bench, Suzi Worsham voiced her disgust. Leaning forward in her seat, she told one reporter that Miriam was the only person she had ever heard Roberto say he didn't like.

Faye Lefler was another defense witness who claimed to have had a run-in with Roberto Villegas. The wife of the manager of the Sarasota Polo Club had also been flown to Virginia from the west coast of Florida to testify about Roberto's "scary" temper.

Miss Lefler, a pretty young blonde in a white cardigan sweater and a string of pearls, told the court that she had met Mr. Villegas in 1989. She said that she had had an ugly encounter with him in the winter of 1994.

"My husband and I reside at the Sarasota Polo Club," Miss Lefler began her testimony. "Roberto was leasing a property fairly near to us. He would play with my husband's team. He was very charming, always smiling, a cheerful person."

Miss Lefler testified that after delivering the low-grade hay that Roberto had requested for his horses, the horseman stormed into the barn where she was cutting the hair of two young children.

"He got out of his truck with his hands raised," Miss Lefler recounted. "He was yelling at me.

" 'What is wrong?' I thought. He walked at a very rapid pace with his hands above his head while he was yelling at me."

As Miss Lefler detailed the encounter, her eyes welled up with tears. " 'What are you trying to do? Are you trying to kill my horses?' he screamed. 'You bitch, I'm going to f---ing kill you, and I'm going to take care of that horse of yours.' "

Under cross-examination, the young woman conceded to Kevin Casey that when she ordered Roberto to leave, he retreated without a fight.

Next, Blair Howard called Katarine Petty, the restaurant manager at Napoleon's restaurant, where Susan and Roberto dined at least two times a week. The thick-bodied brunette described for jurors an altercation she witnessed between Miss Cummings and Mr. Villegas in the parking lot of the cafe. She told the court that Roberto and Susan were her favorite customers, and described how, in the beginning, the two always ordered barbecue rib sandwiches.

"She drank milk and he had coffee," the restaurant manager recalled for the court. "They held hands across the table. They appeared to be a couple just starting out a relationship."

"Did you notice a change in their relationship?" Blair Howard inquired of his witness.

"Yes, Miss Cummings' eating habits changed. She said she didn't want the barbecue sandwich anymore. She ordered grilled cheese, fresh fruit, and hot tea."

She said that Miss Cummings, who, she observed, invariably sat up straight with her hands folded in her lap, always paid the dinner check.

"The bill would lay on the table for a while and no one would touch it," the manager stated. "She would always pay it."

Miss Petty recalled for the jury an argument between the couple that occurred in the restaurant sometime in late July.

"Miss Cummings was sitting with her hands in her lap and he was talking to her. I was clearing a table and I looked at her. She had tears in her eyes. She asked if she could please leave, but he ignored her.

"A few weeks later, another discussion took place. I looked at her eyes, she looked frightened. I was behind the bar, but had walked through and saw them sitting at the table.

"On a break, I was standing on the terrace which overlooks the parking lot. They walked out of the restaurant. They were not holding hands. They were apart from each other.

"She went to the right, he went to the left. She started to get into a small sports car. He quickly turned around and opened the car door. He had his right hand on the car, his fist striking at her on the chest area.

"His fist was like this," Miss Petty demonstrated for the jury. "Maybe he was holding something. Maybe he was hitting her. Then it looked like he threw something at her. He went back to his truck and quickly got in and sped off.

"She sat just like she did in the restaurant, straight up with her hands folded in her lap."

The jury looked on as Miss Petty continued her testimony.

They had already heard about the incident from Susan Cummings. During Susan's testimony, the heiress had described for the court an angry exchange that had occurred between herself and Roberto.

"After we had had dinner at Napoleon's . . . and it was kind of late; we were probably out of the restaurant by quarter to . . . quarter to eleven . . . I had indicated to Roberto that I was going to go home. And as we . . . and he seemed to be very unhappy about that. He showed discontent," Susan had testified.

"And he . . . as we were walking out of the restaurant, I headed toward my car and he headed toward his. And then I . . . as I got in my car, a few minutes . . . a few seconds later, Roberto walked back to my car, opened the door, and punched me and took my shirt and wanted me out of the car and demanded that we go to his house and that he needed to spend some time with me in order to play better the next day."

"Let me just ask you this," Mr. Howard had posed a question. "When you say he needed to spend some time with you in order to play the next day, can you be a little more specific?"

All eyes were on Susan as she recalled what happened next. "Yes, I'm sorry," she began. "What he said is . . . he demanded sex. He said that he would play . . . he would be a much better player if he had sex the night before."

As jurors looked on, Blair Howard had continued with his questions. "When was the first time that evening that he had brought the subject up?"

". . . I think during the course of dinner he had mentioned that I should go with him after dinner," Susan had responded. "And I . . . I told him that I was tired and I preferred . . . I'd rather go home.

"And as we walked out, I headed towards my car and he headed towards his; and then he just turned right back and headed towards me. And at that time, I was already in my car, and he forcefully opened the door and hit me. He punched me on my chest, tugged on my shirt, and said that you know, 'You're not going to tell me what to do. I need to have sex. We need to spend some time together. Why don't we go to my house and spend some time together?'

"And I said, 'I'm not going with you. I . . . you're hurting me. You're punching me. I'm not going to be forced into something like that.' "

As journalists feverishly scribbled the details of Susan's story on their notepads, Blair Howard had addressed his client. "Did he finally leave?"

"He . . . what he did is he took the keys out of my car and I demanded my keys back. He said that I could leave my car here and that I . . . he wouldn't let me go. And I insisted. I said, 'Roberto, there's no way. I'm not going anywhere. I'm just staying right here. I'll just stay right in the parking lot. I would like to have my keys back.'

"He just threw the keys right back at me. They, I think, landed in the car. And he left. He got into his vehicle and spun the wheels and left quickly."

Farrier Harmen vanderWoude testified that twice he witnessed arguments between Miss Cummings and Mr. Villegas while he was working at Ashland Farm. He said he once overheard Miss Cummings offer Roberto $20,000 if he would leave the farm.

Leaning forward in the witness box, his arm resting on the wooden ledge, Mr. vanderWoude said that he visited Ashland Farm again at the end of August. When he arrived, he said, he found Susan on the telephone. The burly blacksmith told the court that he had heard Roberto belittle the heiress and, at one point, saw him slap her on the back.

"We went down to the barn to start shoeing the horses. She seemed nervous and said she was afraid of Roberto. She said he might do something crazy, and she said, 'If I call you, will you come?' I said, 'That's what the police are for.' And she said she didn't know if the police would come."

Mr. Casey approached the witness box where Mr. vanderWoude sat slumped over the microphone. He asked the farrier to recall a conversation he had had with Sheriff's Investigator Lucas on September 8, the day after the shooting.

Reading from Mr. vanderWoude's statement to police, Mr. Casey reminded the witness that he had said, "I never saw what you would characterize as physical violence. I did see Roberto strike Miss Cummings on the back several times, but he was making a point. . . .

"He spoke with Susan in a raised voice, but not a threatening one," Casey read from the official police statement.

"Roberto seemed to be upset because he did not have control over what games he would play," the prosecutor continued to recite Vanderwoude's report. "She owned the horses. She owned the trailer."

Motel employee Nicole Pusker was on hand to tell the jury that she was behind the desk of the Holiday Inn in Pittsburgh on September 5, 1997, when Miss Cummings asked for her own room.

Susan's friend, Elsa Acosta, a local horse owner, told the jury that she had witnessed an argument between Susan and Roberto on Labor Day weekend of 1997. She said that the dispute ended when Roberto placed a horse's lead rope around Susan's neck and declared, "I'll kill her."

Next, Roberto's former girlfriend, Kelli Quinn, reluctantly took the stand. She had been subpoenaed to testify for the defense after Blair Howard's investigators turned up the complaint she had filed against Roberto in 1995. In an emotionless tone, the well-built brunette detailed the incident, telling the court how he had chased after her in his truck, demanding that she pull over and talk to him.

On cross-examination, Mr. Casey tried to establish that after the incident, the two had maintained a close relationship, but the judge did not permit the statement, citing that it was irrelevant to the case.

Another former girlfriend of Roberto's, Kim Volare, said that she had dated the Argentine polo player in Wellington, Florida, in 1989. Her voice cracked as the dark-haired woman described to the court how Mr. Villegas choked her while having sex.

"I was scared," Miss Volare said. "I didn't like it. I was young, I was naïve. I knew it wasn't right. He was harming me."

Landscape contractor Brett Skipper had traveled from his home in Indiana to testify that in 1985, after learning that he'd been fired from his polo team, Roberto "pulled a knife on me" in a hotel parking lot.

After listening to hours of testimony about Roberto's "uncontrollable" temper, jurors would hear from the defense team's final witness.

Santiago Palma had traveled from his native Argentina to testify about a business deal he had made with Roberto in 1995. The well-dressed businessman in the dark-colored, European-style suit recounted for the court how he had paid Roberto nearly $10,000 for a Ford F-350 pickup truck. When Villegas failed to turn over the vehicle or the title to him, Mr. Palma said he confronted the polo player. At that point, he said, Roberto pulled a knife on him and threatened: "Don't get into my business or I'll kill you. You don't know me, you don't know what I'm capable of doing."

Waiting in the wings were defense witnesses that Blair Howard had had flown in to Virginia. Among them was Roberto's ex, Margaret Bonnell, and Sergeant Bob Guierri, the Napperville police officer who had arrested Roberto back in 1987 in connection with a domestic dispute with Bonnell. Deciding that the jury had heard enough testimony about Roberto's bad temper, the defense lawyer thought it best to rest his case.

That afternoon, jurors boarded a bus for Ashland Farm. The fourteen panelists were escorted to the mansion to view the crime scene first hand. Both the defense and the prosecution were convinced that seeing the tiny room where the murder took place would help their cases.

Sheriff's deputies in ten gallon hats and official brown and tan uniforms halted oncoming traffic on Route 211, just where it intersects with the windy two-lane roadway. Blue police lights flashed atop their cruisers as they directed the small procession of unmarked cars and the white van that carried jurors to Ashland Farm.

A group of journalists dressed in lightweight rain gear had

gathered on the grassy shoulder just outside the Cummings's property to observe the field trip to the $2.3-million estate. Judge Penn had denied their requests to accompany the entourage, leaving the reporters and camera crews with no alternative but to watch from a distance.

Susan Cummings and her lawyer led the way in Blair Howard's fancy jeep, with prosecutor Kevin Casey trailing behind in a more modest sports utility vehicle. The motorcade resembled a funeral procession as it idly turned left into the white-pillared entranceway of the grand old estate. A handful of brown horses grazed the well-watered grass as the cortege pulled up to the majestic main house. Several cats scurried across the lawn as the vehicles parked along the rear driveway.

Photographers watched through their zoom lenses as members of the jury stepped out of the police bus, and waited in the rain on the slate walkway near the back door. Susan Cummings stood in the doorway and greeted the panelists as they entered her home and followed the defense attorney through the maze of rooms to the small maid's quarters where the shooting had occurred.

Both Casey and Howard were hopeful that the visit to the murder site would give the jurors new insights into the case, and prompt the panelists to render a decision in their favor.

CHAPTER 22

KEVIN CASEY WAS CONFIDENT HE WOULD WIN A CONVIC-
tion when he strode to the front of Judge Penn's courtroom
to deliver his closing arguments the following morning. The
judge had given Casey and Howard just one-hour apiece to
wrap up, but the prosecutor wasn't worried; it doesn't take
an hour to summarize when the defendant has already confessed.

"It's difficult to know where to begin, since this case
ended, for all intents and purposes, on Friday when Ms.
Cummings took the stand and confessed to first-degree murder," the immaculately-dressed commonwealth's attorney
addressed the court.

"On Friday she got on the stand. At that point she indicated: 'I had my back to Roberto. I knew there was a gun
in this cupboard. I knew it was loaded. I knew it was cocked.
I knew the safety was off.' And in her words: 'I knew it was
ready to fire . . .'

"She didn't say Roberto had the knife in his hand. She
never, ever said she turned around and Mr. Villegas had the
knife in his hand. Yet she would have you believe she was
in imminent danger."

Mr. Casey cited the commonwealth's version of the crime.
"The problem starts with the timing of all this; the condition
of Mr. Villegas when he was found at the scene, the condition of his blood as contrasted with the condition of her
blood. According to her, these incidents happened fairly

close together. The condition of their respective bloods doesn't support that.

"What Ms. Cummings did in the Commonwealth's version is: she went to her bedroom, and in her bedroom she retrieved the pistol which is in evidence. She got that pistol from the holster that was made for that pistol and was kept in the bedroom; and she loaded that pistol with five bullets, with the ammunition that was kept in her bedroom.

"And Ms. Cummings, who is very familiar with guns and this gun in particular, racked it one time to put a bullet in the chamber so it would, indeed, be ready to fire; and then she comes downstairs.

"And I have no doubt that Ms. Cummings, planning to kill her first human on the planet, was a little excited; and she forgot she had already loaded a bullet in the chamber and she racked it again. Gary Arnsten tells us what that does is it throws a bullet out. That bullet lands on the floor.

"Then Ms. Cummings turned the corner into that little kitchen, and she started shooting from that little room at Roberto Villegas, who was all the way across the room. And, of course, that weapon threw shell casings out from the spent bullets; and one of them landed in the hallway, one of them landed right next to the entrance, and two of them landed in the room.

"How did that happen? Because Ms. Cummings was advancing on Roberto. . . . She just killed Roberto Villegas. What is she going to do? Roberto's dead. 'I've got to do something. This doesn't look good for me. . . . Now I need to fix it.'

" 'Well, there's the knife that I found in the truck and took. It's Roberto's knife. Where is that knife? Oh, it's up in my bedroom; it's in my dresser drawer in that plastic bag.'

"So she returns to her bedroom and gets that knife, knowing it belongs to Roberto. She comes back down to the kitchen, removes the knife from its sheath. She places her hand on the counter, and she draws. That's the best way to describe those injuries to her arm. She draws parallel lines, barely breaking the skin. 'Okay. This looks better for me. Roberto attacked me with a knife.

" 'Well, if he attacked me with it, he darn well better have it in some fashion when the police get here.' What to do? Well, there's Roberto. He's dead. He's not going to deny he had the knife: Go to the body and place that knife right here,'' Mr. Casey said, indicating with his hand, "place that knife right there where Roberto's—he's holding that knife. 'The police will believe that.'

"Sadly for Ms. Cummings, too much time had passed and Roberto, despite having lost a great deal of blood, the blood on his arm was dry. So by the time Ms. Cummings placed the knife there, guess what the knife was unable to do? Get any of Roberto's blood on the handle.

"You heard Sergeant Zinn describe in fairly graphic detail the blood that's spewing, dripping, spurting along the wall. And now Ms. Cummings would have us believe that Roberto somehow had this knife, and yet it got no blood on it.

"Consider, if you will, this knife, just blood on the tip,'' Casey said, holding the knife up for the jury to see. "No blood on the blade; which you would expect if you were cutting someone's arm.

"And in the 911 call, what does she say? Well, she admits to the killing, which is nice. But she says, 'He tried to kill me.' Well, how did he do that? She had no significant wounds. She had, by all accounts, some very superficial wounds, and you heard the credible expert testimony about these wounds.

"They were multiple, they were similar, they were clustered, they were parallel, and they were non-life-threatening, all of the characteristics of self-inflicted wounds. That's what Dr. Daniel told you.

"You also heard Dr. Junger testify about the condition of Roberto's blood seen in this picture,'' Mr. Casey said, flashing it before the jury as he continued his closing remarks.

"As near as we can pin down, this photograph was taken at nine-o-six, nine-o-seven, fifteen minutes after the 911 call began. If you believe Ms. Cummings, that's all the time that passed.

"Members of the Fauquier County Sheriff's Office are on the scene taking photographs. The pictures show Roberto's blood already separating. See, the blood serum is already off the blood pool, something that is inconsistent if it had happened fifteen minutes before the call.

"We also presented some evidence about the trajectory of the bullets. We were able to determine that the two bullets that passed all the way through Roberto Villegas passed through in the fashion you saw those dowels sticking through the dummy. The dummy had to be sitting down to have that happen.

"You heard a lot of testimony about what a bad guy Roberto Villegas was, a very bad guy. I will concede one thing. It sounds like he was a bad driver.

"Based on the facts in this case, none of that matters. And it could have been a combination of Charles Manson, Jack the Ripper, and O.J. Simpson sitting in that chair. That didn't give Ms. Cummings the right to do what she did.

"In each case, there was some spark that made Mr. Villegas mad. And he appears to have lost his temper on several occasions; all the way back to 1985. The only thing we didn't have was him losing his temper on the playground as a child. In each case, Mr. Villegas calmed down fairly quickly. In some of the cases, individuals, including women, stood up to him. 'No, Roberto, don't do that. Stop that. Go away.' What did he do in each case? He did it.

"You will recall the unrebutted testimony of Sergeant Zinn. No blood on the table. No blood on the other chair, no blood on the floor where the other chair was. And she would have you believe that is the location she received these wounds in this very awkward fashion that resulted in getting her blood only on the tip and not down the blade [of the knife]. She wasn't cut there when she was cut. Where was she? Where was her blood found? It's over by the counter, over by the sink where she steadied her arm to make those very fine cuts.

"There's one other piece of evidence that you've heard talked about; and that was Ms. Cummings' shoes. And she did cover this in her version of the story. She did say she walked over close to the body.

"Why go near the body? You have to put the knife someplace. I have no doubt she didn't intend to step in blood, but she did. And she picked up a very small bit of blood.

"Why do all these things after Roberto was killed? Well, you wouldn't have to do them if you had acted in self-defense. There's only one reason to do them. You just flat-out blew him away and now you need to fix it somehow. That's what she did."

Returning to his seat, Mr. Casey watched as his opponent rose and walked over to the jury box, where some of the members rocked gently in their chairs.

Positioning himself in front of the panel, Blair Howard began his closing arguments. He had asked Judge Penn for additional time to sum up his case, and with no objection from the prosecution, was granted an extra fifteen minutes to address the jury.

Howard's closing remarks were very much the same as his opening statement. Methodically, he cited the testimony of each of his witnesses, reiterating their stories of Roberto's ill temper. Members of the jury nodded their heads as if in agreement with his reminiscences, paying particular attention when Howard outlined reasons why they should disregard the testimony of the prosecution's key witnesses. He reminded them of Grimsley, the volunteer rescue medic who recanted the written statements he'd made after a visit by Investigator Lamper several days before the trial.

Casey listened. Seated at the long, wooden table, behind a stack of legal books, he jotted down notes and patiently waited for his turn. He knew that he had the advantage. In the commonwealth of Virginia, the prosecution gets one last opportunity to call rebuttal witnesses.

Casey believed that Blair Howard had been attempting to show the jury that Roberto needed a trigger to set off his anger. With Brett Skipper it was the loss of a job, with Santiago Palma it was a confrontation over money, with Faye Lefler it was the low-grade hay.

Calling Jean Marie Turon to the stand, the spry commonwealth's attorney was now laying his trap for the defense.

In a thick Spanish accent, the skinny polo instructor told the court that Roberto had phoned him the night before the match and the two had arranged to take Jean Marie's horses to the banner competition.

"I set aside three of my horses for Roberto to use," Jean Marie testified for the prosecution.

Throughout the case, the defense had been planting the idea that Roberto had flown into a rage when he learned that Susan had forbidden him from using the horses to compete in the most important game of Roberto's season.

Jean Marie was here to prove that Roberto did not need Susan's horses to compete in the match in Potomac.

To drive his point home that Susan had planned Roberto's murder and then after the fact scrambled to cover up the crime, Casey called Erich Junger to the stand for a fourth appearance. The self-assured investigator told the court that during the search of the mansion on Holtzclaw Road, he found no evidence of blood-stains on the table where Susan said she was cut by Roberto Villegas. Dr. Junger also testified that police found no blood on the opposite chair where Susan said she had been sitting when her boyfriend allegedly attacked her with the bone-handled knife.

In his final remarks, Kevin Casey took one last shot at the defense's claim of self-defense. He quickly reviewed the scientific evidence he presented, concentrating on Sergeant Zinn's testimony about the blood spatter.

"There's a point in time, you recall, where Jim Jones and Shawn Walters, members of the Fauquier County Sheriff's Office, take Ms. Cummings upstairs so she can brush her teeth. They collect her shoes . . . And she picks up an article of clothing, and it is a sweatshirt. Later on, it was taken from her at the jail and sent to the lab. Imagine Ms. Cummings' shock and horror when Roberto's blood turned up on that sweatshirt.

"You heard the testimony about the blood that was spurting and spewing around the room. Only one little part of it ended up on her. On her sweatshirt. And she made an all-too-human error of picking up the very same article of clothing she had been wearing earlier that day. That's what explains the pristine nature of her white shirt, which is clear to anybody that she couldn't get at her arm with a sweatshirt on.''

The jury would go away with those final words.

Retiring to a small room in the rear of the courthouse, the jurors began their deliberations. Judge Penn had instructed them on the various charges, advising them that they can choose between first-degree murder, which requires evidence of malice and premeditation, second-degree murder, which requires malice, or voluntary manslaughter, which is committed while under the grip of a strong emotion.

Alternatively, they could find Susan Cummings not guilty by reason of self-defense—but only under certain circumstances, he explained.

''Fear alone, however well grounded, unaccompanied by an overt act, is not enough to justify'' a claim of self-defense, the elder magistrate said in presenting his charge to the jury.

For Susan and her family, the wait seemed like an eternity. The heiress, her mother and sister, and family friend John Aycoth, sat with defense attorneys, Blair Howard and Thomas Hill, in the small guest room they had rented at the Hampton Inn. The 100-room motel, which was just down the road from the courthouse, featured clean and simple accommodations. Business had picked up for the inn during the trial as reporters, witnesses, and even the judge himself, rented rooms there.

As the hours passed, and the jury continued its deliberations, Susan and her sister wondered about the possible outcome. Word that the jurors had asked to retire for the evening and continue their deliberations the following day prompted even more speculation among the members of the Cummings camp.

''What could it mean that they have not returned a verdict yet?'' one of them pondered aloud. ''Do you think it's a good sign or a bad one?''

Meanwhile, friends of Roberto stayed in close touch by telephone. Many were upset over Casey's decision not to paint Roberto in a more positive fashion and wondered why the prosecutor had not called upon them to testify.

In the weeks leading up to the trial, the Worshams, Great Meadow Polo President Richard Vargé, and Roberto's former polo patron, Bill Ylvisaker, had called Kevin Casey to offer themselves as witnesses on Roberto's behalf. Their frustration grew during the trial as Blair Howard called one witness after another to the stand to attack their friend's character. Time after time, they called the commonwealth attorney's office and repeated their offer to testify. But Casey continued to turn them down.

Neither party could have known of the arguments among members of the jury that had gone on behind closed doors. At first, nearly all the jurors had voted to acquit, several members of the panel later divulged. With only three jurors leaning toward a conviction—one of them the jury forewoman—a heated battle broke out over what to do.

As Blair Howard had hoped, many of the women on the jury identified with Susan Cummings and expressed their distress over the treatment she had allegedly endured at the hand of Roberto Villegas.

But one of the male jurors was able to plant some doubt in their minds by demonstrating that the bone-handled knife that Roberto had allegedly used to slice Susan's arm would not even puncture his skin. Repeated attempts yielded similar results.

Questions about Susan's claim of self-defense continued to dog the jury throughout the deliberations. Members were finding it difficult to reconcile Susan's story of how she received her wounds. Ultimately, the jurors felt that they had no choice but to convict.

Word that the jury had returned a verdict caused a flurry of activity in the courthouse. After deliberating for nearly nine hours, the panel announced it was ready to render its decision.

Reporters raced to the lobby phone to alert their editors, and friends of the victim nervously took their places in the upholstered orange chairs of the upstairs gallery. They watched as Susan Cummings rose from her seat and turned to face the twelve men and women who were to decide her fate.

A hush fell over the windowless courtroom. Members of the media flipped open their notepads and began writing furiously as Judge Penn shifted his glance to the jury box.

"Have you reached a verdict," the elder magistrate asked from his seat on the bench.

"Yes we have, your honor," forewoman Marion Bruffy responded in a clear, succinct voice.

Susan's mother and twin sister stood stoically in the first row of the gallery as Deputy Clerk Martha Mitchell read the verdict aloud. They listened as she announced to the court that the jury had found Susan "guilty." The twelve men and women of the jury had found the heiress committed voluntary manslaughter, which carries a penalty of up to ten years in prison.

Standing in between her lawyers, Blair Howard and Thomas Hill, the heiress's face revealed nothing. She remained stone-still, her long, delicate arms at her side, locks of her wavy brown hair falling over the fabric of her brown sport jacket, as Mitchell continued to address the court, telling the judge that on the second charge of Use of a Firearm in the Commission of a Felony, which carries a mandatory prison sentence of three years, the twelve member panel had found Susan "not guilty."

The jury still had a critical task before it: determining Susan Cummings' sentence. Unlike some other states, it is customary under Virginia law for members of the jury to determine how much jail time, if any, a convict should serve.

But, before they would retire behind closed doors, they would hear pleas for leniency from Susan's mother, Irmgard Cummings, and her sister, Diana.

Diana took the stand first. Her voice wavered as she responded to Blair Howard's questions. In a low-pitched, throaty tone, the slender, neatly-attired blonde described how she and her sister had always done things as a pair since their youth.

"My sister and I have always been together," her voice

trembled as she spoke. "We went to the same school together. We've never been apart from each other. We plan to be together forever."

Tears welled up in Susan's eyes as her sister told the court about how she and her fraternal twin had been inseparable since birth, attending the same schools and living together at Ashland Farm.

"My sister and I share a business together," she said, sliding her delicate frame slightly forward in the witness chair. "We work on the farm together. We do just about everything together."

As Diana stepped down, the bailiff called Susan's mother to the stand. It would be the first time since the shooting that Irma Cummings would speak publicly about her daughter. Positioning her lean, well-toned body in the witness box, she began by telling the court that she and her daughter shared a close relationship.

"Well, I always had a wonderful relationship with her," the handsome woman told the packed courtroom.

"Could you tell members of the jury, as a child, just an overview of what kind of child she was growing up?" Blair Howard asked.

"Well, those were twin girls, so, they, you know . . . I . . . they always were playing together. And I did not have a real problem. We have little problems, you know. It was no real major problems. She was very kind and nice and polite to her father and to her mother for . . . you know, in the house we respected each other."

"Did she date much as a teenager?" Howard questioned.

"Yeah," Susan's mother responded.

"Date is a misleading word," the defense lawyer paused. "Did she go out with other young men as a teenager while she was living with you?"

"Well, as a teenager, she had some school friends. But those were school friends. It was not what maybe you call a real boyfriend. As a teenager, you see just school friends. And then she left when she was nineteen."

"Did she ever exhibit to you, ma'am, any affection or love for animals?"

"Yes, very much so, because during the summertime, from the age of three to sixteen, in the summertime we always went to Switzerland. We did not have any dogs and cats. But nearby us there was a barn, so they spent the whole summer, every day they would stay at the barn. They would take some riding lessons and also, oddly enough, neighbors . . . dogs of neighbors would come to our house and even cats included.

"So for one reason or another, we had animals at our house, and they would just play around the house. They would . . . they never wanted to go anywhere and wanted to be at home, and they had a dog and a cat for a reason or another that would stay there."

"What kind of relationship did she have with her father?"

"Her . . . she had a good relationship," Irmgard hesitated. "But her father was traveling a lot, so he was . . . well, he was working very, very hard. And he was traveling a lot with . . . maybe he was gone . . . maybe he was gone six months a year, not six months in a row, but coming back and forth."

"Would Mr. Cummings come and visit his daughters here at Ashland Farm?"

"Oh yes, yes, yes."

"And?"

"He would be the weekend at the farm," Susan's mother spoke in a confident voice, "and during the week he would work in Alexandria."

"And when he was with his daughter, how did they interact together, Susan and . . . ?"

"Oh, she always . . . she always went out with her father on the weekends. And when he was . . . he always asked her, 'Do you like to come with me?' And somehow, a little bit . . . like if she . . . if she would be his mother as she always wanted to look after him and do things for him."

Several of the women on the jury fought back tears as Blair Howard begged the panel for leniency.

"She's made a mistake," the defense counselor pleaded. "That doesn't make her a bad person. That doesn't mean she's a person who should be removed from society."

With Howard's plea, and the testimony of Susan's mother and sister fresh in their minds, jurors once again returned to the deliberation room to decide on a sentence.

Susan and her family remained in the courtroom, waiting together at the defense table while journalists and spectators stood outside, enjoying the warm spring weather. Some paced the small cement area just outside the main entrance to the courthouse. Others sipped coffee and chatted idly, speculating on when jurors might return a decision.

"The waiting, that's the hardest part," Susan's friend Jane Rowe told a reporter for *The Washington Times*. Jane and her daughter had been there for much of the trial, and nervously awaited the jury's decision.

Exactly forty minutes had passed when a court officer announced to the members of the media that the jury had reached a judgment. The journalists looked on from the second row of the gallery as the twelve men and women filed back into Judge Penn's courtroom. They had sat through five days of testimony and spent hours discussing the case among themselves. Many felt that Blair Howard had done an excellent job defending Susan, but they still figured that she'd have to serve some time in prison.

Kevin Casey, bolstered by the jury's decision to return a verdict of voluntary manslaughter, anticipated jail time for the heiress. Before the jury began its second round of deliberations, he had urged the panel to give Susan Cummings a stiff prison sentence. "Do not forget she shot another human being four times," he had told them as they filed out of the courtroom. "I beg you, do not forget Roberto Villegas."

The dapper young attorney stood with his hands clasped behind his back as the forewoman told the judge that the jury had decided to sentence the heiress to "sixty days in the county jail," and to impose a fine of $2,500 for the felony charge of manslaughter. He could not have been pleased when he heard the jury's recommendation and later declined comment on the light sentence.

For the first time since the trial began, Susan Cummings exhibited relief. Turning to one of her attorneys, she reached her arms around Mr. Hill's neck, and smiled as she embraced him. The photographer stationed in the far right corner of the upstairs gallery captured the image on film.

"Miss Cummings will never become president of the United States," Casey sarcastically told the reporters who encircled him as he walked from the courthouse. The obviously discontented attorney declined to comment further on the sentence, prompting reporters to chase after members of the defense team for a sound bite for their evening broadcasts.

Turning their attention to Susan Cummings as she and her legal team appeared on the cement steps of the two-story building, they directed their cameras at the group.

Dressed in a brown blazer and cream-colored jeans, the heiress, flanked by her mother and twin sister, stopped to say a few words to the media before continuing down Ashby Street. "I would like to let you know how deeply appreciative I am," Susan whispered into the microphones. "I feel very happy."

But friends of Roberto were angered by the verdict and did nothing to hide their disappointment from the media.

"He wasn't the type of person who was portrayed in court," Suzi Worsham announced to one weekly newspaper reporter. Suzi and her husband, Travis, had sat together in the last row of the gallery for much of the trial. "We're just sick."

In Buenos Aires, talk of the light sentence flooded the radio airwaves, with contentious announcers ridiculing the Cummings' verdict.

"I honestly thought the justice system in the United States was a model system, something to be admired!" one radio host cried out while discussing the verdict. "This shows how wrong I was. You would get a stronger ticket for a traffic violation than for killing an Argentine!"

"*Even A Louse Deserves A Better Brand of Justice*," read the headline of an editorial that ran in *The Washington Post* later that week. The scathing commentary would not be the last criticism of the case to appear in the news.

EPILOGUE

THE MEDIA SPOTLIGHT REMAINED ON SUSAN CUMMINGS even after she was sentenced to sixty days in the Fauquier County Jail for manslaughter. No sooner had she begun serving her sentence than reports began surfacing that she was being given special treatment behind bars.

Minutes after the verdict was handed down, Circuit Court Judge Carleton Penn ruled that she did not have to begin serving her sentence immediately, as most convicts do. Instead, the elder magistrate allowed her to postpone her jail time so that she could attend a memorial service for her father the following Saturday afternoon in Washington, D.C. His only stipulation was that she report to the jail and begin serving her time immediately following the ceremony.

Susan returned to Ashland Farm that afternoon and enjoyed three days at the estate with her mother and sister before climbing into Diana's car on Saturday morning to make the one-hour trip to Washington to say a final goodbye to her beloved father.

Meanwhile, jail officials were busy preparing for Susan's arrival at the small, red-brick complex. Clearing out a six-bed "dormitory" on the jail's second floor, the officers transferred the five female inmates who were already there to jails in neighboring towns. Officials claimed that the transfer was being done for safety reasons and that they had been worried that some of the other inmates—all of whom had been given much stiffer sentences for their crimes than Susan—might try to harm her.

But the relocation also meant that Susan had the women's cell block literally all to herself, and could enjoy her own private room. Women serving time in the county jail generally had to share an eighteen-by-twenty-foot cell with six bunk beds attached to the wall.

Susan was also provided with her own personal telephone, given unlimited visiting hours for her many guests, and allowed to snack on cookies and a sandwich that were brought in by her mother and sister. The special privileges were not extended to other inmates at the Lee Street facility.

Normally, prisoners are only allowed to see visitors on Saturdays and Sundays, and then for no more than a half-hour. They are not permitted to have more than three visitors, while Susan was entertaining up to six guests a day. Inmates do not have access to a private telephone and they are not allowed to accept food that is brought in to the jail.

Sheriff Joe Higgs, the man who was ultimately responsible for the jail's operation, found himself under attack as news of Ms. Cummings' "special" treatment was reported in *The Washington Post* and other newspapers.

The sheriff insisted that the reason the other prisoners were moved, an action that reportedly cost the taxpayers of Fauquier County two hundred dollars a day, was to protect Miss Cummings.

"When you have a situation where a woman is serving sixty days after killing someone, next to people serving two-year sentences for bad-check writing or forgery, it's understandable that she might not be their favorite person," Sheriff's Major David Flohr, who administered the facility, told the *Post*.

Sheriff Higgs said he allowed Susan to have special visiting privileges for a while so that she could take care of some paperwork stemming from the death of her father. The other privileges, however, were not authorized, he said.

No matter who okayed the "royal treatment," Sheriff Higgs ordered it halted after the story hit the newspapers.

Just as the jail story was beginning to die, Susan Cummings was back in the news again. This time, a number of the horses that were boarded at Ashland Farm escaped from a pasture and ran onto a nearby highway. It was after dark when the animals attempted to cross the busy Route 211 and they were almost instantly struck and killed by motorists in a series of unavoidable accidents. Two of the dead horses belonged to Diana, who was in Monte Carlo with her mother at the time the tragedy occurred. She had gone there to help the middle-aged widow deal with the estate of her deceased father. The other two horses belonged to boarders who demanded an explanation and advised Susan, through her attorney, Blair Howard, that they were holding her accountable.

No one was seriously injured in the collisions. But in one of the crashes, a horse was thrown onto the roof of a car, crushing the vehicle and trapping the owners inside. Police on the scene had to cut the two occupants free. Blair Howard told police that the family believed that a farm worker had accidentally left open a gate to one of the pastures, and said that Susan was deeply saddened by the fateful incident.

The dead horses were Thoroughbreds and warmbloods, a cross between a draft horse and a Thoroughbred. The animals were used for show-jumping and foxhunting and police said they were valued at $40,000.

The media spotlight shone on Susan Cummings for a third time on the day she would be released from jail. After serving only fifty-one days of her sixty-day sentence, the heiress was advised that she was free to go, after having been given time off from her sentence for good behavior.

Word of the shortened sentence outraged some local residents, and prompted members of the media to stake out the jail.

Two weeks later, Susan Cummings was back in the news again as attorneys for Roberto Villegas' mother and sister filed a $103 million wrongful-death suit against her, alleging that she had killed the polo player "without cause or provocation."

One week later, Blair Howard responded to the suit. The papers he filed stated that Susan had acted in "self-defense" and that Roberto had provoked the shooting by assaulting her with a knife—even though the jury had rejected the heiress's claim.

Meanwhile, Susan Cummmings remained at Ashland Farm and tried to put the incident behind her. She continued to ride and tend her horses. But she could not escape the public's continued interest in her story,

Bewildered, she repeatedly asked her attorney why published reports painted her in such an unflattering light. She told him that she simply could not understand why people were saying such mean things about her, and expressed a desire to return to the quiet existence she had once enjoyed.

Blair Howard told her that her life would be forever changed.

SHE LOVED HER SONS...TO DEATH.

Hush Little Babies

THE TRUE STORY OF A MOTHER WHO MURDERED HER CHILDREN

DON DAVIS

Not since the Susan Smith case has a murder so shocked the nation: a beautiful, loving mother is horrified to find her two young sons stabbed to death on her living room floor by an intruder. Hearts go out to poor Darlie Routier, who appeared to live for her children. But overwhelming evidence soon finds Darlie, the neighborhood's "Most Wonderful Mom," guilty of slaying her own innocent children in cold blood...

For six terror-filled years, he couldn't be stopped—until one journalist ingeniously cracked his twisted code...

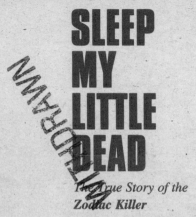

SLEEP MY LITTLE DEAD

The True Story of the Zodiac Killer

Kieran Crowley

The award-winning *New York Post* reporter whose brilliant work helped crack the Zodiac Killer's secret code reveals the inside story—as only he can tell it—of the man who terrorized the streets of New York City for six years, stalking, savagely attacking, and often killing his unsuspecting victims in cold blood.

SLEEP MY LITTLE DEAD
Kieran Crowley
___96339-4 $5.99 U.S./$7.99 CAN.